Paradox® 7

for Windows® 95
Illustrated Standard Edition

Paradox® 7
for Windows® 95
Illustrated Standard Edition

Jan Weingarten
Meta Chaya Hirschl

A DIVISION OF COURSE TECHNOLOGY
ONE MAIN STREET, CAMBRIDGE, MA 02142

an International Thomson Publishing company I(T)P®

Cambridge • Albany • Bonn • Boston • Cincinnati • London • Madrid • Melbourne • Mexico City
New York • Paris • San Francisco • Singapore • Tokyo • Toronto • Washington

Paradox 7 for Windows® 95—Illustrated Standard Edition is published by CTI

Managing Editor:	Marjorie S. Hunt
Product Manager:	Ann Marie Buconjic
Production Editor:	Catherine G. DiMassa
Composition House:	GEX, Inc.
Text Designer:	Leslie Hartwell
Cover Designer:	John Gamache

© 1997 by CTI

A Division of Course Technology — I**T**P®

For more information contact:

Course Technology
One Main Street
Cambridge, MA 02142

International Thomson Publishing Europe
Berkshire House 168-173
High Holborn
London WCIV 7AA
England

International Thomson Publishing GmbH
Königswinterer Strasse 418
53227 Bonn
Germany

Thomas Nelson Australia
102 Dodds Street
South Melbourne, 3205
Victoria, Australia

International Thomson Publishing Asia
211 Henderson Road
#05-10 Henderson Building
Singapore 0315

Nelson Canada
1120 Birchmount Road
Scarborough, Ontario
Canada M1K 5G4

International Thomson Publishing Japan
Hirakawacho Kyowa Building, 3F
2-2-1 Hirakawacho
Chiyoda-ku, Tokyo 102
Japan

International Thomson Editores
Campos Eliseos 385, Piso 7
Col. Polanco
11560 Mexico D.F. Mexico

Trademarks

Course Technology and the open book logo are registered trademarks of Course Technology.

I**T**P® The ITP logo is a registered trademark of International Thomson Publishing.

Some of the product names and company names used in this book have been used for identification purposes only and may be trademarks or registered trademarks of their respective manufacturers and sellers.

Disclaimer

Course Technology reserves the right to revise this publication and make changes from time to time in its content without notice.

ISBN 0-7600-3752-3

Printed in the United States of America

10 9 8 7 6 5 4 3 2 1

From the Illustrated Series Team

At Course Technology we believe that technology will transform the way that people teach and learn. We are very excited about bringing you, instructors and students, the most practical and affordable technology-related products available.

The Development Process

Our development process is unparalleled in the educational publishing industry. Every product we create goes through an exacting process of design, development, review, and testing.

Reviewers give us direction and insight that shape our manuscripts and bring them up to the latest standards. Every manuscript is quality tested. Students whose backgrounds match the intended audience work through every keystroke, carefully checking for clarity and pointing out errors in logic and sequence. Together with our own technical reviewers, these testers help us ensure that everything that carries our name is as error-free and easy to use as possible.

The Products

We show both how and why technology is critical to solving problems in the classroom and in whatever field you choose to teach or pursue. Our time-tested, step-by-step instructions provide unparalleled clarity. Examples and applications are chosen and crafted to motivate students.

The Illustrated Series Team

The Illustrated Series Team is committed to providing you with the most visual introduction to microcomputer applications. No other series of books will get you up to speed faster in today's changing software environment. This book will suit your needs because it was delivered quickly, efficiently, and affordably. In every aspect of business, we rely on a commitment to quality and the use of technology. Each member of the Illustrated Series Team contributes to this process. The names of all our team members are listed below.

Cynthia Anderson	Steven Johnson
Chia-Ling Barker	Susannah Lean
Donald Barker	Nancy Ludlow
Laura Bergs	Tara O'Keefe
David Beskeen	Harry Phillips
Ann Marie Buconjic	Nicole Jones Pinard
Rachel Bunin	Katherine T. Pinard
Joan Carey	Kevin Proot
Patrick Carey	Nancy Ray
Sheralyn Carroll	Elizabeth Eisner Reding
Pam Conrad	Neil Salkind
Mary Therese Cozzola	Gregory Schultz
Carol Cram	Ann Shaffer
Kim Crowley	Roger Skilling
Linda Eriksen	Dan Swanson
Jessica Evans	Marie Swanson
Lisa Friedrichsen	Jennifer Thompson
Michael Halvorson	Sasha Vodnik
Meta Hirschl	Jan Weingarten
Jane Hosie-Bounar	Christie Williams
Marjorie Hunt	Janet Wilson

Preface

Welcome to *Paradox 7 for Windows 95—Illustrated Standard Edition*. This highly visual book offers new users a hands-on introduction to Paradox and also serves as an excellent reference for future use.

Organization and Coverage

This text contains seven units that cover basic through advanced Paradox skills. In these units students learn basic Paradox skills like planning, building, editing, and enhancing Paradox tables. This book also covers creating reports, forms, and queries to help display, print, and analyze information, and much more!

About this Approach

What makes the Illustrated approach so effective at teaching software skills? It's quite simple. Each skill is presented on two facing pages, with the step-by-step instructions on the left page, and large screen illustrations on the right. Students can focus on a single skill without having to turn the page. This unique design makes information extremely accessible and easy to absorb, and provides a great reference for after the course is over. This hands-on approach also makes it ideal for both self-paced or instructor-led classes. The modular structure of the book also allows for great flexibility; you can cover the units in any order you choose. Each lesson, or "information display," contains the following elements:

Introduction — Concise text that introduces the basic principles discussed in the lesson and integrates the brief case study scenario. Procedures are easier to learn when concepts fit into a framework.

Numbered steps — Clear step-by-step directions explain how to complete the specific task. When students follow the numbered steps, they quickly learn how each procedure is performed and what the results will be.

Reference tables — These are quickly accessible summaries of key terms, toolbar buttons, or keyboard alternatives connected with the lesson material. Students can refer easily to this information when working on their own projects at a later time.

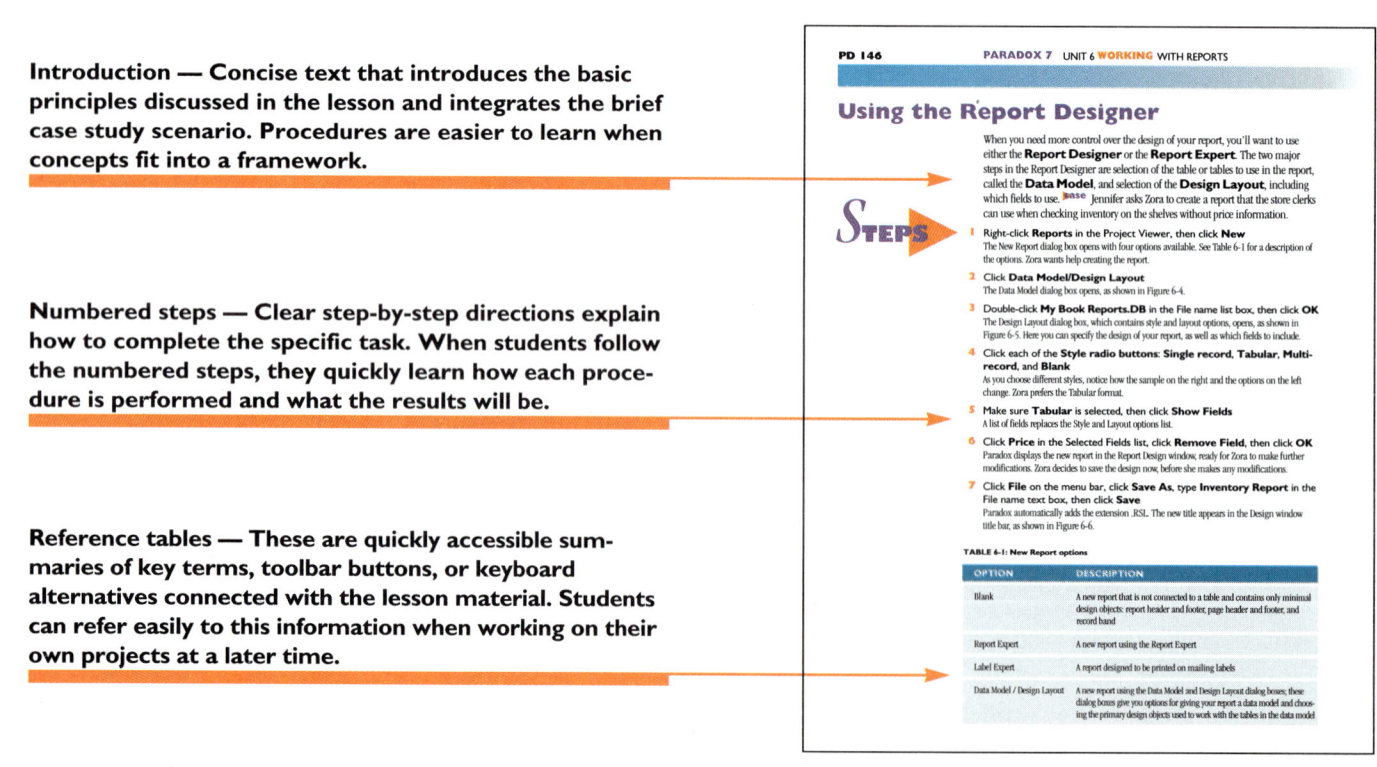

Other Features

The two-page lesson format featured in this book provides the new user with a powerful learning experience. Additionally, this book contains the following features:

- Read This Before You Begin Paradox 7 Page – This page provides essential information that both students and instructors need to know before they begin working through the units.
- Real-World Case – The case study used throughout the textbook is designed to be "real-world" in nature and representative of the kinds of activities that students will encounter when working with Paradox. With a real-world case, the process of solving the problem will be more meaningful to students.
- End of Unit Material – Each unit concludes with a Task Reference that summarizes the various methods used to execute each of the skills covered in the unit. The Task Reference is followed by a meaningful Concepts Review that tests students' understanding of what they learned in the unit. The Concepts Review is followed by a Skills Review, which provides students with additional hands-on practice of the skills they learned in the unit. The Skills Review is followed by Independent Challenges, which pose case problems for students to solve. The Independent Challenges allow students to learn by exploring and develop critical thinking skills. The Visual Workshops that follow the Independent Challenges in Units 2-7 also help students to develop critical thinking skills. Students are shown completed tasks and are asked to recreate them from scratch.

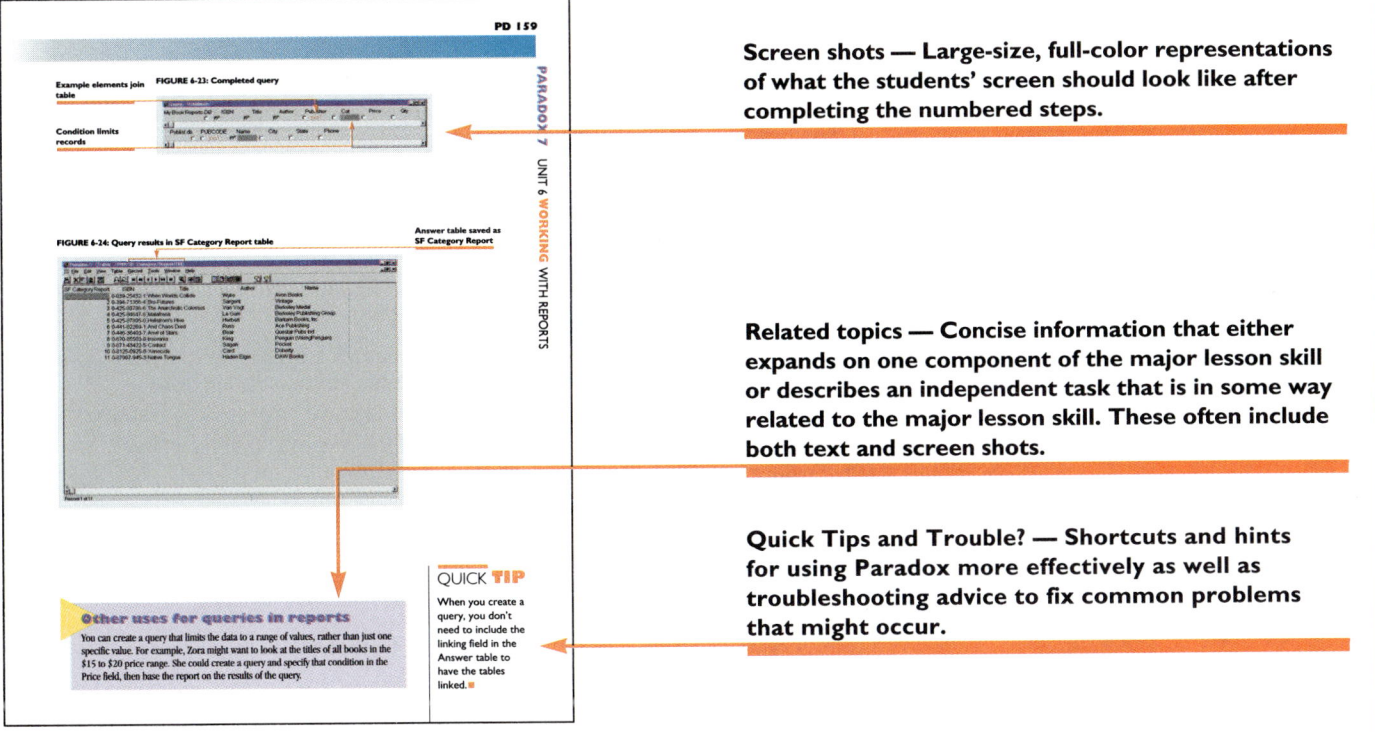

Screen shots — Large-size, full-color representations of what the students' screen should look like after completing the numbered steps.

Related topics — Concise information that either expands on one component of the major lesson skill or describes an independent task that is in some way related to the major lesson skill. These often include both text and screen shots.

Quick Tips and Trouble? — Shortcuts and hints for using Paradox more effectively as well as troubleshooting advice to fix common problems that might occur.

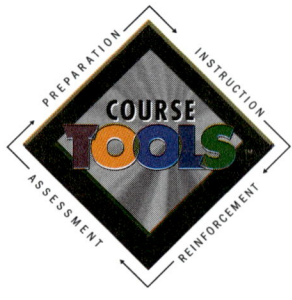

CourseTools

CourseTools are Course Technology's way of putting the resources and information needed to teach and learn effectively into your hands. With an integrated array of teaching and learning tools that offer you and your students a broad range of technology-based instructional options, we believe CourseTools represent the highest quality and most cutting edge resources available to instructors today. CourseTools can be found at http://coursetools.com. Briefly, the CourseTools available with this text are:

Student Disks

To use this book students must have a Student Disk. See the inside front or inside back cover for more information on the Student Disk. Adopters of this text are granted the right to post the Student Disk on any stand-alone computer or network.

Course Online Faculty Companion

This new World Wide Web site offers Course Technology customers a password-protected Faculty Lounge where you can find everything you need to prepare for class. These periodically updated items include lesson plans, graphic files for the figures in the text, additional problems, updates and revisions to the text, links to other Web sites, and access to Student Disk files. This new site is an ongoing project and will continue to evolve throughout the semester. Contact your Customer Service Representative for the site address and password.

Course Online Student Companion

Course Online Student CompanionOur second Web site is a place where students can access challenging, engaging, and relevant exercises. They can find a graphical glossary of terms found in the text, an archive of meaningful templates, software, hot tips, and Web links to other sites that contain pertinent information. We offer student sites in the broader application areas as well as sites for specific titles. These new sites are also ongoing projects and will continue to evolve throughout the semester.

Instructor's Manual

This is quality assurance tested and includes:

- Solutions to all lessons and end-of-unit material
- Unit notes which contain teaching tips from the authors
- Extra Independent Challenges
- Transparency Masters of key concepts

Solutions Files

This disk has been quality assurance tested and contains solutions to all end-of-unit material and extra Independent Challenges.

Course Test Manager

Designed by Course Technology, this cutting edge Windows-based testing software helps instructors design and administer tests and pre-tests. This full-featured program also has an online testing component that allows students to take tests at the computer and have their exams automatically graded.

Brief Contents

Contents

UNIT 4   **Working with Tables**   *PD 81*

TABLES

Paradox® 7 for Windows® 95

Read This Before You Begin
Paradox 7 for Windows 95

Using Your Own Computer

If you are going to work through this book using your own computer, you need a computer system running Windows 95, Paradox 7 for Windows 95, and a Student Disk. You will not be able to complete the step-by-step exercises in this book using your own computer until you have your own Student Disk. This book assumes the Paradox settings described above.

To the Student and the Instructor

This book assumes that the Text Object Expert is off. To verify this, click Edit, Preferences, then the Experts tab, and make sure the Run Experts When Creating Objects on Documents is *not* checked.

The exercises and examples in this book feature sample Paradox files stored on the Student Disk provided by the instructor. The Student Disk contains all the files students need to complete the exercises in the book. See the inside front or inside back cover for more information on the Student Disk.

The data files to be used with the text are stored in folders on the Student Disk. Before students can work through the book, the files contained in each folder should be transferred to high density 3.5 inch disks. Please refer to the README.DOC file on the Student Disk for complete instructions. Instructors can make the data files available to students on high density 3.5 inch disks; you may choose to make this disk available to students, having them copy the data files themselves onto separate high density disks; or you may post the files to network or standalone workstations. The book assumes that students will be working through the units using files from the high density 3.5 inch disks, each disk containing files from the appropriate folder. This disk division minimizes the possibility that students will run out of disk space as they alter, create, and save data files in the units. *NOTE: the above folders contain Windows 95 file-names. You will need to perform the copy operations on a Windows 95 computer in order to avoid truncated filenames.* See the README.DOC file for more information.

The instructions in this book assume Paradox has been installed using the Typical installation during the Setup program. It is also assumed the students know which drive and folder contain the Student Disk files, so it's important that disk location information is provided before the students start working through the units. If students have any difficulties, see your instructor or technical support person for further information.

UNIT 1

OBJECTIVES

- ▶ Define database software
- ▶ Launch Paradox 7 for Windows 95
- ▶ View the Paradox screen
- ▶ Set the working directory
- ▶ Open and view a table
- ▶ Explore table properties
- ▶ Use the Table View toolbar
- ▶ Get Help and exit Paradox

Getting
STARTED WITH PARADOX 7 FOR WINDOWS 95

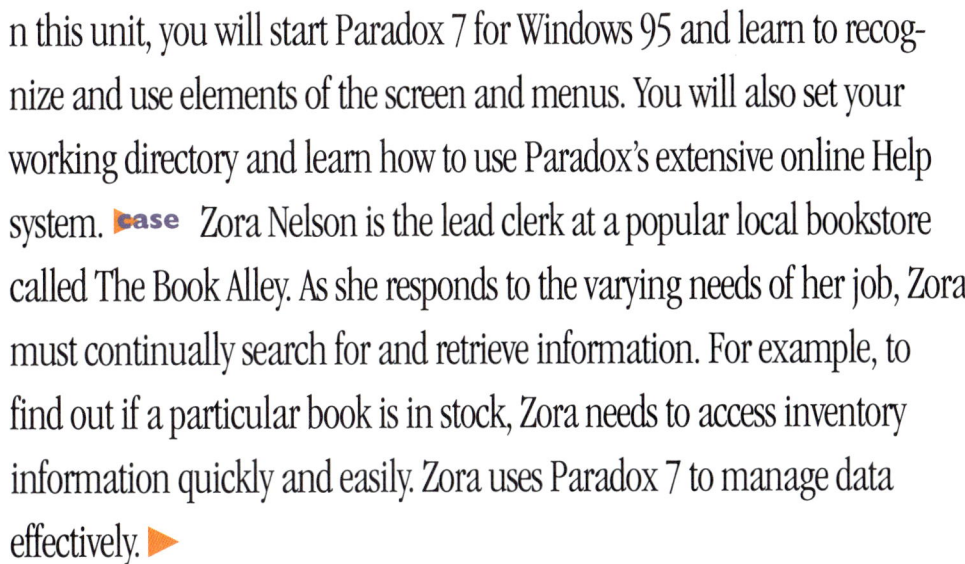

I n this unit, you will start Paradox 7 for Windows 95 and learn to recognize and use elements of the screen and menus. You will also set your working directory and learn how to use Paradox's extensive online Help system. ▶ **case** Zora Nelson is the lead clerk at a popular local bookstore called The Book Alley. As she responds to the varying needs of her job, Zora must continually search for and retrieve information. For example, to find out if a particular book is in stock, Zora needs to access inventory information quickly and easily. Zora uses Paradox 7 to manage data effectively. ▶

Defining database software

Although you might not be aware of it, you already use databases every day when you consult lists of information, such as an address book or a dictionary. The **database** Zora uses in her job includes lists of books in stock, books on order, publishers, and major customers. In Paradox, each list becomes a **table** and the information about each item in the table is a **record**. Each record contains specific data, such as a book's title, author, price, and so on. These data items are called **fields**. Figure 1-1 illustrates the components of a database. The power of a **relational database management system** like Paradox lies in its ability to quickly locate data, retrieve and present data in any format, link information in related tables, and change the table as needs change. Figure 1-2 shows a sample of the inventory list Zora had to create manually at The Book Alley before she switched to Paradox. Figure 1-3 shows the same inventory list created using Paradox.  **case**   Zora likes working with Paradox because it allows her to:

- **Enter data quickly and accurately**
  In the past, Zora has been plagued by inconsistent entries made by different staff members. With Paradox, Zora can create standard forms which will require employees to enter data in a particular format.

- **Locate and retrieve data quickly**
  Zora can ask Paradox to locate and retrieve specific information. If Zora's boss wants to know how many books by a certain author were sold in the last quarter, Zora can retrieve the information in no time.

- **Change and update data easily**
  If a publisher's address changes, Zora can enter the new address once and have Paradox update it automatically in all the tables in the database. If the management decides to increase prices by 10%, Zora can run a simple calculation and have all the prices automatically increased throughout the database.

- **Modify the structure of a table**
  If a publisher adds a World Wide Web page as a tool to place orders, Zora can add a field to the publisher table to capture the Web page address. As business needs change, Zora can modify the structure of the appropriate table.

- **Sort data**
  Zora can sort data to rearrange the records in a logical order, such as alphabetic or numeric. If a customer requests a list of science fiction books sorted alphabetically by title, Zora can easily oblige.

- **Create eye-catching reports**
  Zora can create reports that look at the data in different ways. For the monthly sales meeting, she can produce an inventory report that includes pictures, graphs, and other design elements to enhance the effectiveness of the report.

**FIGURE I-1:
Components of a
database**

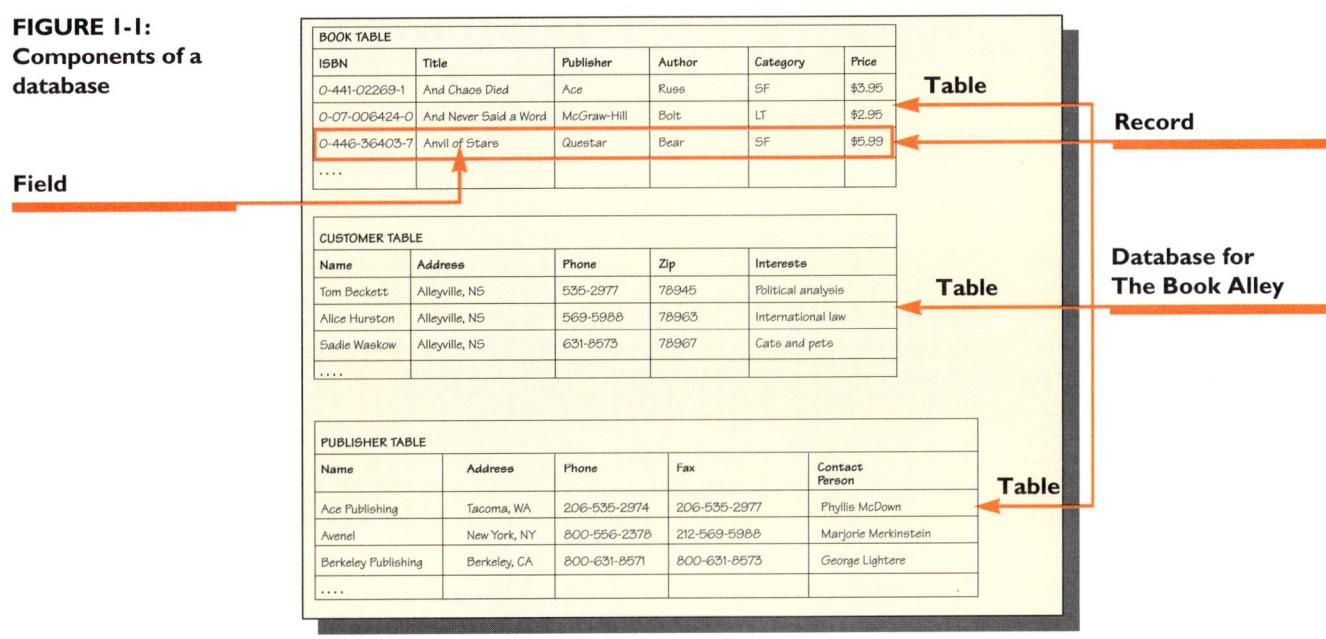

FIGURE I-2: Manual inventory list

```
BOOK TABLE
ISBN              Title                    Publisher       Author       Category      Price
0-441-02269-1     And Chaos Died           Ace             Russ         SF            $3.95
0-07-006424-0     And Never Said a Word    McGraw-Hill     Bolt         LT            $2.95
0-446-36403-7     Anvil of Stars           Questar         Bear         SF            $5.99
. . . .
```

**FIGURE I-3:
Inventory list in a
Paradox table**

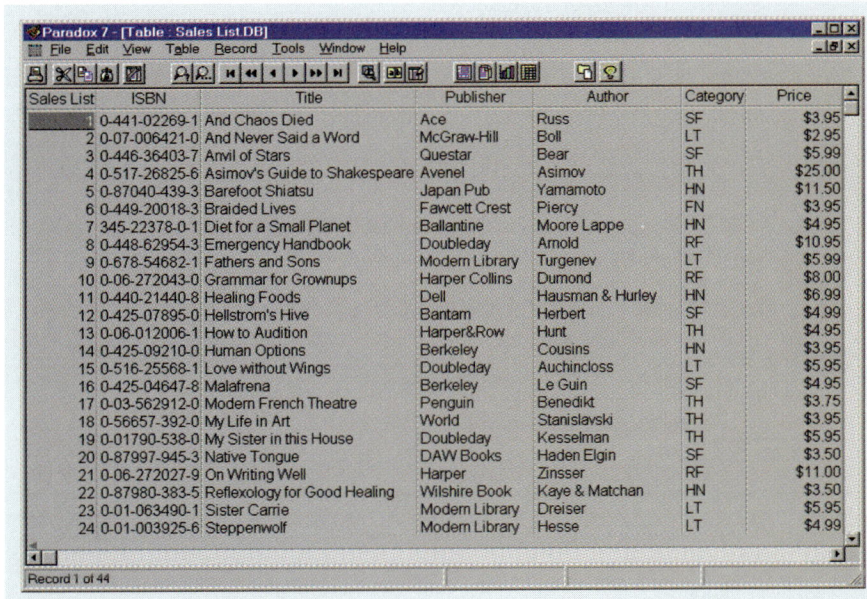

Launching Paradox 7 for Windows 95

To launch Paradox 7, you use the Windows 95 taskbar. You click on Start, then Programs, and then Paradox 7. If you are using a computer on a network, you might need to use a different starting procedure depending on the environment. Check with the lab supervisor. **case** Zora launches Paradox to familiarize herself with the program.

1   Make sure the Windows 95 desktop is open, then insert your Student Disk in the appropriate disk drive

2   Click the **Start button** ![Start] on the taskbar
The Start menu appears on the desktop.

3   On the Start menu, point to **Programs**
Each of the menus remains open as you point, as shown in Figure 1-4. Depending on the programs installed on your computer, the programs you see on the Programs menu might be different from the ones shown in the figure.

4   On the Programs menu, click **Paradox 7**, click **Paradox 7** again (if necessary)
Depending on your installation, you might have to first click Paradox 7 which is next to the folder icon, and then click Paradox 7. The Startup Expert appears, as shown in Figure 1-5, unless a previous user has **disabled** it (turned it off). You can click the Don't show the Startup Expert again check box, but don't disable this feature without checking with your instructor first. For more about experts, see the related topic "Using Paradox experts." Zora isn't ready to start a database, so she cancels the Startup Expert.

5   Click **Cancel** to close the Startup Expert
The Startup Expert dialog box closes, and the Paradox window appears with the Project Viewer open. In the next lesson Zora will familiarize herself with the elements of the Paradox window.

FIGURE 1-4:
Paradox 7 program selected

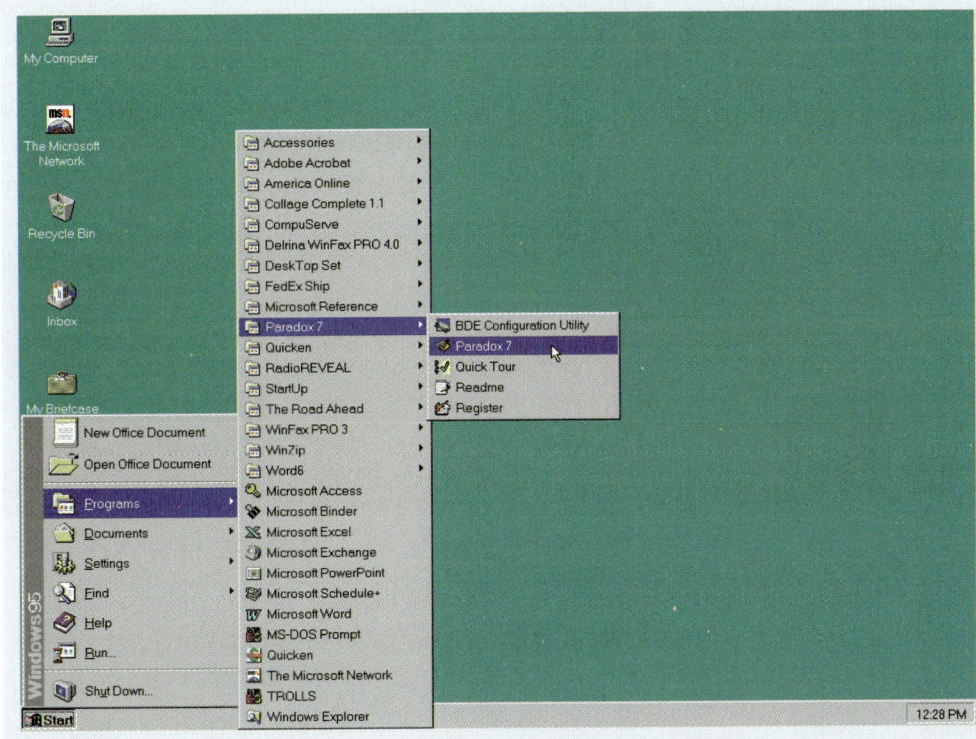

FIGURE 1-5: Paradox Startup Expert

Using Paradox experts

Paradox experts provide easy-to-follow steps that help you quickly perform common Paradox tasks. Paradox 7 provides a number of experts to walk you through these tasks: Creating charts, databases, forms, mailing labels, reports, and tables in addition to experts that assist in merging information and importing text.

TROUBLE?

You might see a dialog box with the message "Working directory is invalid or undefined. Using Startup directory instead." If you see this dialog box, click OK to start Paradox. ■

Viewing the Paradox screen

When you launch Paradox, the Project Viewer appears inside the Desktop window, as shown in Figure 1-6. The Paradox Desktop is made up of many **objects**, such as the menu bar, title bar, and toolbar. For more information on menus and toolbars see the related topic "Different menus and tools for different tasks."

Compare the descriptions below to Figure 1-6 to familiarize yourself with the objects on the Paradox screen.

- The **Desktop** is the main Paradox workspace. When you open tables, forms, reports, or other objects, they all appear on the Desktop.

- The **title bar** displays the application name, Paradox 7. The text in the title bar is a property of the Desktop.

- The **menu bar** contains items from which you choose Paradox commands. As with all Windows applications, you choose a menu item by clicking it with the mouse or by pressing [Alt] plus the underlined letter in the menu name.

- The **toolbar** gives you easy access to many of the commands available in Paradox. To choose a tool, simply click it with the left mouse button.

- The **Project Viewer** allows you to work with and manage your Paradox files. From the Project Viewer, you can create new tables or open existing ones, rename or delete files, and perform many other file management functions.

- The **status bar** at the bottom of the screen displays useful information about the current file or the action in progress. In Figure 1-6, notice that the mouse pointer is positioned on the button at the left edge of the toolbar ▦, and the status bar displays a message that describes what happens if you click the button.

- As you move the mouse pointer over a button on a toolbar, the name of the button, called a **ToolTip**, appears below or above the button, as shown in Figure 1-6.

Title bar

Menu bar

Open Table button

ToolTip

Project Viewer
(your file list might
be different)

Toolbar

Status bar

Desktop

FIGURE I-6: Paradox Desktop

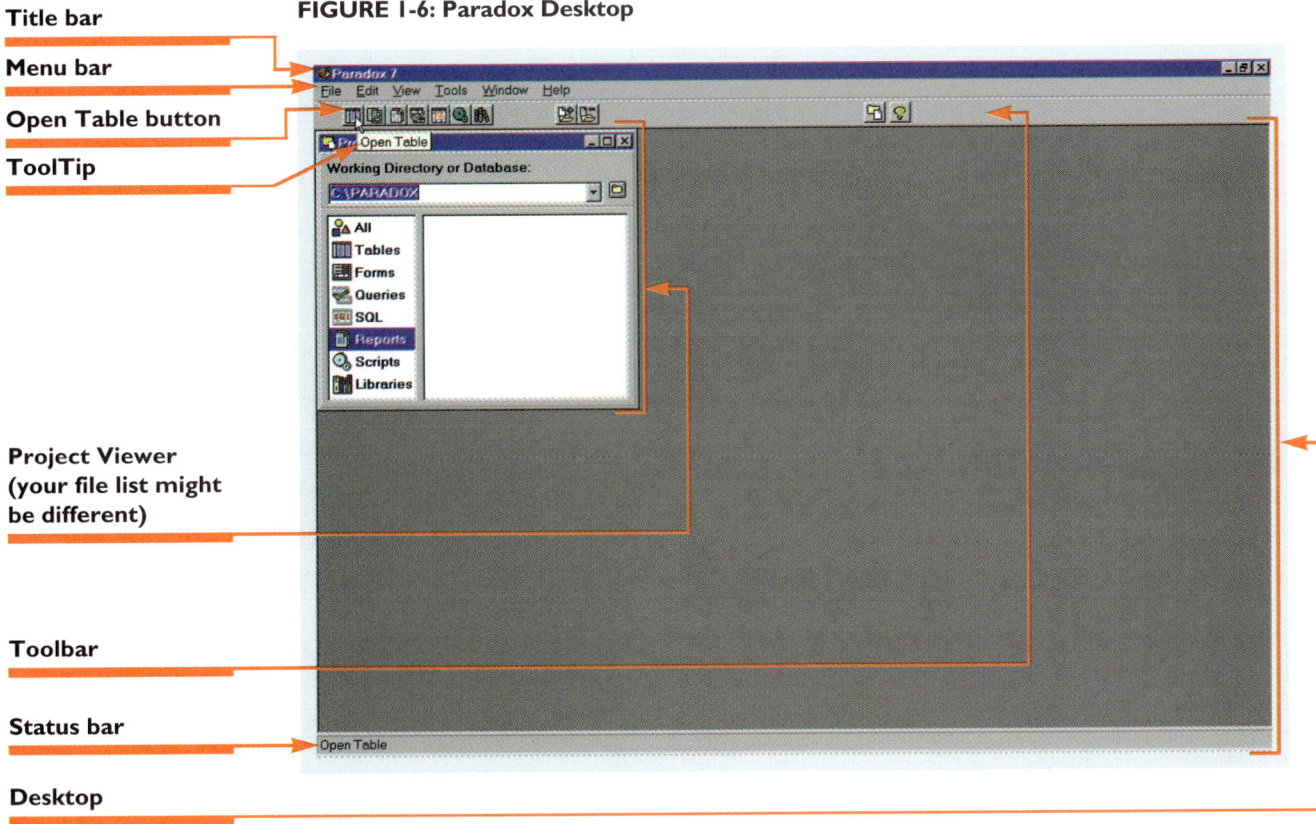

Different menus and tools for different tasks

The techniques for using menus and tools are the same throughout Paradox, but the available options change depending on the task you're performing and the type of window that's open. Each type of Paradox window has its own set of menu and toolbar items. Right now, you are looking at the Project Viewer window, which has options for opening files and changing the way your Desktop looks. Other views include Table and Form View.

QUICK **TIP**

To get the best view of the Paradox Desktop, maximize the window (if it isn't already) by clicking the Maximize button  in the Paradox window.■

Setting the working directory

The **working directory** is the default directory Paradox uses to open and save files. You can set as many working directories as you need to manage your files. The advantage of working directories is that you have predefined a path, a set of folders in which to keep files, so that you can quickly move to the specific work area of your choice. This saves the time of tediously choosing folders every time you want to open or save tables, for example. The working directory also controls which files are displayed during open and save operations. **case** Zora's computer contains the database for the bookstore, as well as the database for the cafe located in the bookstore's atrium. To avoid confusion, the bookstore and cafe databases are stored in separate working directories. For easy access to the bookstore files and to make sure all of her changes are saved to the correct directory, Zora always selects the bookstore's directory as her working directory before she begins work.

1 Click the **Project Viewer Browse button** 🗔, as shown in Figure 1-7
The Directory Browser dialog box opens, as shown in Figure 1-8. Next, Zora could simply type the directory name in the Directories text box, but she finds it easier to choose from a list. That way she doesn't have to remember the exact name.

2 Click the **Drive (or Alias) arrow** ▾, as shown in Figure 1-8
A list of available drives appears.

3 Click the letter corresponding to the drive containing your Student Disk
The drive and any directories it contains are shown in the Directories list. "A:" appears in the Directories text box. (If you are using a different drive, you will see that drive letter instead of "A.")

4 Click **OK**
The Working Directory or Database text box now displays "A:\"

FIGURE 1-7: Project Viewer Browse button

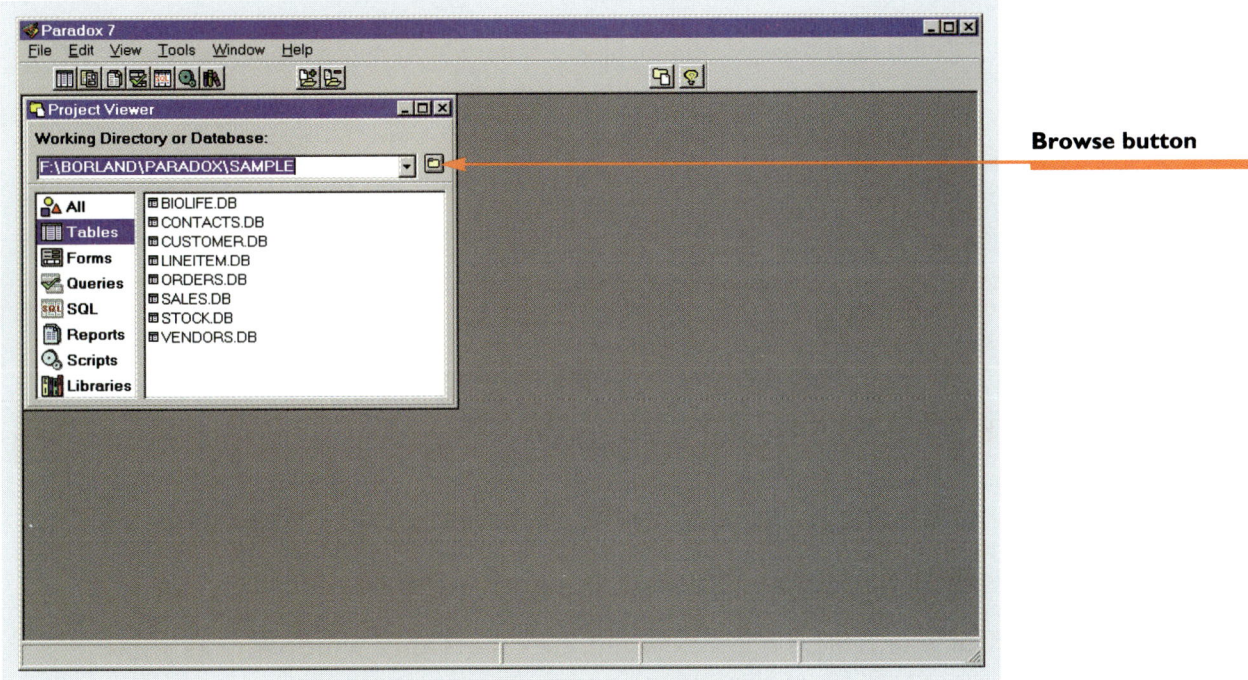

Browse button

FIGURE 1-8: Directory Browser dialog box

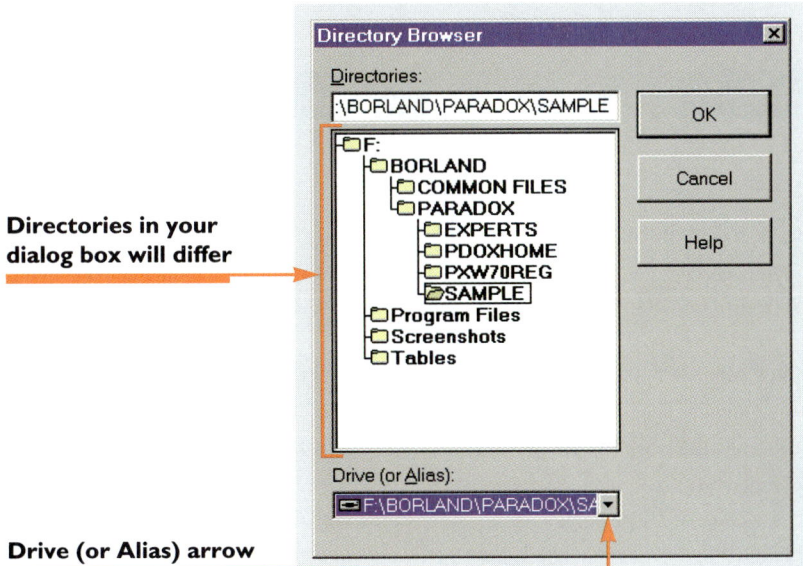

Directories in your dialog box will differ

Drive (or Alias) arrow

Opening and viewing a table

Tables are the basic building blocks of Paradox databases. After you create a table, you can use it to store and retrieve data, and to organize data into eye-catching reports. ►**case** Now that Zora understands the basic elements of the Paradox screen, she proceeds to open a table and explore the Table View window. As you'll see, the Table View window displays data in rows and columns.

1 Verify that the Project Viewer is open, if it isn't, click the **Project Viewer button** 🔳 on the toolbar, then click **Tables**
The Project Viewer displays a list of tables as shown in Figure 1-9.

2 Double-click **Book Inventory.DB**
This opens the table containing a list of books. For each book, the table includes an entry for ISBN (short for "International Standard Book Number"), Title, Publisher, Author, Category Price, and Quantity. Don't be concerned if you see asterisks in some of the columns. When you maximize the table in the next step, the asterisks will be replaced with data.

3 If your table is not maximized, click the **Table window maximize button** 🔲
Make sure you click the Table window maximize button, and not the Paradox window maximize button. Your screen should now match Figure 1-10. Follow along as Zora learns some of the basics about tables, using Table 1-1 as a guide.

TABLE 1-1: Elements of a Paradox table

ELEMENT	DESCRIPTION
Table	A collection of records
Table name	Appears in the Table window title bar and in the upper-left corner of the table area
Toolbar	Contains buttons that help you work with tables; clicking a toolbar button is a shortcut to many menu options
Record numbers	Numbers in the leftmost column that indicate the position of each record within the table
Field name	Attributes of the table entity; for example, the Book Inventory table is made up of the field names ISBN, Title, Publisher, Author, Category, Price, and Quantity
Field value	The data contained in one field of a record; for example, the Author field value for record number 15 is "Chang"; the highlighted area shows your current field value position; in Figure 1-10, the current field value position is record number 1
Record	Contains an entire set of field values for one entity; in Figure 1-10, all of the information for the book Modern French Theatre (the ISBN, Title, Publisher, Author, Category, Price, and Qty fields) make up a record
Status bar	Displays useful information about the current file or the action in progress; in Figure 1-10, notice that the left side of the status bar tells you that record #1 is currently highlighted (selected) and that 46 records are contained in the table; as you work through the lessons in this book, keep an eye on the status bar for important messages

FIGURE I-9:
Project Viewer

Double-click here

Project Viewer

Your file list might
differ

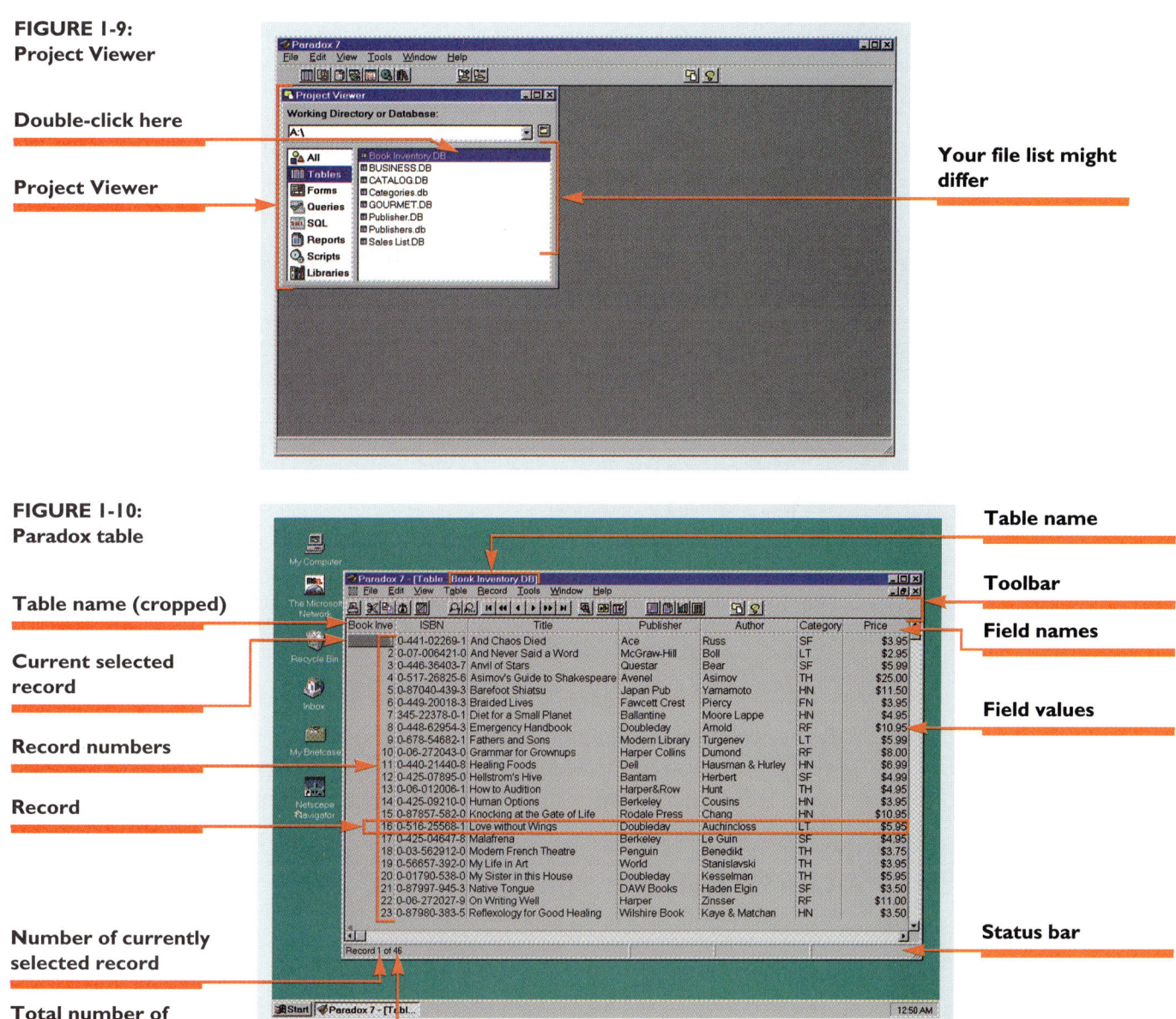

FIGURE I-10:
Paradox table

Table name (cropped)

Current selected
record

Record numbers

Record

Number of currently
selected record

Total number of
records in table

Table name

Toolbar

Field names

Field values

Status bar

TROUBLE?

If you don't see
Book Inventory.DB
in the Project Viewer
list, you might have
selected the wrong
directory, or the
Project Viewer might
not be displaying the
tables list. If neces-
sary, repeat Steps 1
through 4 in the
previous lesson.

Exploring table properties

All the objects in your table have properties that you can change to suit your needs. Some properties relate to appearance and others indicate actions you can perform with the object. To display a list of the properties associated with an object, you simply right-click the object. ▶**case** Zora decides to view various properties to familiarize herself with some of the objects in her table. She does not change any properties now.

I Move the mouse pointer over the **Title column heading**
The mouse pointer changes to 🖰.

2 Right-click the **Title column heading**, then click the **Alignment** tab to make it foremost in the dialog box
The Title_Heading Properties dialog box opens, as shown in Figure 1-11. This dialog box shows the three properties of the column heading—General, Alignment, and Font. Zora knows she could click any of them to change the way the Title column heading appears in the table. This Properties dialog box will be useful when Zora wants to enhance the appearance of her table.

3 Click the **Close button** ⊠ in the Title_Heading Properties dialog box
Now Zora decides to see the properties associated with a field.

4 Right-click in one of the ISBN fields (not the heading)
A context-sensitive menu displays the options Filter, Properties, Data Dependent, and Copy as shown in Figure 1-12. Notice that some options are dimmed, indicating that the items are not available at this time.

5 Click **Properties**
The ISBN Properties dialog box displays the General, Alignment, and Font properties.

6 Click the **Close button** ⊠ in the ISBN Properties dialog box
The ISBN dialog box closes. Zora investigates the Table View toolbar next.

FIGURE 1-11: Title_Heading Properties dialog box

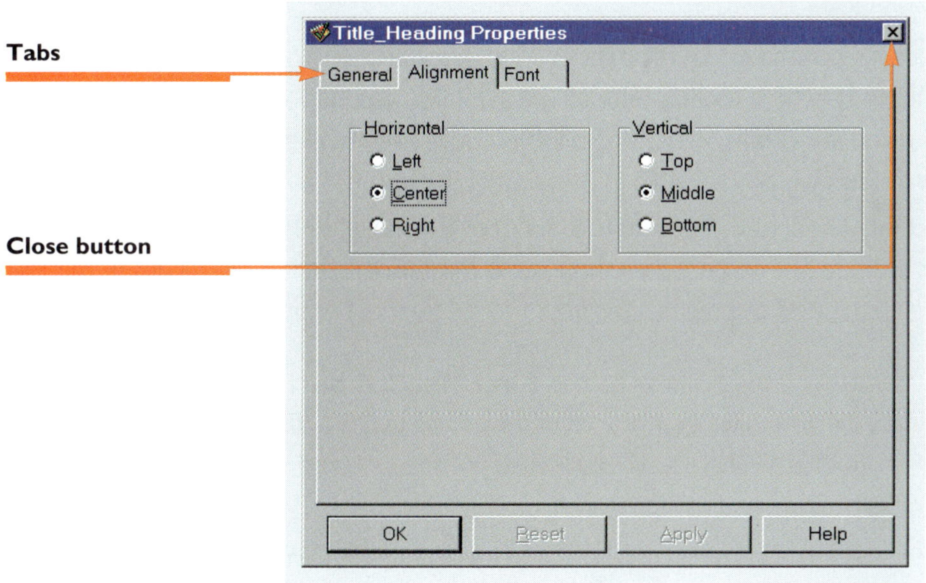

Tabs

Close button

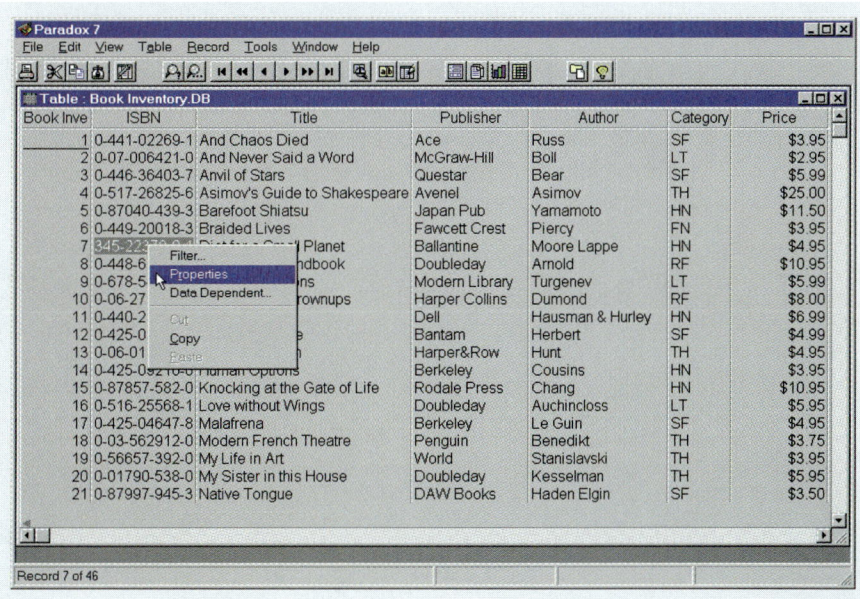

FIGURE 1-12: Context-sensitive menu

Using the Table View toolbar

Paradox's **toolbar buttons** provide quick access to many commonly used commands. Which toolbar buttons are available depends on your current task. When you are viewing or editing a table, you see the toolbar in Figure 1-13. **case** Zora wants to be able to move quickly through the records in the Book Inventory table. In order to do this, she uses the navigation buttons on the Table View toolbar. She can use these buttons to move to the first or last record in the table, to the next or previous record, or to see the next or previous screen of records.

1. Move your mouse pointer to the **First Record button** ▌◀ on the toolbar
   Notice the status bar message that describes the button's purpose. Zora uses this button to make sure that the first record in the table is selected.

2. Click ▌◀
   The highlight moves to record number one (if it wasn't already there), indicating that the first record is selected. The field in which the highlight initially appears depends on the field you selected at the end of the previous lesson. Now you can select the next record.

3. Click the **Next Record button** ▶ on the toolbar
   The status bar indicates that the next record is now highlighted, or selected.

4. Click the **Last Record button** ▶▌ on the toolbar
   The highlight moves to the last record in the table, as shown in Figure 1-14.

5. Click the **Previous Record button** ◀ on the toolbar

6. Click ▌◀
   The highlight returns to the first record, as shown in Figure 1-15

FIGURE 1-13: Table View toolbar

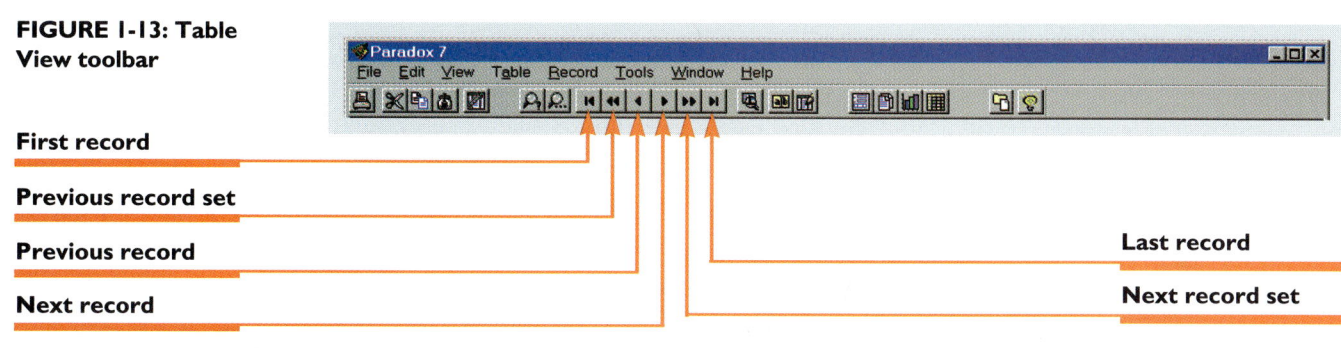

First record

Previous record set

Previous record

Next record

Last record

Next record set

FIGURE 1-14: Last record highlighted

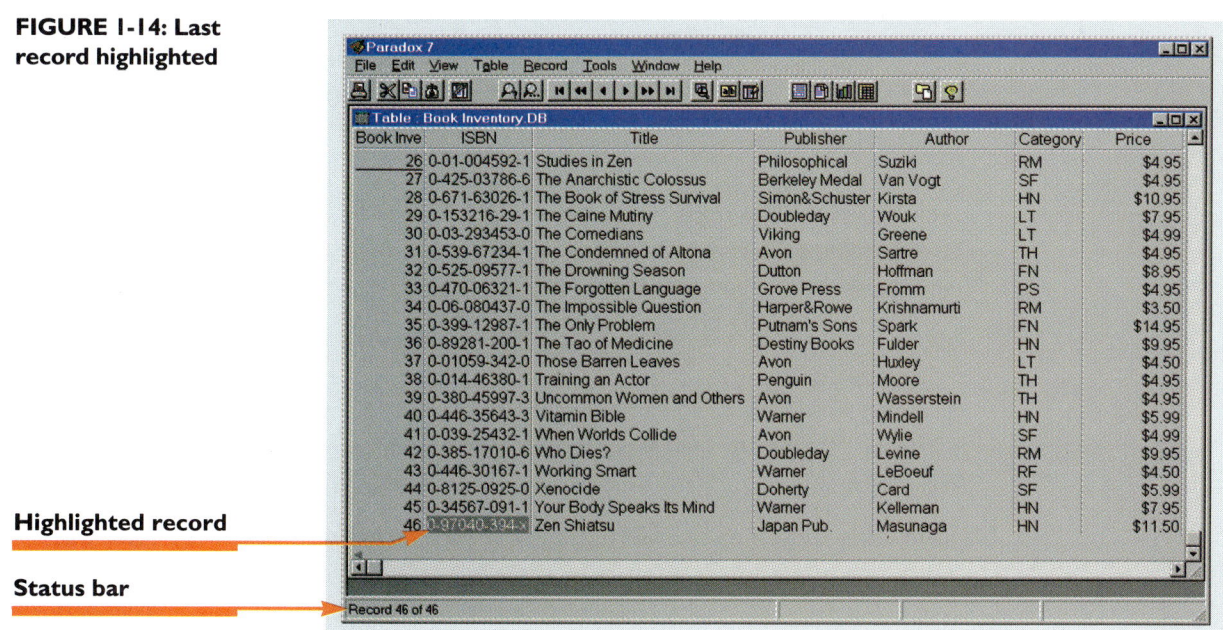

Highlighted record

Status bar

FIGURE 1-15: First record highlighted

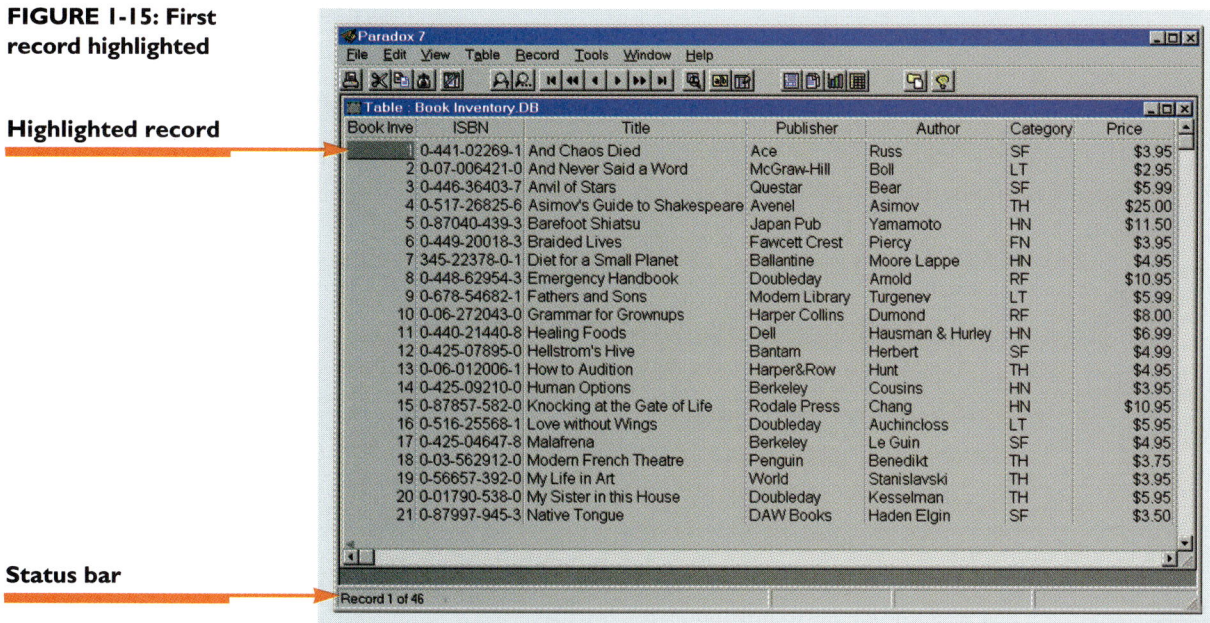

Highlighted record

Status bar

Getting Help and exiting Paradox

Paradox features an extensive online Help system that gives you immediate access to definitions, explanations, and useful tips. The Paradox Help system operates like the Windows 95 system. Help information appears in a separate window that you can resize and refer to as you work. Then, when you are done working with Help and a table, close Help and the table, close the database, and then exit Paradox. The way data are saved in database programs is different from other programs in that changes are saved immediately. See the related topic "Dynamic record updating" for more information. Always close tables before you exit Paradox. If you plan to turn off your computer, you should exit both Paradox *and* Windows 95. ▶case   Whenever Zora has questions about a Paradox topic such as the toolbar, she can access the Paradox Help system.

1   Click **Help** on the menu bar, click **User's Guide Topics**, then click the **Contents** tab to make it foremost in the dialog box
The Contents of Help topics are listed. Zora is interested in the What's New topic.

2   Double-click **What's new**, click **What's new in Paradox 7**, then click **Display**
The new features of Paradox 7 appear, as shown in Figure 1-16. Notice that there are phrases underlined, indicating that there is more information about that topic in another window. Zora wonders what the User's Guide says about changing properties and preferences.

3   Move the pointer to the phrase **properties and preferences** until the pointer changes to 🖑, then click it
The discussion of tabbed dialog boxes is familiar because you are currently using them. Now Zora wants to go back to the previous screen.

4   Click **Back** on the Help button bar
You return to the list of What's New in Paradox 7. For a list of handy Paradox Help buttons. Zora returns to the table of contents next.

5   Click **Contents** on the Help button bar, then double-click **What's New**
This returns you to the index listing and collapses the subheadings of What's New, as shown in Figure 1-17. From this screen you can investigate any of these topics in the same manner. For now, Zora is ready to leave Help.

6   Close all the Help windows
The Help windows close and you return to the bookstore table. Zora is ready to exit Paradox.

7   Click **File** on the menu bar, then click **Close**
The File menu appears. The Book Inventory table closes. Zora is ready to exit Paradox.

8   Click **File** on the menu bar
The File menu appears as shown in Figure 1-18. Notice that not all the commands are available in this menu–why?

9   Click **Exit**
The Paradox window closes and you return to the Windows 95 desktop. Zora is now comfortable with the Paradox 7 environment.

FIGURE 1-16: What's New Help window

For more related information ▶

Click to see more information on these topics ▶

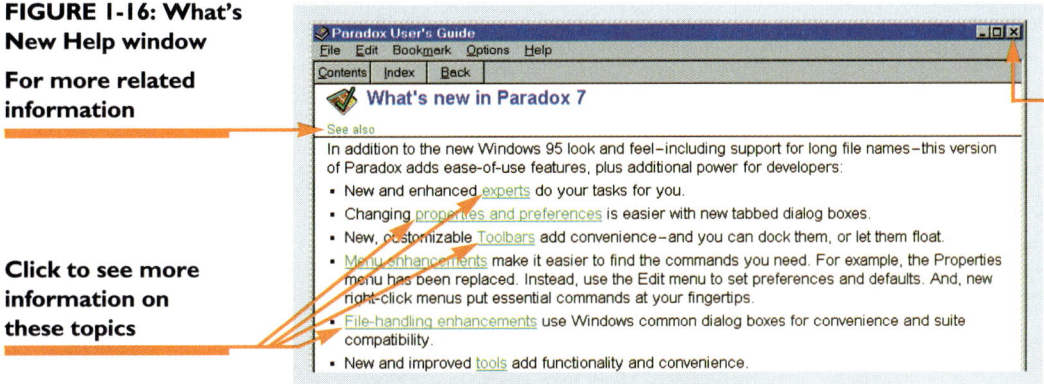

Close button ◀

FIGURE 1-17: Help Contents

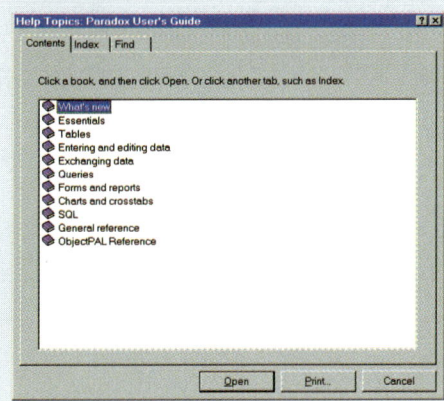

FIGURE 1-18: Exiting Paradox with the File menu

Close button ▶

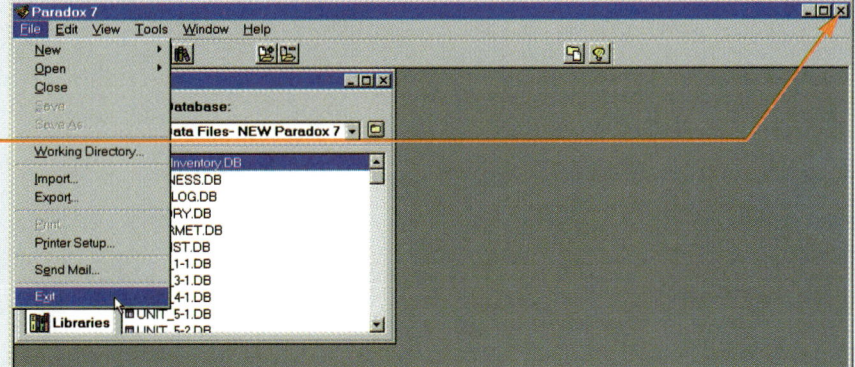

Dynamic record updating

Every time you make a change or addition to a table, the update is immediately saved. This is called dynamic record updating, which means that the changes to the table occur as you enter them, not at a later time. You might recall that when you type words in a word processor or enter numbers in a spreadsheet, the update is not saved until you explicitly save the file. However in a database program tables are updated as you use them. This is done so that the database is kept current and so that the most relevant information is supplied to the users.

QUICK **TIP**

The Project Viewer is maximized whenever you maximize the Table window. That's why when you closed the maximized table, you found that the Project Viewer was also maximized.■

TASKREFERENCE

TASK	MOUSE/BUTTON	MENU	KEYBOARD
Browse through directories to assign a working directory	📁	Click File, Working Directory, then click the Browse button	
Close a table	Click the table Close button	Click File, then Close	
Exit Paradox	Click the Close button	Click File, then Exit	[Alt][F4]
Get Help		Click Help, then User's Guide Topics	
Move to First Record, Previous Record Set, Previous Record, Next Record, Next Record Set, and Last Record	⏮ ⏪ ◀ ▶ ⏩ ⏭	Click Record, then First, Previous Set, Previous, Next, Next Set, or Last	First-[Ctrl][F11] Previous Set-[Shift][F11] Previous-[F11] Next-[F12] Next Set-[Shift][F12] Last-[Ctrl][F12]
Use Project Viewer	🗂	Click Tools, then Project Viewer	
View object properties - on field name	Move the mouse until it changes to 🖫 then click the right mouse button	Click Table, then Heading Properties	[Ctrl][H]
View object properties - on field values	Click the right mouse button, then click Properties	Click Table, then Data Properties	[Ctrl][M]

CONCEPTSREVIEW

Label each element of the Paradox window shown in Figure 1-19.

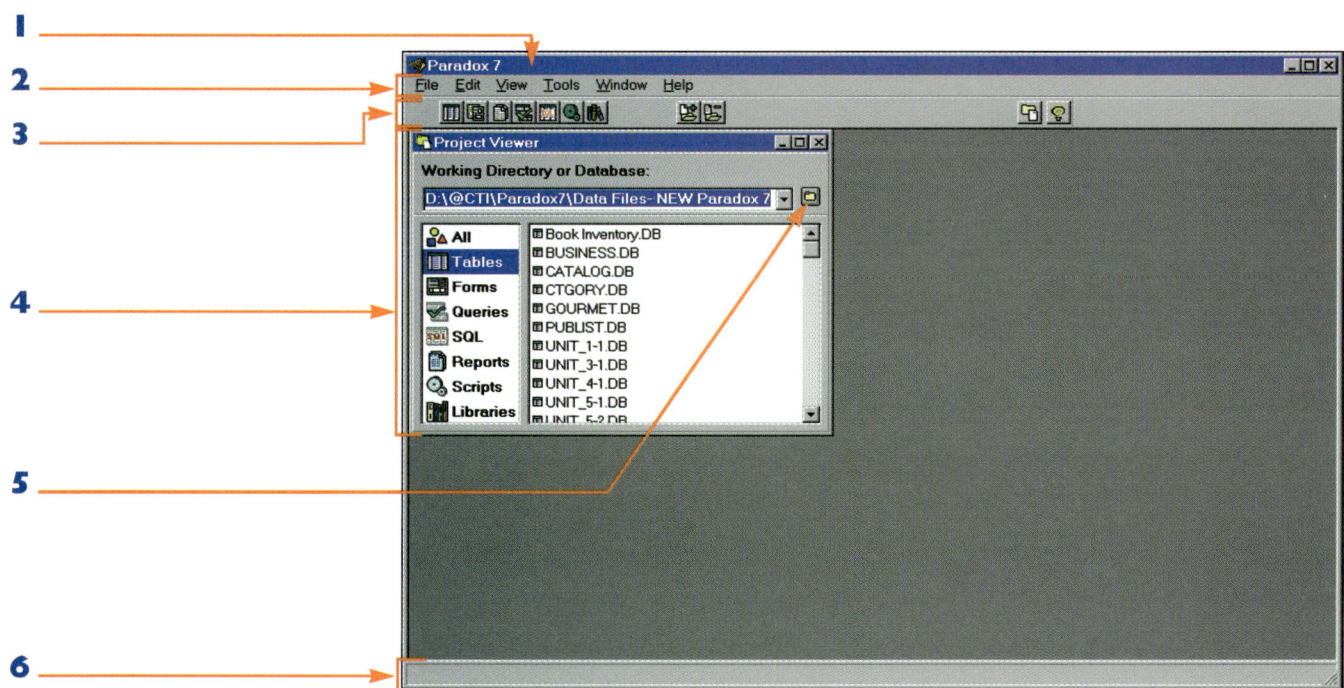

1
2
3
4
5
6

FIGURE 1-19

Match each statement with the term it describes.

7 An attribute of an entity

8 A collection of records

9 A set of buttons that give you quick access to Paradox commands

10 An entire set of field values for one entity

11 A screen area that displays useful information about the current action

12 The position of a record within a table

13 A characteristic of an object that you can change

a. Status bar

b. Record

c. Record number

d. Field name

e. Table

f. Property

g. Toolbar

Select the best answer from the list of choices.

14 To store and retrieve data quickly and efficiently, you should use a:

a. Spreadsheet

b. Word processor

c. Desktop publisher

d. Database management system

15 The purpose of the Project Viewer is to:

a. Plan projects

b. Manage Paradox files

c. Combine separate Paradox tables into one project

d. Automate the creation of project grids

16 It is important to set the working directory:

    a. Because Paradox won't let you create a table if you don't

    b. Because that's where Paradox keeps all its forms

    c. To make sure Paradox is working

    d. To help you organize your files

17 Buttons used as shortcuts for commands are contained in the:

    a. Title bar

    b. Menu bar

    c. Toolbar

    d. Status bar

18 To move the highlight to the next record, you would:

    a. Click File

    b. Click the Next Record button

    c. Click the Next Record Set button

    d. Click the Project Viewer button

19 When you click File on the menu bar, you see the:

    a. Table structure

    b. Project Viewer

    c. File menu

    d. Current file

20 The buttons on the toolbar:

    a. Offer shortcuts to common operations

    b. Are always the same

    c. Have options that can't be accessed from the main menu

    d. Are available only when you use the Project Viewer

21 As you move the mouse pointer over a button on a toolbar, the name of the button appears above or below and is called a:

    a. title bar

    b. ToolTip

    c. button description

    d. StatusTip

22 To display as much of a table as can fit in the Paradox window you:

    a. Maximize the table window

    b. Click Best Fit from the View menu

    c. Maximize the Paradox window

    d. Restore the table window

23 To display a listing of topics that you can search in Help you click:

    a. Contents

    b. Listing

    c. Back

    d. Index

SKILLSREVIEW

1 Launch Paradox 7 for Windows 95.

  a. Make sure your computer is on and Windows 95 is running.

  b. Click the Start button, point to Programs.

  c. Click Paradox 7, then Paradox 7 again, if necessary.

  d. Cancel the Startup Expert, if necessary.

2 View the Paradox screen.

  a. Click each option on the menu bar and look at the resulting menu.

  b. Pass the mouse pointer over the toolbar and read the descriptions in the status bar.

  c. Identify the types of files the Project Viewer displays by clicking All.

  d. Click on Tables, Forms, Queries, SQL, Reports, Scripts, and Libraries.

  e. Move the pointer over the icons and note the names in the status bar.

3 Set the working directory.

  a. Make sure the Project Viewer is open.

  b. Open the Directory Browser dialog box.

  c. Change to the common files directory, then close the Directory Browser dialog box.

  d. Open the Directory Browser dialog box.

  e. Close the Directory Browser dialog box.

  f. Change the directory to one that you have listed in the Directory Browser dialog box.

  g. Change the working directory back to A:, or the directory that contains your Student Disk.

4 Open a table and identify its elements.

  a. Make sure the Project Viewer is open and A: is the working directory.

  b. Open the Book Inventory table.

  c. Make a list of the objects that comprise the table, using Table 1-1 as your guide.

  d. Add to the list the new toolbar buttons that appear when you open a table.

  e. Maximize the Table window.

  f. Minimize the Table window.

  g. Size the window to fit your needs.

5 Explore table properties.

  a. Hold the mouse pointer on the border between two column headings until the pointer changes to a rectangular shape.

  b. Right-click the mouse to display the Properties dialog box for that heading.

  c. Click the General tab to display a color palette.

  d. Change the color to pink, click Apply.

  e. Change the color to gray, click Apply.

  f. Click OK.

6 Use a toolbar button.

  a. Make sure the Book Inventory table is on the screen.

  b. Use the Next Record button to move the highlight to the next record.

  c. Click the Previous Record button.

  d. Click the Next Record button.

  e. Click the Last Record button.

  f. Click the First Record button.

7 Practice using the Help system.

  a. Select User's Guide Topics from the Help main menu.

  b. Click the Index tab.

  c. Search for help on the Project Viewer.

  d. Read all the information you can about the Project Viewer.

  e. Note how to set Project Viewer preferences.

  f. Return to the Index by clicking the Index button.

  g. Close Help by clicking the Close button.

8 Exit Paradox.

  a. Open the File menu.

  b. Use the Exit option to exit Paradox.

  c. Launch Paradox again, by clicking Start, choosing Programs, clicking Paradox 7, then clicking Paradox 7 again, if necessary.

  d. Exit using the keyboard by pressing [Alt][F4].

  e. Launch Paradox.

  f. Exit using the mouse by clicking the Close button.

INDEPENDENT
CHALLENGE 1

Paradox provides online Help that explains procedures and gives you examples. Explore the User's Guide topics in Help by looking up all of the topics covered in this unit: launching Paradox, viewing the Paradox screen, setting the working directory, opening a table, exploring table properties using toolbars, getting Help, and exiting Paradox. List three additional pieces of information you learned from Help that you didn't learn in this unit.

INDEPENDENT
CHALLENGE 2

Database management software is widely used in almost every industry. Consider the following businesses and describe at least one table that might be used in each of them. Describe the purpose of the table, then list likely fields for each table.

- Travel office
- Art supply store
- Retail clothing store
- Web page consulting firm
- Construction contractor
- Grocery store
- Direct mail household catalog company
- Landscape architecture firm

UNIT 2

Building
A TABLE

Now that you are familiar with the Paradox Desktop and know how to use toolbars, you are ready to plan and create a table structure and then add data. A **table structure** is similar to a blank address book, which contains lines for fields such as name, address, and phone number. After you create the table structure, you can enter data into the table (just as you would enter your friends' addresses into a blank address book). When you create a table structure, you assign names to each field in the table and specify the type and amount of data you plan to store in each field. Once you create the table structure, you must save it before you actually enter data into the table. **case** Zora wants a table that can maintain an inventory of books in stock. Before she sits down at the computer, she determines what information she needs from the table.▶

Planning a table

It's important to know how you will use a table before you begin to build it. The time you spend planning will mean less time spent later redesigning and restructuring tables, and possibly deleting and reentering data. The first step is to clarify the purpose of the table. **case**   Zora uses the following guidelines to plan her book inventory table.

1   **Define the purpose of the table by getting input from people who use the data**
Before Zora goes any further, she conducts a brainstorming session with the clerks, bookkeepers, and management personnel. She asks them how they would ideally like to use the data concerning books and what some of the problems are with the current manual system. She also asks the users for any reports they need that deal with book inventory.

2   **Using this input, identify the specific type of information users need**
Based on her needs and the needs of the other users, Zora identifies six critical pieces of information for the table: ISBN (International Standard Book Code Number), title, author, category, price, and quantity sold. For example, Zora needs quick access to quantity and pricing information for each book in stock.

3   **Divide data into fields and estimate the size of the fields**
Each piece of information Zora needs to know about the books in her inventory is a separate field in the table. Some fields will contain names, and others will contain numbers (price and quantity). She will also create a field that contains a code identifying the book. She looks at her list of books and decides that the longest title contains 25 characters and the longest author's name contains 20 characters. The ISBN is always 13 characters, and the category field will contain only two characters. She doesn't have to worry about the sizes of the Price and Quantity fields, because Paradox will assign those automatically.

4   **Sketch the table structure**
Based on the input she has received and her own estimates, Zora sketches the design shown in Figure 2-1.

FIGURE 2-1: Table design for the book inventory table

Plan for the Book Alley Inventory Table

Field	Type	Size	Purpose
ISBN	Text	13	Uniquely indentifies books
Title	Text	25	Name of book
Author	Text	20	Name of author
Category	Text	2	Book category code
Price	Money		Retail price of book
Quantity	Number		Number in stock

QUICK **TIP**

Keep your table as simple as possible. Don't try to include all your information in one table. It's more efficient to divide the data among several tables. For example, there's no need to store an author's full name and address in the book inventory table, along with the book information. You can store that information in a separate author table in the database. Paradox allows you to retrieve the information from both tables when you need it.■

Creating a table

Now that you've planned the structure of the inventory table, you can create it. If you already had a similar table, you could use its structure as a basis for this one. See the related topic "Borrowing a table structure" for more information. ▶**case** Zora begins by creating a folder for her Paradox files and then setting her working directory.

1   **Launch Paradox, if it's not already running, and insert your Student Disk in drive A:**
    You might use a different drive, depending on your environment. Consult your instructor. You will save the Paradox files in a new folder.

2   **Click Tools on the menu bar, click Utilities, then click Add**
    You can use Paradox Tools to help you manage files and folders as well as database structures.

3   **Click the Look in list arrow, click 3½ Floppy (A:), click 🗀, then type My Paradox Files**
    The new folder is now named, as shown in Figure 2-2.

4   **Click OK, then click the Close button ⊠ in the dialog box**

5   **Set the working directory to the appropriate drive and folder**
    Now all your Paradox files will be saved to the same folder.

6   **If the Project Viewer isn't open, click the Open Project Viewer button 🗗 on the toolbar**
    Using the Project Viewer is the easiest way to open the dialog box that you use to create a new table structure.

7   **Right-click Tables on the left side of the Project Viewer**
    Right-clicking a table object displays two options: New and Open. If you wanted to open an existing table, you could click Open to display the table in the Table View window. In this case, though, you want to create a new table.

8   **Click New**
    The Create Table dialog box opens, as shown in Figure 2-3. You can specify a table type other than Paradox 7 in this dialog box. In this case, Zora wants to create a Paradox 7 table.

9   **Select Paradox 7, if necessary, then click OK**
    The Create Paradox 7 Table dialog box opens, as shown in Figure 2-4. Zora is ready to define the table structure.

**FIGURE 2-2:
Create My Paradox
Files folder**

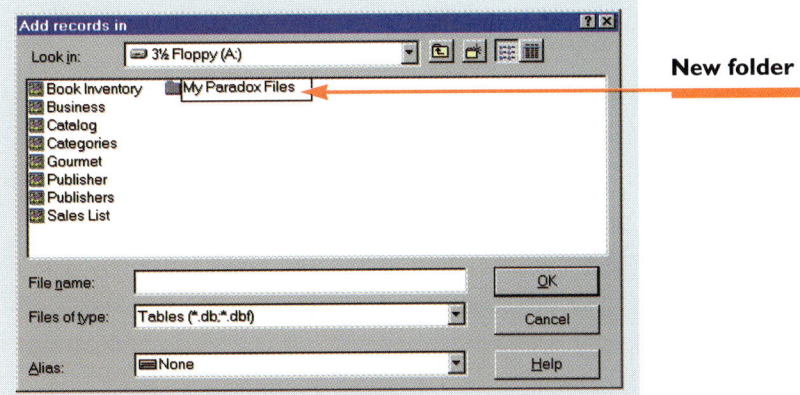

New folder

**FIGURE 2-3: Create
Table dialog box**

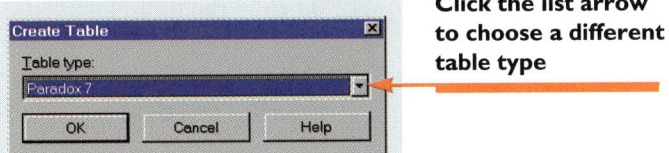

**Click the list arrow
to choose a different
table type**

**FIGURE 2-4: Create
Paradox 7 Table
dialog box**

Field roster

Borrow button

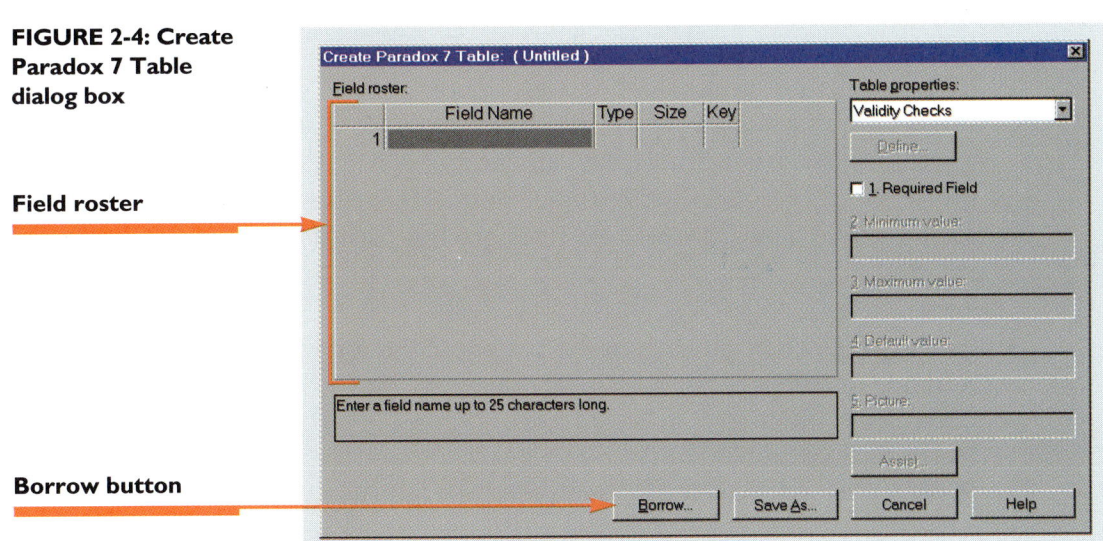

Borrowing a table structure

If you already have a table similar to the one you want to create, you can save time
by borrowing the structure of the existing table. In the Create Paradox 7 Table dialog box, click Borrow to open the Borrow Table Structure dialog box. Click the
table whose structure you want to borrow, then click OK. If the table you want isn't
shown in the Source Table list, change directories by clicking the Look in list
arrow. After you find the table whose structure you want to borrow, click Open to
return to the Create Paradox 7 Table dialog box.

Adding field names

The Create Paradox 7 Table dialog box is where you define the structure of the new table. The most important part of the Create Table dialog box is the **Field roster**, which is arranged in rows and columns. Each row defines one field in your table. Using the Field roster, you give each field a unique name, indicate what type of data you plan to enter into the field, and how many characters you want reserved for the data. To correct errors in the Field roster, see the related topic "Correcting mistakes in Field roster entries." **case**   The **field name** identifies the information you will store in the field. For example, the ISBN field will contain the International Standard Book Number. Table 2-1 lists the rules for naming fields in a Paradox table.

Following these rules, Zora enters the field names she created during her planning session.

1   Type **ISBN** in the first row of the Field Name column
The highlight indicates your current cursor position but it disappears when you begin to type the field name. Watch the bottom of the Field roster box for instructions on completing the current entry.

Now that you've entered the field name for the field that will contain the ISBN number, you can enter the field names for the remaining fields.

2   Press [↓]
A second row appears in the Field roster, with the cursor in the Field Name column. Your screen should look like Figure 2-5. Once you enter the first field in a new structure, you can no longer borrow the structure from another table. The Borrow button dims to show that the option is not available.

3   Type **Title**

4   Pressing [↓] to begin each new row, enter the following field names:
Author (in row 3)
Category (in row 4)
Price (in row 5)

5   Press [↓] for the last time, then type **Qty** in Row 6
Your screen should now look like Figure 2-6.

TABLE 2-1:
Rules for naming fields

TOPIC	RULE
Size	A field name can contain up to 25 characters
Capitalization	The first letter of a field name is automatically capitalized, even if you enter the field name in lowercase
Duplicates	Field names in a table must be unique; do not use a field name more than once in a table.
Spaces	A field name can include spaces, but not as the first character in the field name
Allowed characters	A field name can include almost any printable character, including letters, numbers, and keyboard symbols; the following characters should not be used, because they have special meanings to Paradox: [,] {, } (,) and (- or]); you can use the number sign (#) with other characters but not by itself

FIGURE 2-5: One field name entered

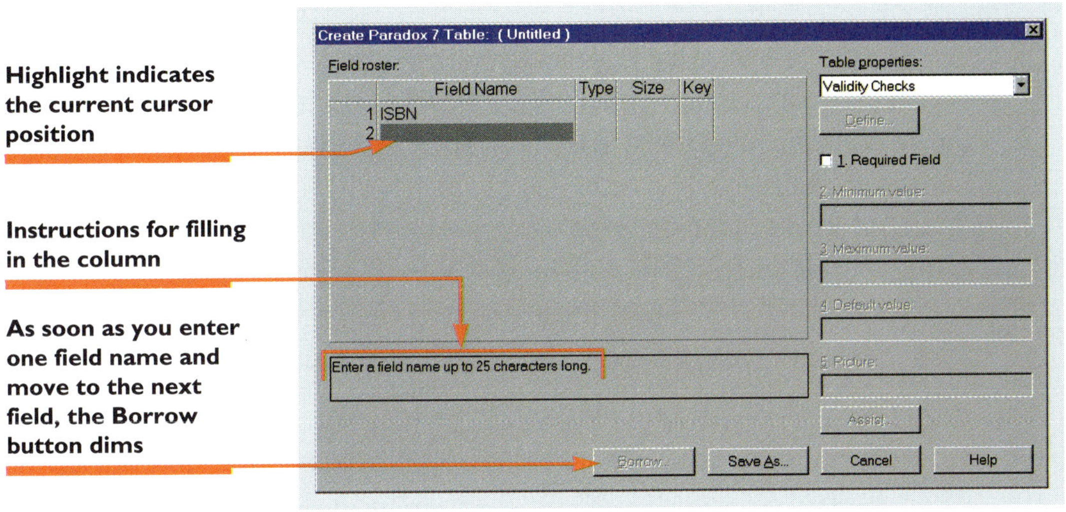

Highlight indicates the current cursor position

Instructions for filling in the column

As soon as you enter one field name and move to the next field, the Borrow button dims

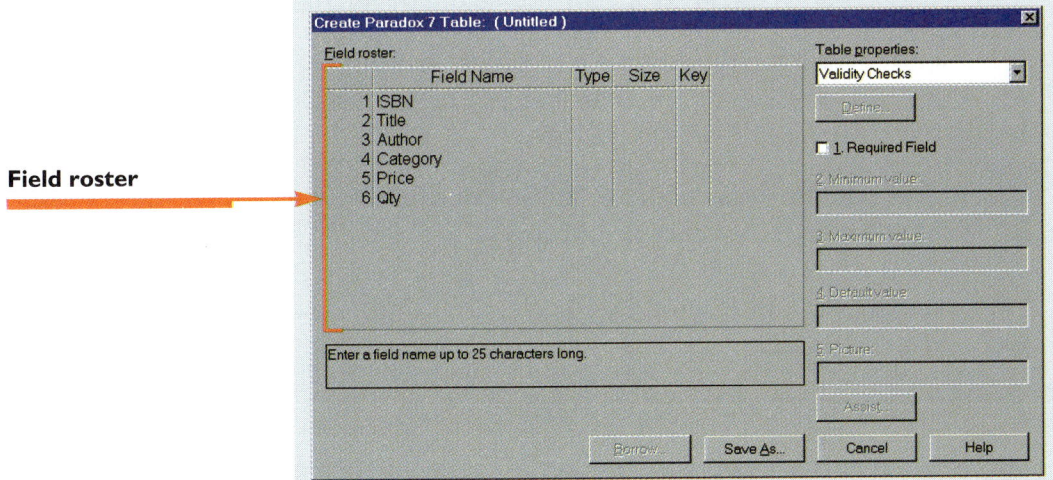

FIGURE 2-6: Six field names entered

Field roster

Correcting mistakes in Field roster entries

If you make a mistake in the Field roster, click the entry containing the mistake and type the correct entry. If you want to change only part of an entry, double-click instead. This places an insertion point in the entry. Use the mouse or arrow keys to move to the position you want, and add or delete text as necessary. To delete an entire field from the roster, click anywhere in that field's row, then press [Ctrl][Del].

Specifying field type, size, and key

Now that you've entered the field names, you can specify a type and size for each field in the table. As shown in Table 2-2, a **field type** indicates the intended use for the information stored in the field. The **field size** defines the maximum number of characters you expect to store in each field. Specifying field size is important because if the size is too small, you won't be able to enter complete data whereas if you specify more than you need, you waste disk space. ▶**case** Zora begins with the ISBN field. Because she can't remember the exact name of the field type she wants, she decides to choose it from a context-sensitive menu.

1   Click in the **first row** of the Type column, then right-click
    A menu opens, as shown in Figure 2-7. The ISBN field will contain characters (numbers and dashes), so Alpha is the appropriate field type. Notice that the "A" in Alpha is underlined.

2   Click **Alpha**
    An "A" (the underlined letter from the menu) appears in the first row of the Type column, indicating that the ISBN field is an Alpha field. For the remaining Alpha fields, Zora will simply type the letter "A."

3   Press [↓] and type **A** to specify the field type for the Title field

4   Repeat Step 3 for the Author and Category fields
    Next, Zora specifies the field type for the Price field. Because she doesn't know which letter or symbol to type, she right-clicks the field type.

5   Right-click the **Type column** in the Price field row to display the context-sensitive menu, then click **$ (Money)**
    Making the Price column a Money field ensures that the numbers stored in this field will appear as currency, with a dollar sign and two decimal places. Unlike Alpha fields, Money fields can be used in calculations.

    Next Zora specifies the field type for the Qty field.

6   Right-click the **Type column** in the Qty field, then click **Number**
    Because Zora has specified the correct field types for the Price and Qty fields, she will be able to use the data stored in those fields for various calculations. For example, she could multiply the quantity of books sold by the price to calculate a total sale value for a particular title.

    Your screen should look like Figure 2-8.

FIGURE 2-7:
Context-sensitive
menu for Type

Instead of choosing
from the menu, you
can type the under-
lined letter or symbol

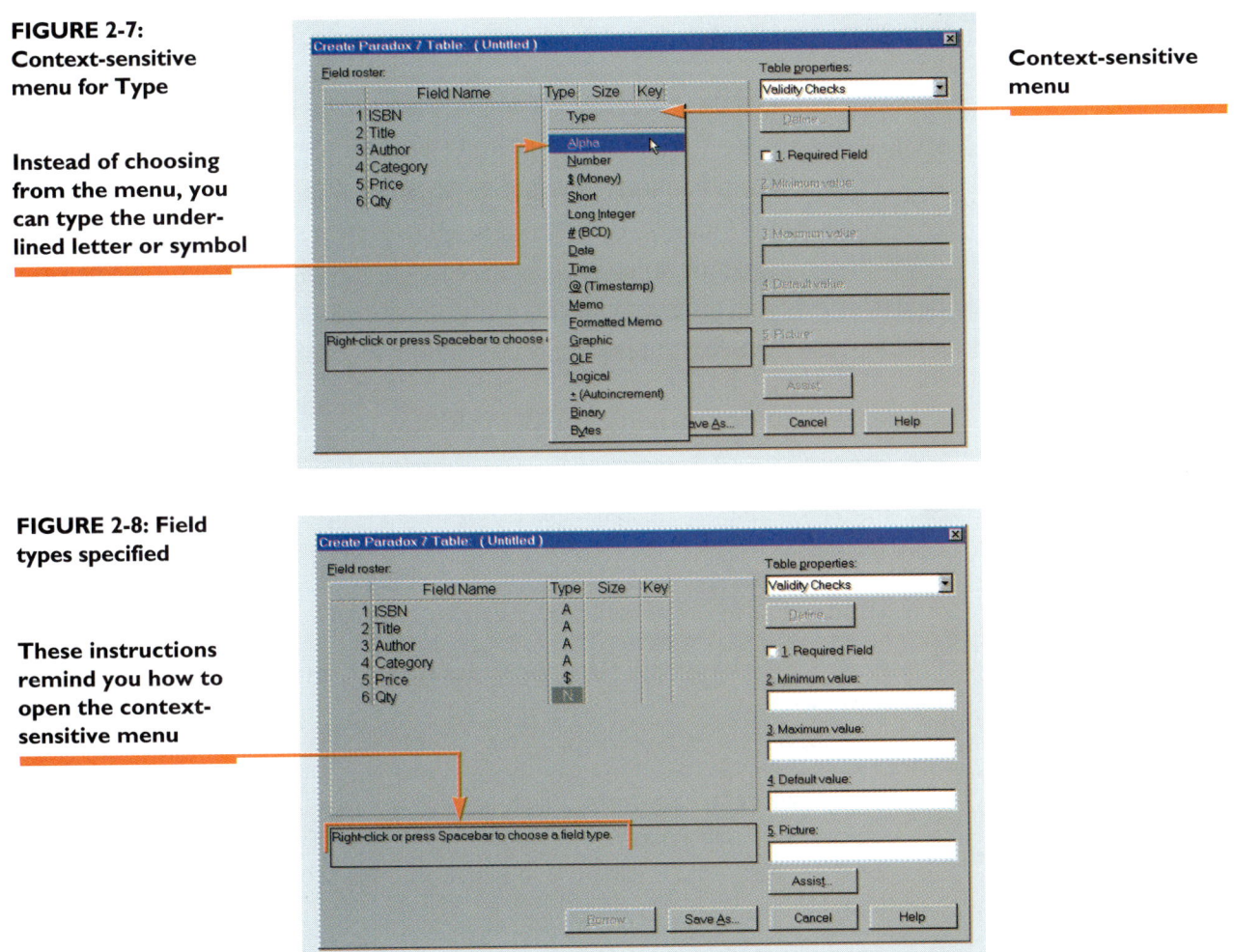

Context-sensitive
menu

FIGURE 2-8: Field
types specified

These instructions
remind you how to
open the context-
sensitive menu

TABLE 2-2: Common field types

FIELD TYPE	PURPOSE	RULES FOR DATA STORED IN THIS FIELD TYPE
Alpha	Names, titles, ZIP codes, any text or numbers that won't be used in calculations	Any combination of letters and numbers, up to 255 characters
Number	Numbers that will be used in calculations	Only numbers, commas, a minus sign, and a decimal point
Money	Values stored in a Money field are displayed with a dollar sign and two decimal places	Same as Number field
Date	Dates that include the day, month, and year	Any valid date (including BC dates) through December 31, 9999
Memo	Any text that won't fit in an Alpha field	Any characters; size is limited only by available disk space
Graphic	Any graphic image (scanned photographs, clip art, charts, etc.)	Any object or image that can be pasted from the Windows Clipboard

Specifying field type, size, and key continued

Specify sizes for all the Alpha fields now. Each record in a table must be unique in some way. You can ensure uniqueness by assigning a **key**. The key might be a single field or a combination of fields. See the related topic "Creating a composite key" for more information. The key is also called a **primary index** because it determines the order in which records are stored in the table. You indicate the key field by entering an asterisk in the Key column for that field. When you begin entering data, Paradox will not allow you to enter duplicate data into the key field.

7 Click the **Size column** in the ISBN field row

8 Type **13**

Field size is not the same as column width. Field size refers to how much data can be entered while column width refers to display only.

Zora has determined the size of the Alpha fields based on her knowledge of the business.

9 Pressing **[↓]** add the field sizes for Title, Author, and Category, as shown in Figure 2-9

Next Zora enters the size of the Price field.

10 Click the **Size column** in the Price field row, then look at the message area below the Field roster

The message ,"Field Size is not allowed for this field type," tells you that you can't specify a size for a Money field.

11 Click the **Size column** in the Qty field row, then look at the message area below the Field roster

As you can see, Paradox determines the sizes of both Number and Money fields. Your screen should look like Figure 2-9.

Zora is now ready to identify the key field.

12 Click the **Key column** in the ISBN field row

You can press any character to set or remove a key.

13 Press **[Spacebar]**

An asterisk appears in the Key column, as shown in Figure 2-10. The key field must be the first field in the Field roster. Zora has completed defining the table structure and is ready to save it.

FIGURE 2-9: Field sizes defined

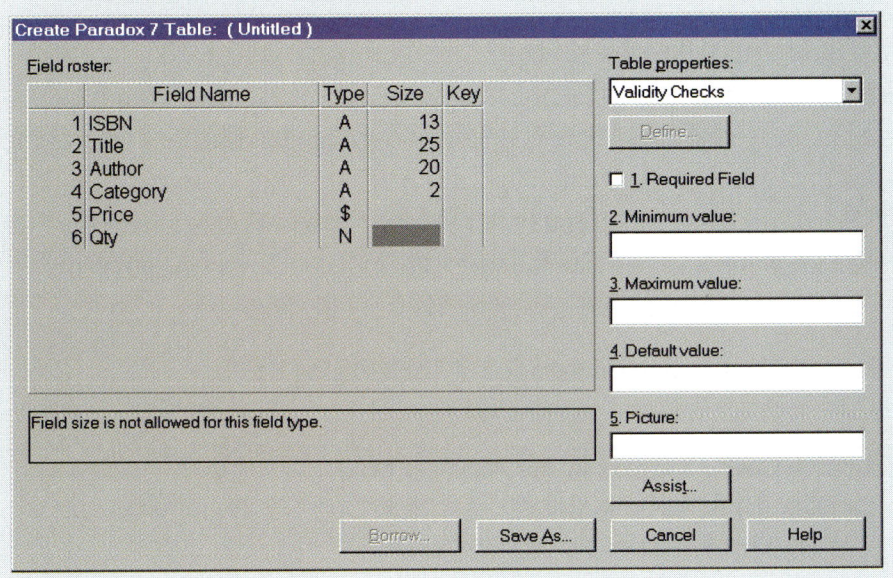

FIGURE 2-10: ISBN field is the key field

Asterisk indicates
a key field

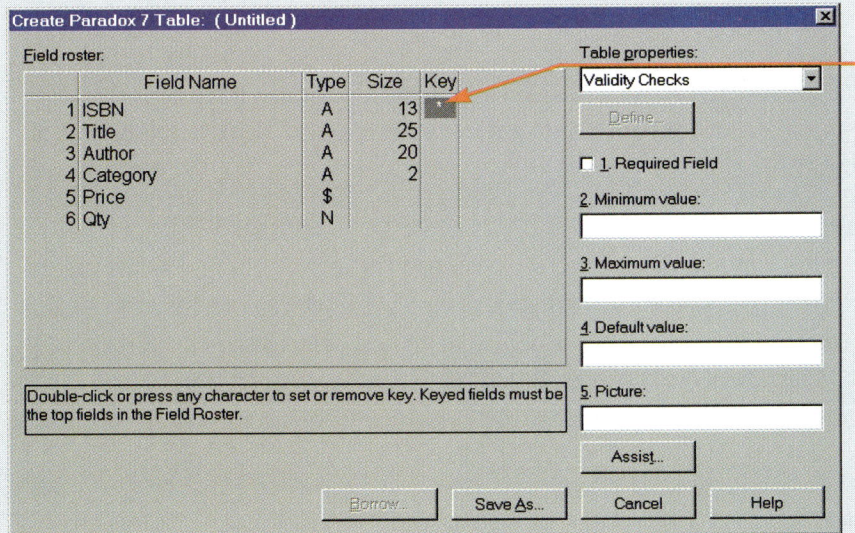

Creating a composite key

In a table that doesn't have a naturally unique field like the ISBN in Zora's table, you can create a key by combining two or more fields. For example, in a list of major customers, Zora might have more than one customer named Jones. In this case, she could combine the last name with the first name and middle initial to create a **composite key** that *will* be unique. The only restriction is that the fields used in the composite key must be the first ones listed in the Field roster.

TROUBLE?

If you accidentally press [↓] and add a new field to the Field roster when you have no more fields to add, you can simply press [↑] and the blank field row disappears.■

QUICK **TIP**

You can also enter all the information for one field at once by pressing [Tab] to move across the row. Then press [↓] to move down to the next field.■

Saving a table structure

Once you have created the table structure, you must name and save it before you can begin to enter data. The difference between the Save and Save As commands is explained in the related topic "Save and Save As commands." Choose a table name that is descriptive and remember that the table name can include spaces. Paradox will add the .db file extension. If you have made any errors or omissions in the roster, Paradox will not let you save the structure until you correct the problem. ▶**case** Zora decides to name her new table "Books at the Book Alley."

1 Click **Save As** in the Create Paradox 7 Table dialog box
The Save Table As dialog box opens, as shown in Figure 2-11.

2 Make sure **WORK:** appears in the Alias list box
This indicates that the file will be saved to your working directory. (Recall that you set your working directory before you created the table structure.)

3 Type **Books at the Book Alley** in the File name text box
You don't have to add a file extension because Paradox automatically adds a .db extension to all table filenames. The saved file will contain an empty structure with no data.

4 Click the **Display Table check box** in the Options section of the dialog box
This tells Paradox to display the table as soon as you save its structure. If you don't check this box, the structure is saved, but you have to perform an extra step to open the table before you can enter data.

5 Click **Save**
The Books at the Book Alley.db table opens, as shown in Figure 2-12. The field names you entered in the Field roster appear across the top of the table. If you can't see a field it's because there isn't enough room on the screen to display all the fields. The message in the status bar indicates that the new table contains no records yet.

FIGURE 2-11: Save
Table As dialog box

Working directory
you selected earlier

Enter the table
name here

Make sure this box
is checked

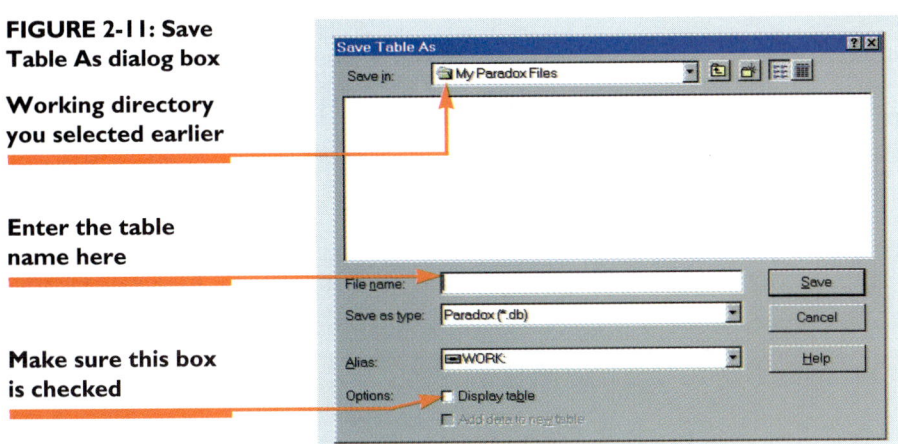

FIGURE 2-12: Books at
the Book Alley table

Table name appears in
the document window
title bar

There are no records
because you haven't
entered any data yet

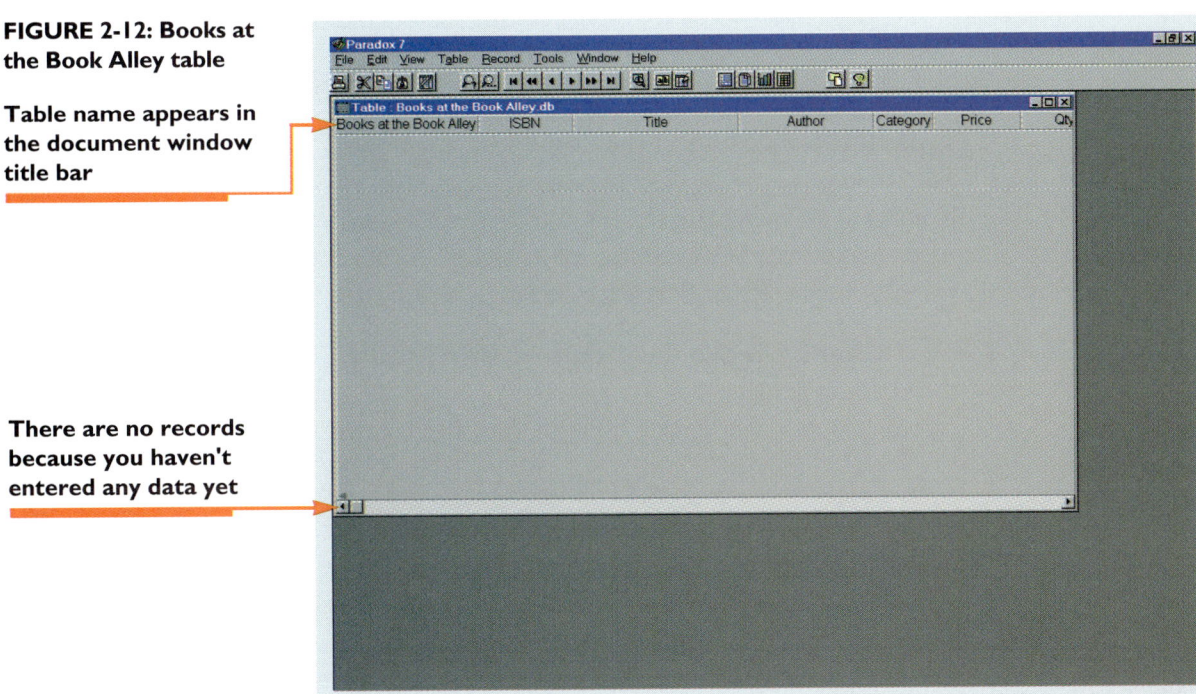

Save and Save As commands

You use the Save command to save a file with its existing filename, and you use the
Save As command to save a copy of the file with a different filename or when you
save a new table.

TROUBLE?

If you did not set
the correct working
directory before you
created the table
structure, you can
save your file to a
different directory
by clicking the Drive
(or Alias) arrow and
choosing a new
directory.■

Adding records

Adding new records to a table is a simple matter of moving from field to field and typing the data in each field. When you first open a table, Paradox protects the data by allowing you to view the data only. If you want to make any modifications to the table data, such as add new records or change existing data, you must switch to Edit mode. When you finish editing the data, you switch back to table view and all the changes are saved to your disk. **case** Zora just received a book shipment, and she needs to add seven new records to her book inventory table.

1 Click the **Edit Data button** 🖻 on the toolbar, then maximize the screen
The word "Edit" appears in the status bar, indicating that Paradox is in Edit mode. To learn more about the "Locked" message that also appears in the status bar, see the related topic "Locked records." Keep in mind that you cannot use Edit to modify the table structure, only the data stored in the table. To add a new record, you must first move to the last record in the table.

2 Type **0-441-02269-1** in the ISBN field, then press **[Tab]** to move to the Title field
If you make a mistake typing the data, you can correct it while you are still in the field. Simply use the Backspace or Delete keys to delete a mistake, then type the correction. In the next lesson, you will learn how to correct data in table records after you have moved to another field.

3 Type **Chaos Died** in the Title field, then press **[Tab]** again to move to the Author field
Zora continues entering the data, using the Tab key to move between fields.

4 Type **Russ** in the Author field, type **SF** in the Category field, type **3.95** in the Price field, then type **1** in the Qty field
You do not need to type a dollar sign when entering the price because Paradox automatically supplies it for a money field. You will also notice that the Qty field shows values with two decimal places, for example 1.00, when they should be integers. Paradox automatically formats numeric fields with two decimal places. Zora changes the Qty field property in the next lesson.

5 Press **[↓]** to complete the entry in the Qty field
A blank row appears, ready for you to enter another new record. Compare your screen to Figure 2-13.

FIGURE 2-13: One record entered

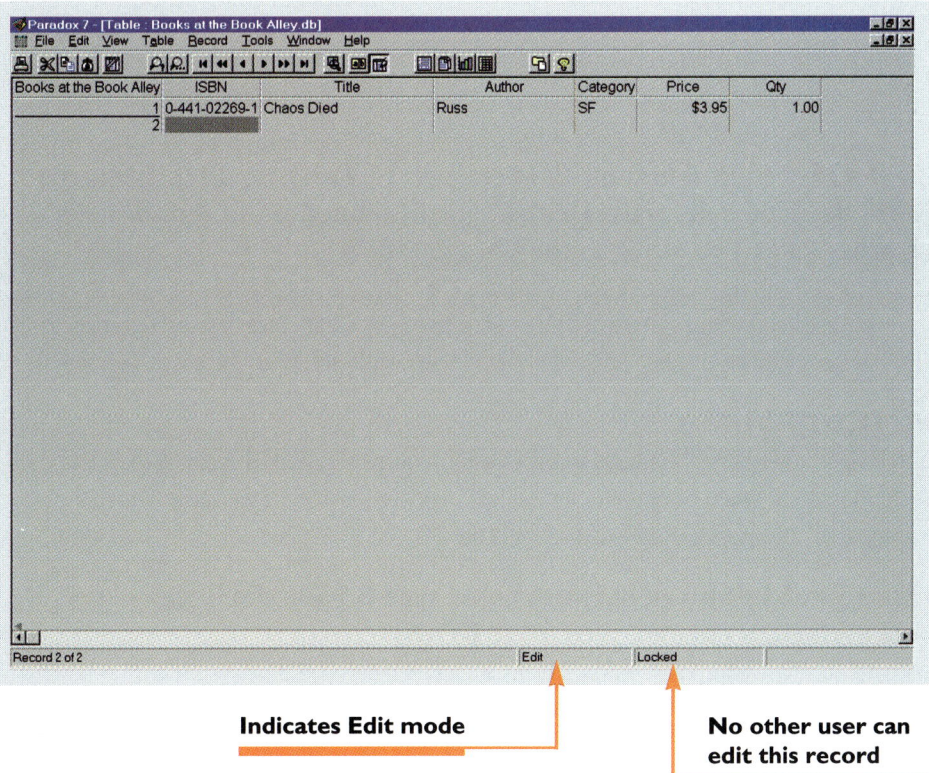

Indicates Edit mode

No other user can edit this record

TROUBLE?

If you notice errors after you've left a field, you can cancel all changes to the current record by clicking Edit on the menu bar, then clicking Undo. This cancels any changes that have been made in any field in the record. If you were creating a new record, the entire record is deleted. If you want to change only a portion of a record, use one of the editing techniques described in the next lesson.■

QUICK TIP

You can also press [F9] to toggle between Edit mode and table view.■

Locked records

When you are editing a record, you will see the word "Locked" in the status bar. Paradox automatically makes a record unavailable to another user (locks it) when you are editing a record. This is to protect records against more than one simultaneous update, creating unpredictable results. For example, if bank records weren't locked for update, money could be posted and withdrawn at the same moment, with the possibility of erroneous end results. When you leave the record, Paradox posts the changes (saves to disk) and unlocks the record making it available to another user.

Adding records, continued

6 Type **0-425-07895-0** in the ISBN field, press **[Tab]**, type **Hellstrom's Hive** in the Title field, press **[Tab]**, type **Herbert** in the Author field, then press **[Tab]** to move to the Category field

This book belongs in the Science Fiction Category (SF). Because the record immediately above is in the same category, you can use a shortcut key to copy the data into the new record. Once again, you need to press one key, and then hold it down while you press the other.

7 Press **[Ctrl][D]**

The code SF is automatically entered in the Category column. [Ctrl][D] is called the **Ditto key** combination. When the data for a new field matches the data in the same field in the previous record, use [Ctrl][D] to avoid retyping data.

8 Pressing **[Tab]** to move between fields, type **8.95** in the Price column, type **2** in the Qty column, then press **[Tab]**

The second record is added and automatically sorted by ISBN. Compare your screen to Figure 2-14. Zora is ready to continue entering records.

9 Pressing **[Tab]** to move between fields enter the following data describing books, do *not* press **[Tab]** after the last record

0-671-88448-4	Mama	McMillan	FN	5.99	3
0-938190-64-4	Healing with Whole Foods	Pitchford	HN	24.95	2
0-553-07245-5	Long Quiet Highway	Goldberg	LT	19.95	5
0-8195-6011-1	Centering	Richards	RM	13.95	3
0-2767-1791-1	Jules and Jim	Truffaut	TH	10.95	1

Now that you've finished entering the new records, you should exit Edit mode. That way you won't accidentally make other changes to the table as you scroll through the records.

10 Click the **Edit Data button** 🖼 on the toolbar to exit the Edit mode, then scroll left until you see the record number column

When you exit Edit mode, you see the message in the status bar: "Record has been posted." This means that Paradox has saved the changes to your disk. Compare your screen to Figure 2-15.

FIGURE 2-14: Two records entered

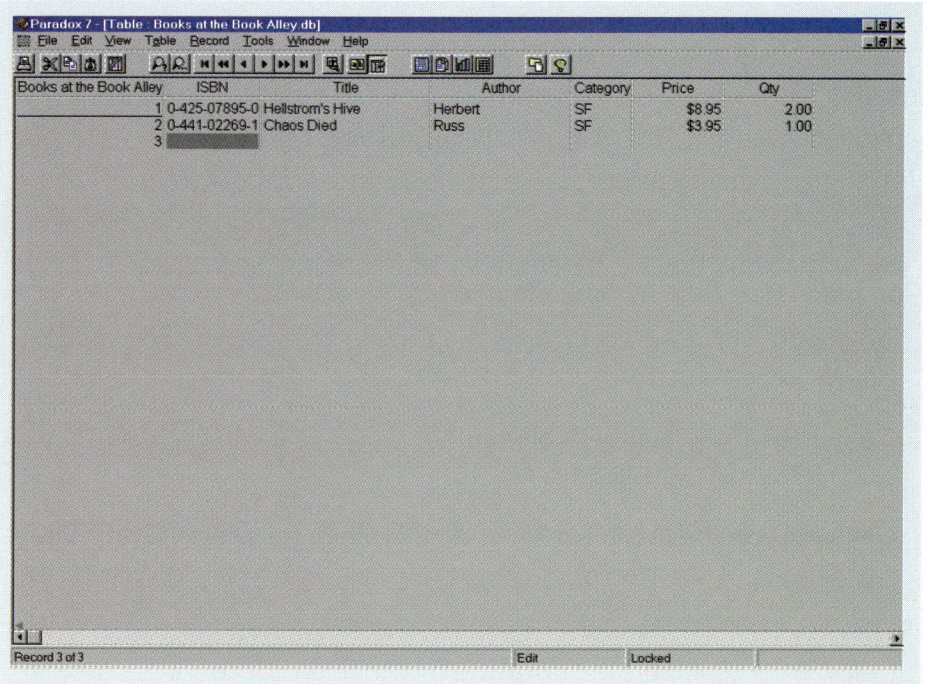

FIGURE 2-15: Seven records entered

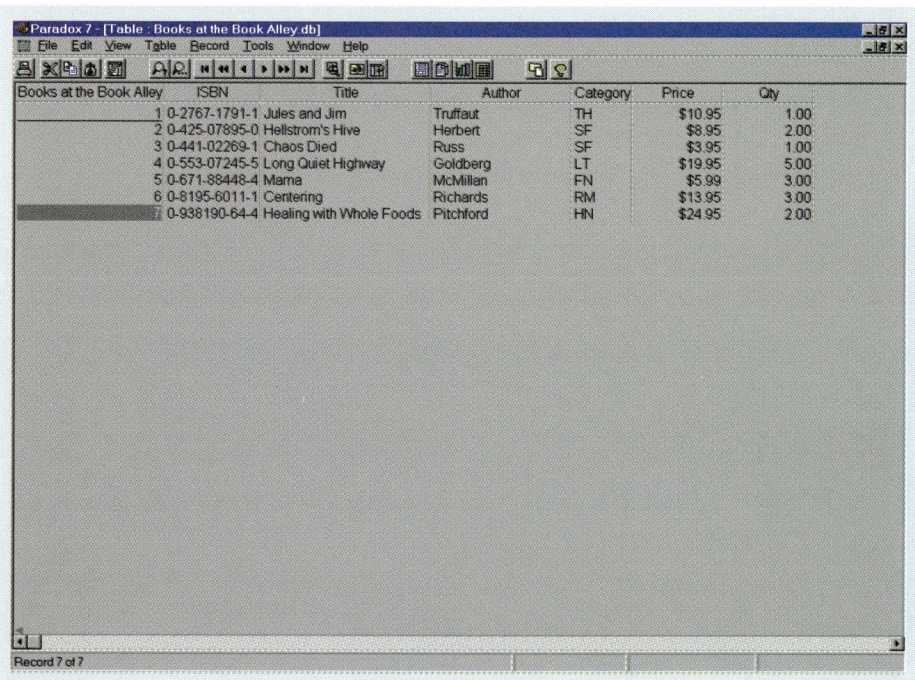

Editing records

You can delete entire records that are no longer needed from your table. But keep in mind that once you delete a record, there is no way to recover it. For more information about canceling edits, see the related topic "Using Undo." When you delete a record, Paradox moves the records below it up to close the gap. ▶case Zora just found out that *Centering* is out of print and there are no copies on the shelves, so she wants to delete its record from the book inventory table.

1 Click the **Edit Data button** 🖼 on the toolbar to switch to Edit mode
   The status bar indicates that the Edit mode is active.

2 Click **6** in the record number column
   The record for *Centering* is the current record.

3 Click **Record** on the menu bar, then click **Delete** (or press **[Ctrl][Del]**)
   The record is deleted, as shown in Figure 2-16. Notice the number of records remaining in the table. Zora realizes that a title is misspelled.

4 In the Title column find **Jules and Jim** and double-click to select **and**, then type **et**
   You can edit any field by simply clicking the field and typing. Now Zora wants to change the way Qty is displayed. It should be an integer because books don't exist as fractions.

5 Move the cursor to any value in the Qty field, right-click the mouse, click **Properties**, then click the **Format tab**

6 In the Format list box, click **Integer**, then click **OK**
   The Qty field data is now displayed as integers, as shown in Figure 2-17, although this doesn't affect the way it prints. Zora is satisfied with the table now and is ready to print it.

FIGURE 2-16: Table
with *Centering* deleted

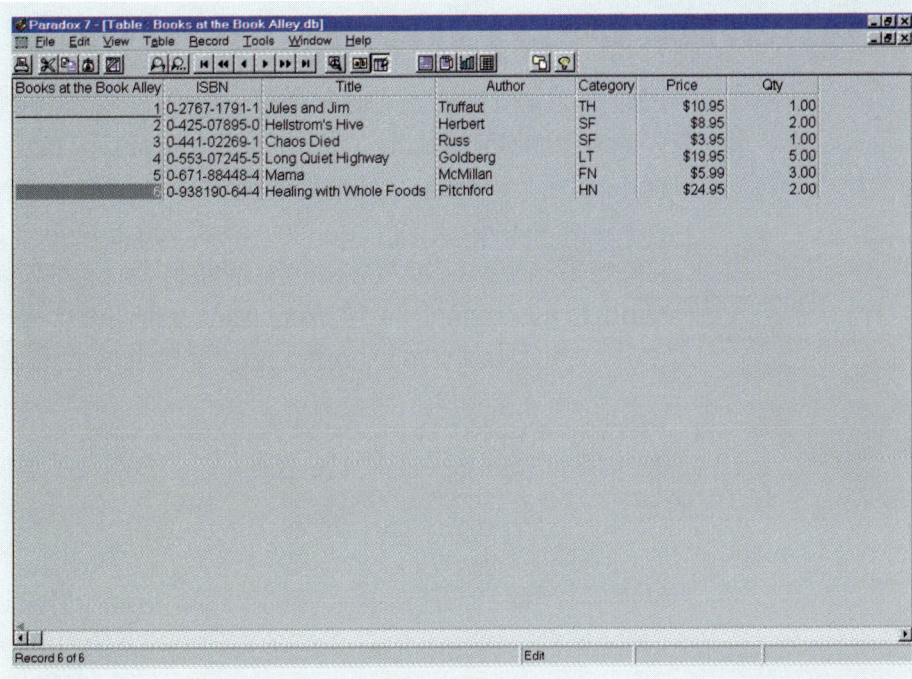

FIGURE 2-17:
Corrections made to
Books at the Book
Alley table

Edit mode

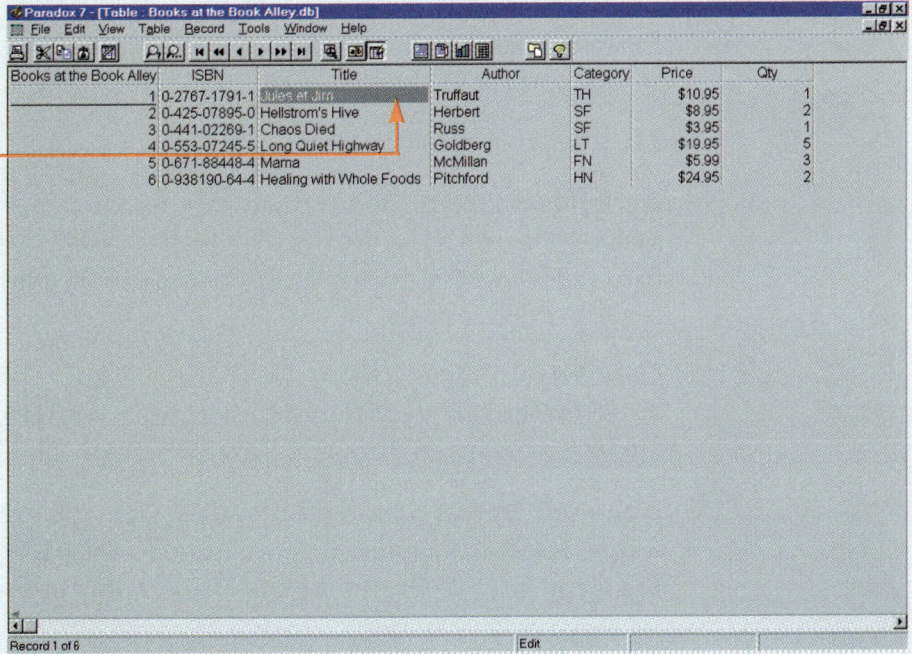

Using Undo

You can use the undo feature to reverse all changes to fields in the current record. Because Paradox updates data as soon as you move off a record, you must use Undo before you leave the record. To discard changes to a single field, press [Esc] before you leave the field. Paradox restores the original contents of the field. But remember, you cannot use undo to retrieve a record you have deleted. Once you delete a record in a Paradox table, there is no way to get it back except to enter it again.

Printing and copying a table

It's a good idea to print a table after you complete data additions and changes so you can double-check the information. The printed table is known as a **report,** and in this lesson you'll print your table using a default report format. It's also a good idea to make a copy of a table when you print it, so that you have a copy in reserve. That way, when you edit the table in the future you will always be able to return to the original. **case** Zora wants a printed copy of the table so she can review it and show it to her colleagues for their comments.

STEPS

1   Make sure Books at the Book Alley.db is open
The table you want to print must be open.

2   Click the **Print button** 🖫 on the toolbar
This opens the Print File dialog box shown in Figure 2-18. The default setting, All, prints the entire table. The 1 setting in the Copies box prints one copy. The Overflow handling options refer to treating data that won't fit on the standard page. For now, accept the default settings by clicking OK.

3   Click **OK** to print the entire table
Paradox prints the table in a default report format, as shown in Figure 2-19. For more information about printing a wider table, see the related topic "Printing in landscape orientation."

Zora is happy with her printed table.

4   Click **File** on the menu bar, then click **Close**
A dialog box appears noting that view properties have changed and asking if you want to save them. Paradox is noting that you changed the display of Qty data to integer format. Because this is useful, save the properties.

5   Click **Yes**
The Books at the Book Alley table closes and you return to the maximized Project Viewer window. Next Zora makes a copy of her table as a backup.

6   Right-click **Books at the Book Alley** from the Project Viewer, click **Copy,** select the appropriate drive and folder from the Save in list box, then type **COPY-Books at the Book Alley** in the File name box
Compare your screen to Figure 2-20.

7   Click **Copy**
Now there are two copies of the same table so next time you edit the Books at the Book Alley table, you can return to the original if you need to. Before leaving her desk, Zora exits Paradox.

8   Click **File** on the menu bar, then click **Exit**
Paradox closes.

FIGURE 2-18: Print File dialog box

Your printer might be different

Default options will print 1 copy of the entire table

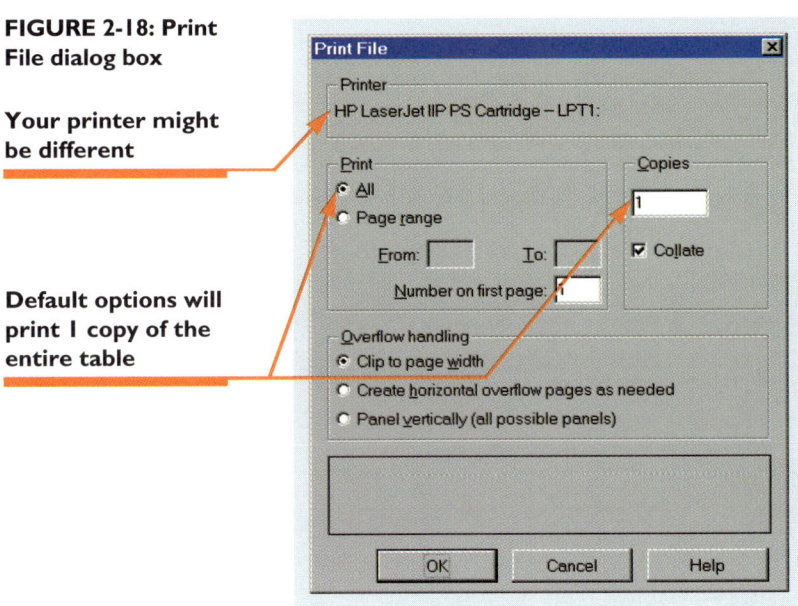

FIGURE 2-19: Books at the Book Alley printout

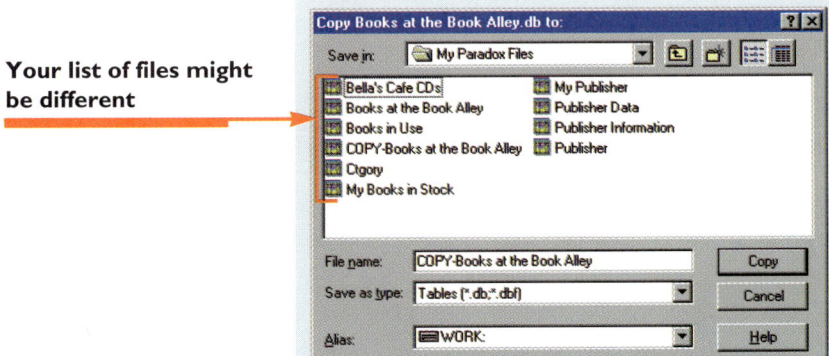

ISBN	Title	Author	Category	Price	Qty
0-2767-1791-1	Jules et Jim	Truffaut	TH	$10.95	1.00
0-425-07895-0	Hellstrom's Hive	Herbert	SF	$8.95	2.00
0-441-02269-1	Chaos Died	Russ	SF	$3.95	1.00
0-553-07245-5	Long Quiet Highway	Goldberg	LT	$19.95	5.00
0-671-88448-4	Mama	McMillan	FN	$5.99	3.00
0-938190-64-4	Healing with Whole Foods	Pitchford	HN	$24.95	2.00

FIGURE 2-20: Copy dialog box

Your list of files might be different

QUICK TIP

Because a Paradox table often includes several related files, always use Paradox's Copy command because it copies all the related files.■

QUICK TIP

The Project Viewer window remains maximized after you close a maximized table.■

Printing in landscape orientation

If the table is wide you might want to print it in landscape orientation. To do this, click Print from the main menu, click Printer Setup, then click the Modify Printer Setup button. In the Properties dialog box click the Paper tab to put it foremost, then click the Landscape radio button in the Orientation area. Click OK twice to return to the table and then print as usual.

TASKREFERENCE

TASK	MOUSE/BUTTON	MENU	KEYBOARD
Assign a key			Double-click in key field or press any character to set or remove asterisk
Copy table with data	Right-click name in Project Viewer, click Copy, type in new name, then click Copy	Click Tools, click Utilities, click Copy, select table to copy, click OK, type new table name, then click Copy	
Create new folder		Click Tools, click Utilities, click Add, click the New Folder button 📁.	
Edit records	Click 📇	Click Table, then click Edit Data	[F9]
Print a table	Click 🖨	Click File, then click Print	[Alt] [F4]
Save a table structure	Click Save As in Create Paradox 7 Table dialog box		
Specify field type	Right-click Type field for context-sensitive menu		

CONCEPTSREVIEW

Describe the purpose of each of the elements of the Create Paradox 7 Table dialog box shown in Figure 2-21.

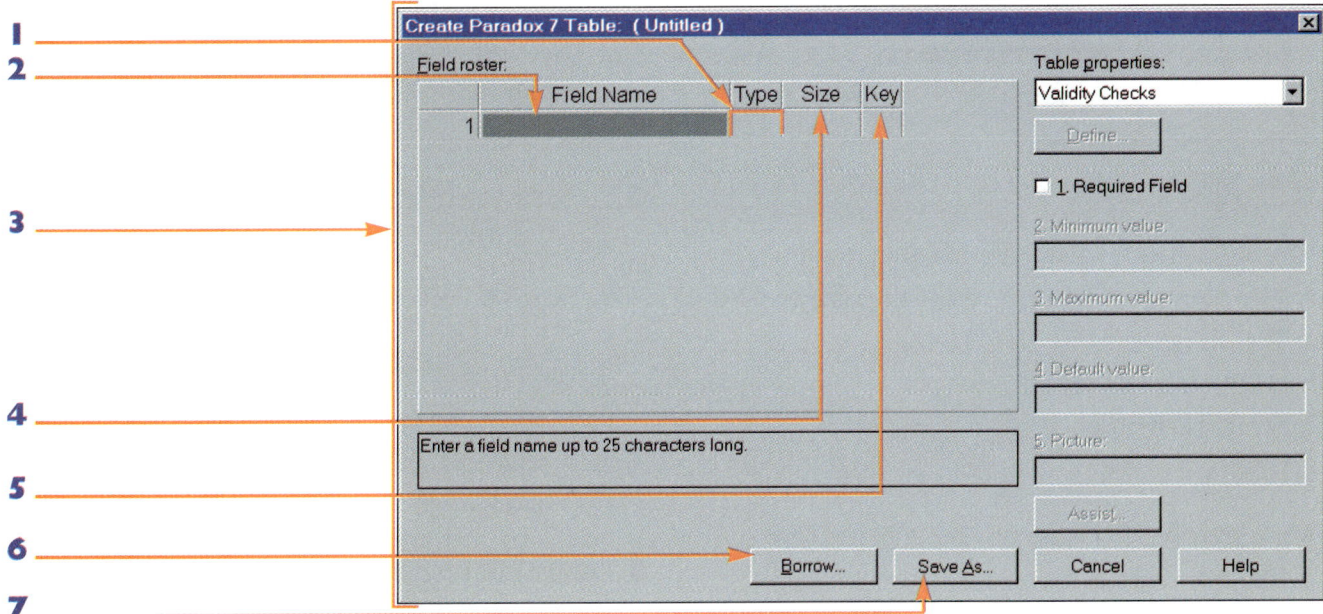

FIGURE 2-21

Match each of the following terms with the statement that describes its function.

8 Ensures that each record is unique

9 Lists all the fields in a table's structure

10 Identifies the information in a field

11 Can't be used in calculations

12 Opens a table after the structure is saved

13 Required before you can enter data into a table

14 Mode for adding new records

a. Alpha field

b. Field name

c. Table structure

d. Edit mode

e. Field roster

f. Display table check box

g. Key field

Select the best answer from the list of choices.

15 The first step in planning a table is to

   a. Decide who is going to use the table

   b. Determine what you want out of the table

   c. Figure the maximum number of characters in each field

   d. Settle on a name for the table

16 Context-sensitive is

   a. A feature that lets you view the type and size for any field

   b. A menu that displays choices relevant to the object when you right-click the object

   c. A separate utility program that automates the process of creating tables

   d. A feature that lets you zoom in on an object and magnify it

17 Money and Number fields

    a. Are limited to 100 characters

    b. Can contain numbers and dollar signs

    c. Can be used in calculations

    d. Have nothing in common

18 When you right-click Tables in the Project Viewer window, you will see

    a. A list of table files in the working directory

    b. The Directory Browser dialog box

    c. The context-sensitive menu

    d. The Table Type dialog box

19 What do you have to do before you add a new record?

    a. Make sure you have all the correct data, because it's difficult to go back later and change it

    b. Plan the field structure

    c. Switch to Edit mode

    d. Switch to field view

20 Which key or keys do you press to move to the next field?

    a. [Tab] is the only key you can use

    b. [Spacebar] and [Tab] both work

    c. [Spacebar] and [Enter] both work

    d. [Tab] and [Enter] both work

21 What does the Ditto key, [Ctrl][D], do?

    a. Copies all of the data from the previous record into a new record

    b. Copies data from the previous field into the same field in a new record

    c. Makes a copy of your table

    d. Appends data from one table into another table

SKILLSREVIEW

1 Plan a table that will maintain an accurate accounting of the balance in your checking account.

    a. Decide on the type and size for the following fields: check or deposit number, description, check amount, deposit amount, and balance.

    b. Sketch the table structure.

    c. Mark check or deposit number as the key field on your sketch.

    d. Explain why you chose that field as the key.

2 Create the table structure.

    a. Launch Paradox, if necessary.

    b. Set your working directory, if necessary, then open the Create Paradox 7 Table dialog box.

    c. Enter the necessary field names.

    d. Specify the field type for each field.

    e. Specify the field size for each field.

    f. Assign a key field.

3 Save the table structure.

    a. Click Save As in the Create Paradox 7 Table dialog box.

    b. Make sure you have selected the proper directory.

    c. Type "Home checking" in the File name text box.

    d. Click Display table check box.

    e. Click Save and view the empty table structure in the Table View window.

4 Add records.

    a. Click the Edit Data button.

    b. Enter your checks for the last month, using [Tab] to move between fields. Add at least 6 records. Don't worry about spelling errors.

    c. Use the Ditto key, [Ctrl][D], whenever you can.

5 Edit records.

  a. Review the check records and make corrections where appropriate.

  b. To edit a single word or letter, double-click the word or letter.

  c. To correct a field by retyping it completely, click the field once and type.

  d. Look at the format of the fields and if you need to change a number format, right-click the field, click Properties, click Format, choose the format from the format list, then click OK.

6 Print and copy a table.

  a. Make sure the Home checking table is open.

  b. Click the Print button on the toolbar.

  c. Click OK to print the entire table.

  d. Click File on the menu bar, then click Close.

  e. Click Home checking in the Project Viewer.

  f. Right-click Home checking, click Copy.

  g. Select My Paradox Files from the Save in list.

  h. Type COPY Home checking, then click Copy.

  i. Click File on the menu bar, then click Exit.

INDEPENDENT
CHALLENGE 1

Marcia Famiglia of Famiglia's Pasta Store wants you to help keep track of her pasta inventory. You suggest creating a table that will include the pasta brands, types, prices, and number of units in stock. Plan and design a table structure. Create the table, name it Famiglia's Pasta, add one record and print the table. Be prepared to turn in your design sketch.

To complete this independent challenge:

1 List the fields that should be included in the Famiglia's Pasta table.

2 Estimate the maximum number of characters for each field.

3 Identify the field type for each field. Make sure that all fields that will be used in calculations are either Number or Money fields.

4 Draw a sketch of your table design, including the name, size, and type for each field.

5 Identify the key field, if any, and explain why you chose that field.

6 Launch Paradox, if necessary.

7 Create the Famiglia's Pasta table based on your sketch.

8 Add 6 records.

9 Print and save the table.

INDEPENDENT
CHALLENGE 2

The Madison Public Library is planning to loan toys to low-income families. Julie Regenbogen volunteered to take charge of the project. She must catalog the library's toy collection in a way that will help her know where each toy is and, if loaned out, when it is due back. Design a table for Julie to use.

To complete this independent challenge:

1 Sketch a design for the loan table including field names, types, and sizes. Identify the key field.

2 Launch Paradox, if necessary.

3 Create the table structure.

4 Save the structure as "Toys at Library" in the My Paradox Files folder on your Student Disk.

5 List some ways Julie might want to see the data displayed in the Toys at Library table (for example, in order of date of return, all toys that are overdue, and so on).

6 Add 5 records.

7 Print and save the Toys at Library table.

INDEPENDENT
CHALLENGE 3

As sole proprietor of your business, Sports Unlimited, you must keep a current list of your customers to notify them of pending sales and promotions. Your table includes the customer's name, address, phone number, and the date he or she became your customer. Each record has a unique customer number. Customers have expanded and moved to larger buildings, changed their names, or even gone out of business. Your Student Disk contains a table named PD 2-1. Begin by making a copy of the table.

To complete this independent challenge:

1 Launch Paradox and select the appropriate drive and folder as the working directory.

2 Right-click PD 2-1 in the Project Viewer, click Copy, save it as "COPY Sports Unlimited," then click Copy.

3 Open the table and click the Edit Data button.

4 Press ▶️ to move to the end of the list. Notice the total number of records in the table.

5 Press ◀️.

6 Make the following changes to customer records:
   - Customer Diving for Treasure has a new post office box number: 675.
   - The phone number for Blue Sports has changed to 503-555-3369.
   - American Surfing Supply has gone out of business.

7 Enter the following new customer records:

Cust ID	Company	Street	City
R-100	Rustic Supplies	P.O. Box R79	Olympia
W-231	Washburn Water Co	12 Upjohn Dr.	Lafayette
H-103	Happen' Hikes	345 Win Rd.	Ithabrillo

State	ZIP	Phone	First Cont
NM	87116	505-266-9888	5/5/96
NM	87106	505-898-9645	7/8/96
NM	85905	505-854-8211	8/8/96

8 Print the revised table, then close the table. (*Hint:* Print the table in landscape orientation.) Remember you can start the edits over by using the copy of the table. If you do decide to use the copy, be sure to make another copy first, so that you can always go back to the original table.

INDEPENDENT
CHALLENGE 4

As director of a popular local cafe and magazine shop, Bella's Café, you know that the music played on the sound system at Bella's Café is important for sales and customer satisfaction. You decide to better organize the CD list and track the CDs that are played. Begin by making a copy of PD 2-2.

To complete this independent challenge:

1 Launch Paradox and select the appropriate drive and folder as the working directory.

2 Right-click PD 2-2 in the Project Viewer, click Copy, save it as "COPY Bella's Cafe CDs," then click Copy.

3 Open the Bella's Cafe CD table and click the Edit Data button.

4 The artist name, Wolfgang Amadeus Mozart, has been misspelled, for the record title, Odyssey. Correct the last name.

5 The artist is omitted from Opera Excerpts Vol 1. Add the artists Guiseppe Verde and Richard Wagner.

6 Edit the words of the title, Karajan Conducts Favorites, so each beginning letter is capitalized.

7 Three CDs have incorrect categories listed. Change the following titles to Classic: Karajan Conducts Favorites, Odyssey, and Opera Excerpts Vol 1.

8 Print the revised table, then close the table. (*Hint:* Print the table in landscape orientation.) Remember you can start the edits over by using the copy of the table. If you do decide to use the copy, be sure to make another copy first, so that you can always go back to the original table.

VISUALWORKSHOP

As the owner and director of Gallery Receptions, Inc, you produce receptions for art and performance space galleries in the Southwest. You are responsible for all the details of hosting successful opening nights. One of the key ingredients is delicious food and you have an inventory of what you know art lovers like. Using Figure 2-22 as your guide, create a table structure, name it Gallery Gourmet, add the records to the table, and print it. (*Hint*: If you don't define a key, Paradox will create one.)

Cust ID	Item No	Description	Quantity	Price
1023-B	V-163	Marinated Artichokes	12.00	$10.95
1023-B	D-201	Three-Cheese Dressing	10.00	$8.50
1023-B	S-281	Cream of Avocado Soup	6.00	$12.00
1023-B	S-152	Jellied Borsch	8.00	$10.00
1023-B	M-123	Greek Meat Balls	4.00	$15.00
2167-D	M-146	Caramelized Ham with Walnuts	6.00	$8.50
2167-D	F-216	Russian Salmon Pie	15.00	$10.00
2167-D	P-006	Curried Turkey with Almonds	5.00	$7.50
2167-D	P-104	Pecan-Stuffed Pheasant	7.00	$15.00
2167-D	S-056	Orange Ginger Sauce	10.00	$9.50
2167-D	B-302	Swedish Orange Rye Bread	12.00	$3.50

FIGURE 2-22

Manipulating
DATA

*I*n this unit you will learn how to find the data that you want from a table. You'll learn a simple locate method and you'll learn how to extract data using queries. A **query** is a question you ask about a table which displays only specific records or fields. The answer to your query is called an **Answer table** which can be treated like any other Paradox table. You will learn how to create a query, modify and save the answers produced by the query, then save the query itself. You will also use a query to link two tables and extract data from both tables at once. **case** Zora Nelson needs to field customer questions and at the same time produce a book list that includes only the ISBN, Title, and Author fields. She also plans to use a query to link the book inventory table with a table that lists the names and addresses of all the publishers she orders from regularly. ▶

Locating a record

If your table has a lot of records, it can be time-consuming to find the one you want to change. You can locate a record with a specific value in a field, or a specific record number. When you tell Paradox to find a record by value, for example, a particular title, it searches the records until it finds the first record with that value in the specified field. The cursor then moves to that record, which becomes the current record. None of the found records are saved in a special table, but you can move quickly and easily around the table. ▶case The first call of the day is from a customer who wants a copy of *The Comedians*. Zora must find out if the book is in stock and if it is, tell the customer the price.

1 **Launch Paradox, if it's not already running, insert your Student Disk in drive A:\, and set the working directory to the appropriate folder**
You might use a different drive, depending on your environment. Consult your instructor.

2 **Using the Project Viewer, copy PD 3-1 and save it to the appropriate directory folder as My Books in Stock.DB**
Zora is searching for a particular title. She will first click in the search field to simplify the process.

3 **Double-click My Books in Stock.DB, click anywhere in the Title field (except the data), then click the Locate Field Value button 🔍 on the toolbar**
This opens the Locate Value dialog box shown in Figure 3-1. For more information about the options in this dialog box see Table 3-1. Because you clicked in the Title field before opening this dialog box, "Title" is already displayed in the Field text box. To search for a value in another field, click the Field list arrow to display a list of fields to select from. Now Zora is ready to tell Paradox which value in the Title field she wants to find.

4 **Type ..Comedians in the Value text box**
The two dots (..) are a **wildcard** that stands for any character or characters. Zora is sure that the word "Comedians" is somewhere in the title, but it might be preceded by "The." So she uses the wildcard character before "Comedians" to ensure that Paradox will find any record that includes the word.

5 **Click OK**
As shown in Figure 3-2, *The Comedians* is now the current record. Zora scrolls right and looks at the Qty column and sees that there is one copy in stock and the price is $4.99. Zora provides this information to the customer.

6 **Click the First Record button ◄◄ on the toolbar**
You are back at the beginning of the table. Zora wants to create a book list with fewer fields next.

7 **Close the table**

FIGURE 3-1: Locate Value dialog box

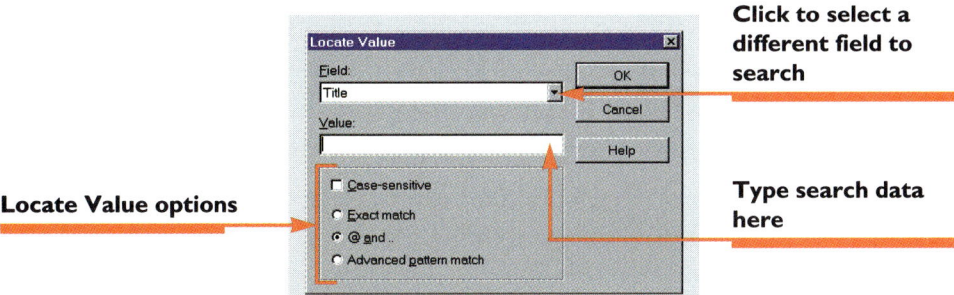

Click to select a different field to search

Locate Value options

Type search data here

FIGURE 3-2: Locate found _The Comedians_

Locate button

Locate Next button

Current record

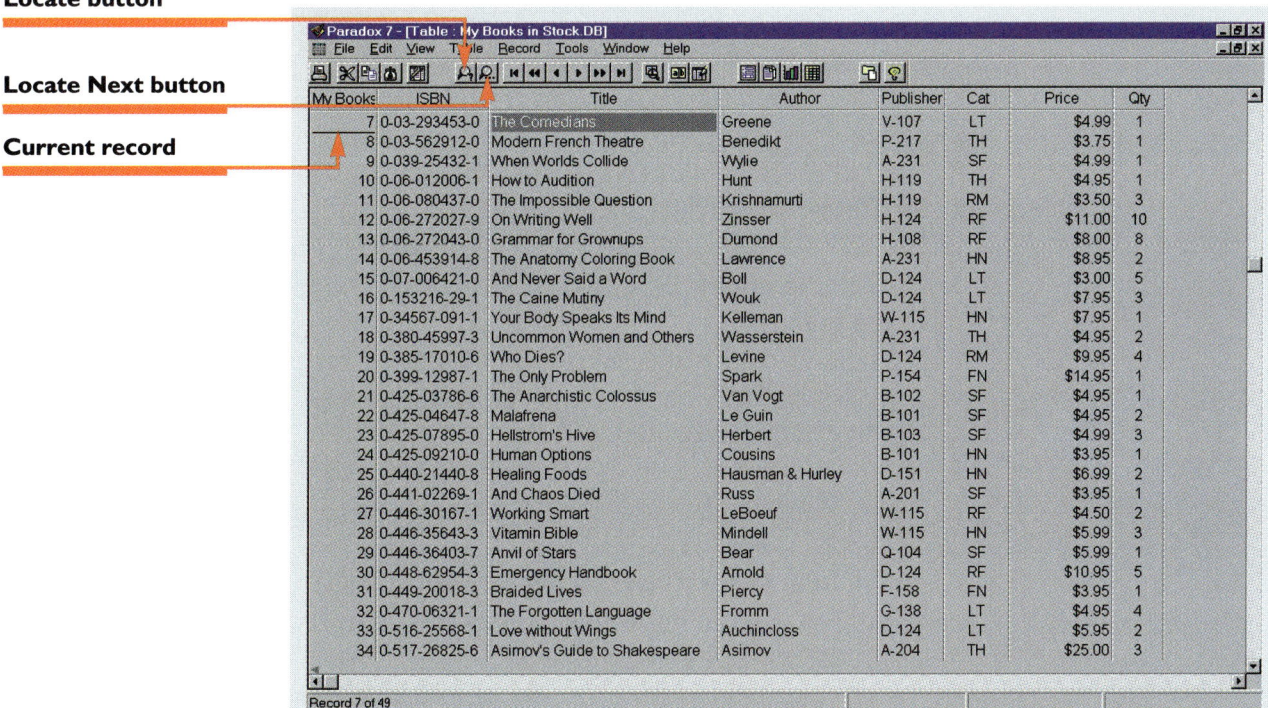

TABLE 3-1: Locate Value options

CHOOSE:	FOR LOCATE OPTIONS
Check Case-sensitive	If you want to search for the text exactly as you typed it, including capitalization
Exact Match	If you want to search for a match, character by character, without the use of wildcards
@ and ..	If you want to use either or both of these wildcards in your search; @ stands for any character, and .. stands for any number of characters, including none
Advanced pattern match	If you want to use an extended list of wildcards in your search, for example, ^ denotes the beginning of a field while $ denotes the end of a field

Creating and running a query

A more permanent way to find records is to create queries. You create a query by displaying a **query image** that shows all the fields in the table. In this lesson, you will learn how to create and run a simple query. 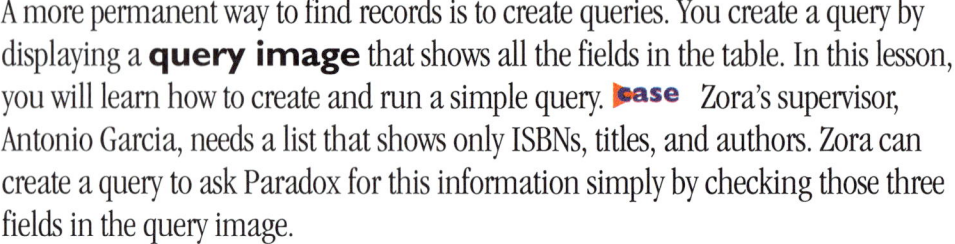 Zora's supervisor, Antonio Garcia, needs a list that shows only ISBNs, titles, and authors. Zora can create a query to ask Paradox for this information simply by checking those three fields in the query image.

1   Click **File** on the menu bar, click **New**, then click **Query**
    Paradox opens the Select File dialog box shown in Figure 3-3. This is where Zora will tell Paradox which table to query.

2   Double-click **My Books in Stock**
    This opens the query image for the selected table. The table fields are arranged in a **table skeleton** in the query image. The title bar now reads "Query:<Untitled>," indicating that this query is new and has not yet been named and saved. Now Zora selects the ISBN, Title, and Author fields by placing a check mark in the small box (called the **check box)** below each field name.

3   Right-click the **check box** below **ISBN**, then choose the top check mark from the menu
    Right-clicking the check box displays all the check options. These check marks are used to set some specifications for the Answer table, as explained in Table 3-2.

4   Click the **check boxes** below **Title** and **Author**
    Figure 3-4 shows check marks in the ISBN, Title, and Author fields. The query that Zora has created asks Paradox the question: "What information is stored in the ISBN, Title, and Author fields?" Now Zora is ready to run the query.

5   Click the **Run Query button** ⚡ on the toolbar
    Paradox extracts the ISBN, Title, and Author fields from the My Books in Stock table and displays them in a temporary table named :PRIV:ANSWER.DB, as shown in Figure 3-5. The records are in ISBN order because ISBN is the key. Now Zora can print the Answer table.

6   Click the **Print button** 🖨 on the toolbar, then click **OK**
    The Answer table prints. Now that she has printed the results she needs, Zora can close the :PRIV:ANSWER.DB table without saving it.

7   Click **File** on the menu bar, then click **Close**
    The :PRIV:ANSWER.DB table window closes, but the query image remains open.

TABLE 3-2: Types of check marks

CHECKMARK	DESCRIPTION
☑	A plain check mark displays all unique field values in ascending order (no duplicate entries)
☑+	Check Plus displays all field values (including duplicates) without sorting them
☑↓	Check Descending is just like the plain check mark except that it displays field values in descending order
☑G	Check GroupBy is used for SET queries, which are beyond the scope of this book

FIGURE 3-3: Select File dialog box

Your list of files might differ

Select the file you want to query

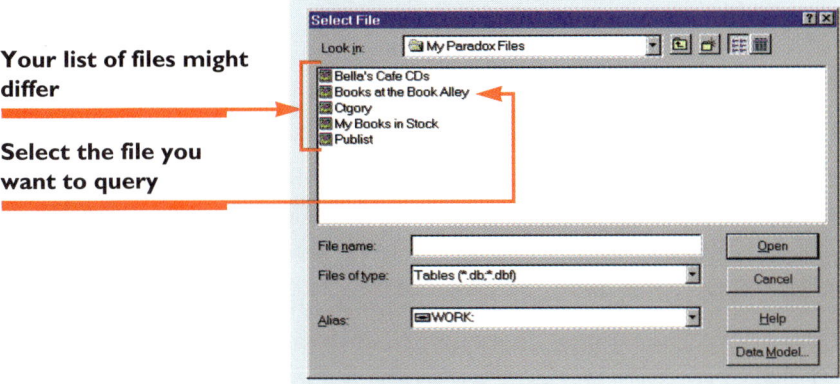

FIGURE 3-4: Completed query image for the ISBN, Title, and Author query

Checked fields will be included in the Answer table

Field condition box

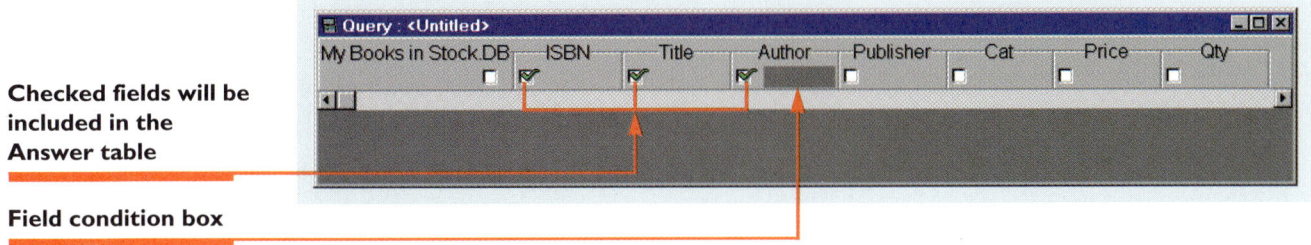

FIGURE 3-5: Answer table displays the ISBN, Title, and Author fields for all books

Includes fields you checked in the query image

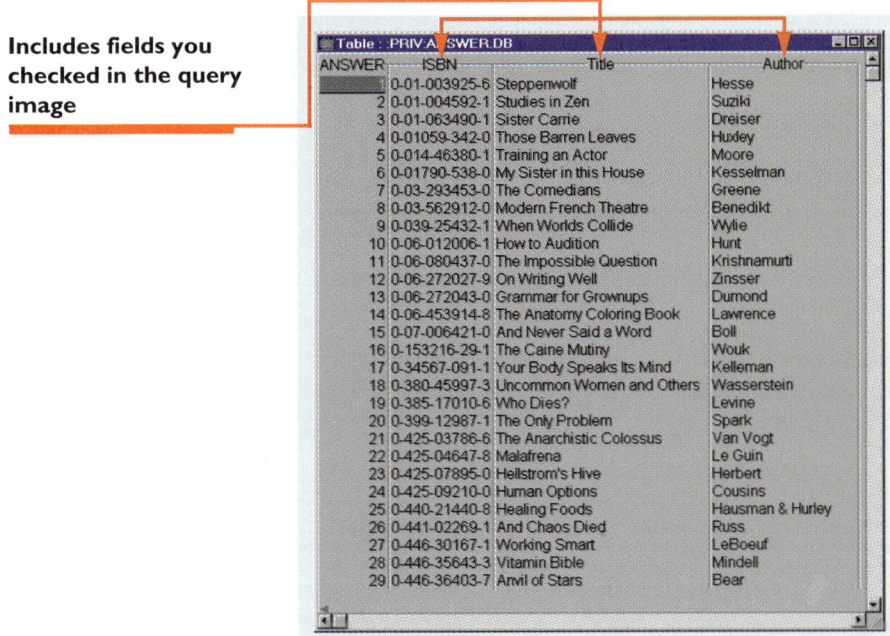

QUICK **TIP**

The check marks toggle on and off, so if you check a box by mistake, just click the box again to delete the check mark. If you want to include all the fields in the Answer table, click the box below the table name and check marks will appear in all the fields. ■

Selecting specific records

The query you created in the previous lesson displayed the ISBN, Title, and Author fields for all the records in the original inventory table. You can also limit the records in the Answer table if you add selection conditions to the query image. A **selection condition** filters out the records that don't meet the criteria you specify in the query. For example, you can add a selection condition that would extract records for books with a price of at least $10.00. ▶**case** Because The Book Alley is now specializing in health and nutrition books, Antonio would like to see a list of only those books. Zora changes her query to limit the records to those with HN in the Cat field.

1 Click the **check box** below **Cat**
   Now four fields are checked in the query image. Next Zora adds the selection condition in the Cat field to extract only health and nutrition books.

2 Click the shaded area (the field condition box) under the **Cat field name**
   The darker shading disappears and the insertion point appears in the space. Selection conditions are case-sensitive, which means that Paradox considers HN, hn, hN, and Hn to be different values. Be careful to enter a condition value that is compatible with the data in the field. In this case, Zora uses uppercase characters to match the uppercase category codes in the inventory table.

3 Type **HN** (the abbreviation for health and nutrition)
   Figure 3-6 shows the modified query image.

4 Click the **Run Query button** 🗲 on the toolbar
   The new Answer table is much shorter than the one created in the previous lesson because it includes only health and nutrition books. Zora sees that the Cat field is unnecessary in this Answer table, because all the books are in the same category. She decides to remove that field. Instead of closing the Answer table, she finds it easier to drag the Answer table window down so she can view both the Answer and query windows at the same time.

5 Click the **Answer table title bar** and drag the window down until you can see the query image above it, then click the **query window title bar**
   If a title bar doesn't appear because the window is maximized, simply click the **Restore button** ▣ first, then move the Answer table. The query window is now the active window.

6 Click the **Cat field check box**
   The check mark is removed but the selection condition remains.

7 Click 🗲
   The Answer table opens, as before, but without the Cat field as shown in Figure 3-7. Now the table is ready to be printed.

8 Click the **Print button** 🖨 on the toolbar, then click **OK**
   Now that she has the list she needs, Zora closes the Answer table.

9 Click **File** in the menu bar, then click **Close**
   The Answer table closes and the Query image remains open as shown in Figure 3-8.

FIGURE 3-6: Modified query image

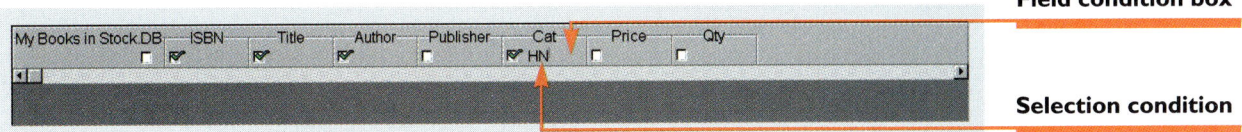

Field condition box

Selection condition

FIGURE 3-7: Answer table without Cat field

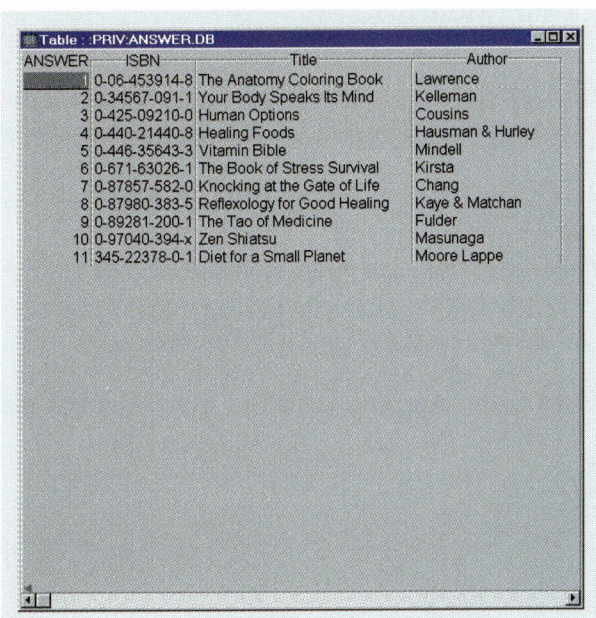

FIGURE 3-8: Query image without Cat field

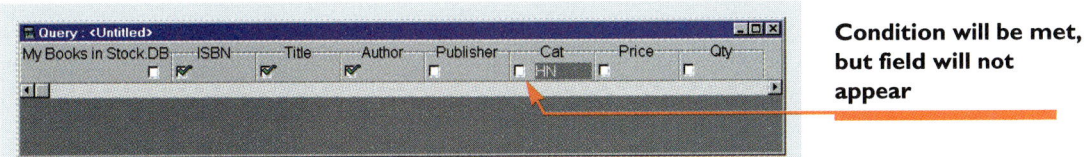

Condition will be met, but field will not appear

QUICK **TIP**

If you can't see the window you want, click Windows and select the window you want on top.■

Sorting query results

In the previous lessons, the records in the Answer table appeared in the same order as they appear in the original inventory table. Now you'll learn how to specify the order of the records in the Answer table. You can sort the Answer table by one or more of the fields you checked in the query image. **case** Zora wants to recreate her list of the ISBN, Title, and Author fields for all the records, but this time she wants the records in alphabetic order by title. First she removes the selection condition that limited the list to health and nutrition books, then she specifies the record order for the Answer table.

1 Click the **Cat field condition box** if necessary and delete **HN**
In order to produce a sorted Answer table, Zora specifies the order before she runs the query.

2 Click the **Sort Answer Table button** [icon] on the toolbar, then click the **Sort tab**
The Query Properties dialog box opens, as shown in Figure 3-9. The list of available fields includes only those fields you have checked in the query image. To sort by one of the fields, you simply select the field name and move it to the Sort order list.

3 Click **Title** in the Answer fields list, then click the **right arrow**
Title moves to the Sort order list, as shown in Figure 3-10.

4 Click **OK**
The Query Properties dialog box closes and you return to the query image. Paradox will sort the Answer table when you run the query.

5 Click the **Run Query button** [icon] on the toolbar
The Answer table shown in Figure 3-11 is sorted in alphabetic order by title. Zora wants to print the new alphabetized list for Antonio.

6 Print the **Answer table**, then close it
The Answer table closes, and you return to the query image.

FIGURE 3-9: Query Properties dialog box

Click to select
Title field

Click to move selected
field to Sort order list

Sort tab

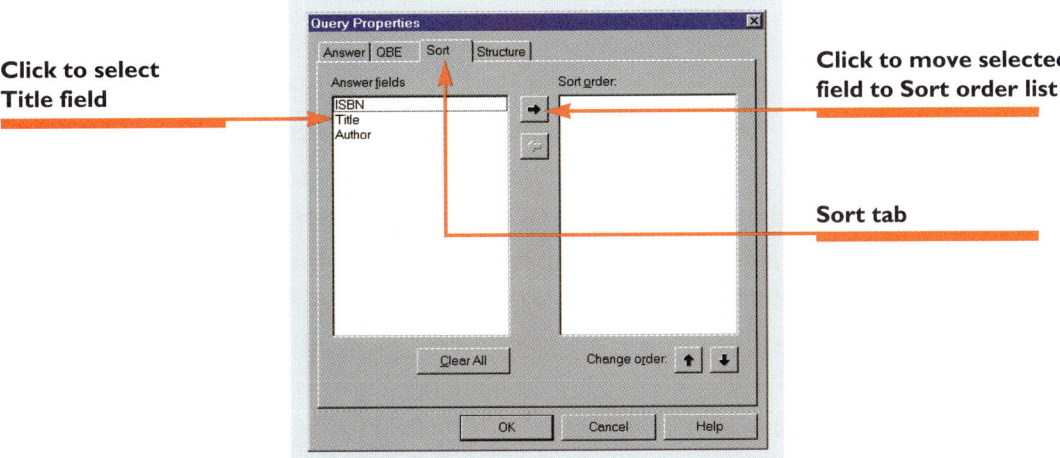

FIGURE 3-10: Query Properties new sort order

Paradox will sort
the Answer table by
title when you run
the query

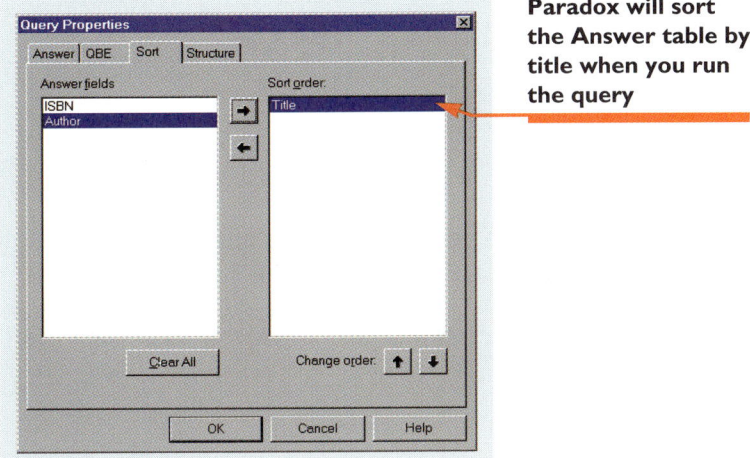

FIGURE 3-11: Answer table sorted by title

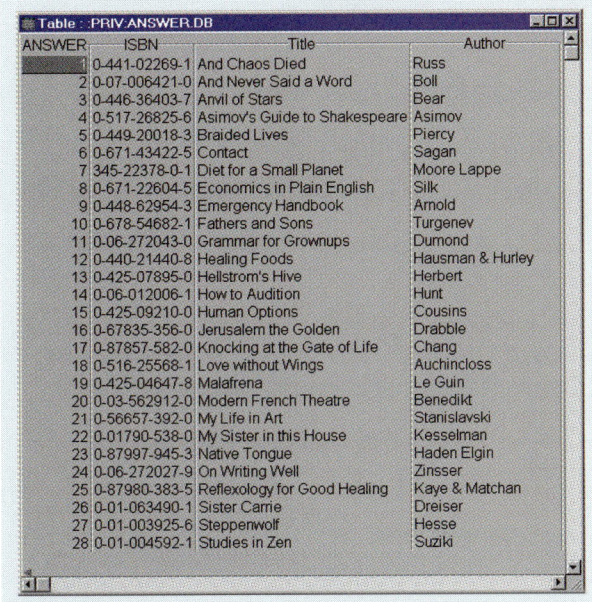

QUICK **TIP**

You can also open
the Query
Properties dialog
box by clicking
Properties on the
menu bar, then click-
ing Answer Sort.■

Modifying the Answer table

So far in this unit, each time you ran a query, the new query results simply replaced the previous Answer table. But if you want to use the information in the Answer table later, it's best to tell Paradox *before you run the query* that you want to save the Answer table with a new name. While you are specifying a name for your Answer table, you can also make some decisions about how you want the data in the table to be displayed. For example, you can rearrange the fields in the Answer table so that they appear in a different order than in the original table. ▶**case** Zora wants to save the results of the query she created in the last lesson so she can use the data later. In addition, she wants to rearrange the fields in the Answer table in order to make the Title field the leftmost column.

1 Click the **Query Properties button** 🖼 on the toolbar, then click the **Answer tab**

The Query Properties dialog box opens with the Answer tab foremost, as shown in Figure 3-12. The Table name box shows the default Answer table name, :PRIV:ANSWER.DB. Zora wants to save the Answer table as Titles List.DB.

2 Double-click the **Table name box,** delete the current name, then type **Titles List**

The new name also appears in the Answer image. Now Zora changes the appearance of the Answer table by modifying the Answer table image.

3 Click the **Structure tab**, click **Title**, then click the **Up Arrow** 🔼 once

The title moves to the top of the list, so it will appear to the far left. Zora wants the next field to be author.

4 Select **Author** and click the **Up Arrow** 🔼 once

Title and author are now at the top of the list, as shown in Figure 3-13.

5 Click **OK** to close the Query Properties dialog box and return to the query image

Now Zora can run the query that will actually produce the Answer table.

6 Click the **Run Query button** ⚡ on the toolbar

The result of the query, Titles List.DB, is shown in Figure 3-14. Now Zora prints her Answer table.

7 Print the **Titles List table**

The table is now in a useable form for Zora and Antonio.

8 Close the **Titles List table**

The Titles List table closes. Notice that the new filename, Titles List.DB, appears in the list of tables in the Project Viewer. The query image remains open.

FIGURE 3-12: Query Properties dialog box with Answer tab fore-most

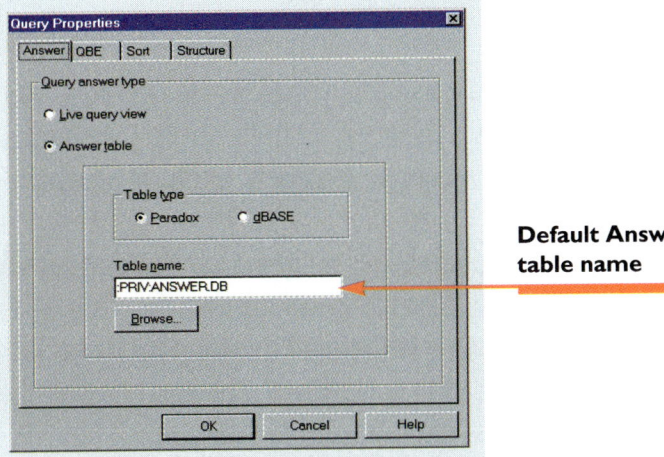

Default Answer table name

FIGURE 3-13: Structure tab with changes to the Answer table

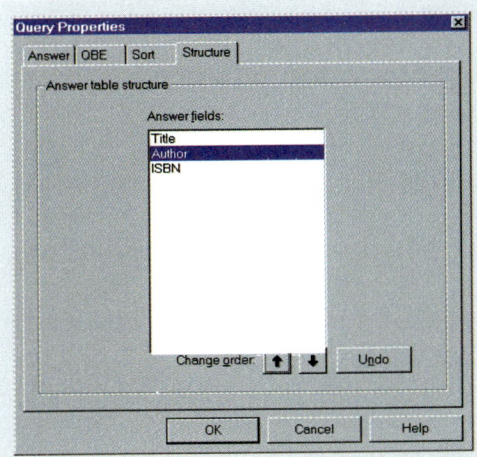

FIGURE 3-14: Modified Answer table now named Titles List.DB

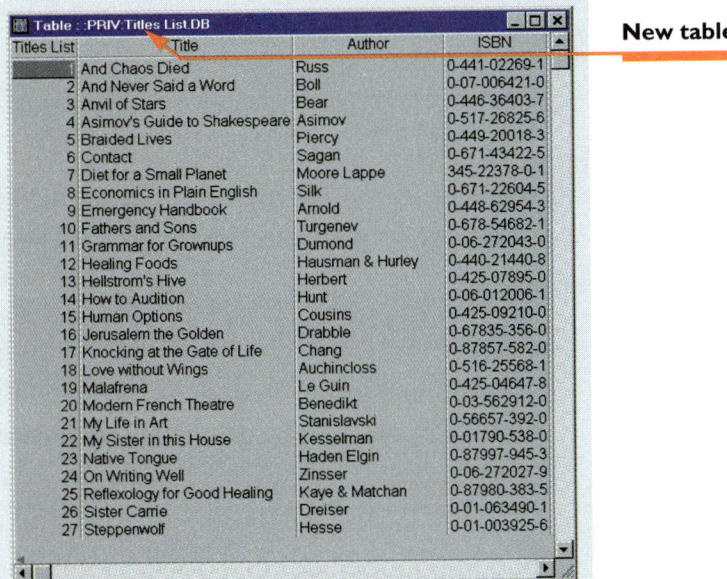

New table name

Saving a query

After designing a query that you expect to use often, you can save it. Later, you can modify or run the query from the Project Viewer just like any other file. For information about running a query you have previously saved, see the related topic "Running an existing query." **case**   Zora expects to print the list of health and nutrition books every month. She decides to save the query design so she won't have to recreate it each time she needs it. She will modify the previous query to extract only health and nutrition books (as before), then save her query with the name Health & Nutrition. She also needs to change the Answer table name from Titles List to Health & Nutrition.

1 Click the **Cat field condition box** and type **HN**
This will filter out all books not in the health and nutrition category, as before. Zora leaves the same fields checked. Now she needs to specify a new name for her Answer table.

2 Click **Query** on the menu bar, click **Properties**, then click the **Answer tab**
The Query Properties dialog box opens with the Answer tab foremost. The name Zora specified for her previous Answer table, Titles List.DB, appears in the Table name box.

3 Click the **Table name box**, delete the existing name, then type **Health & Nutrition**
Paradox automatically adds the .DB file extension. Zora liked the layout of her last Answer table, so she doesn't make any changes to the answer image.

4 Click **OK**
Now Zora is ready to save her query.

5 Click **File** on the menu bar, then click **Save As**
The Save file as dialog box opens, as shown in Figure 3-15. Notice that the default file extension for a query is .qbe.

6 Type **Health & Nutrition** in the File name text box
Paradox will automatically assign the .qbe extension to your saved query.

7 Click **Save**
Now Zora can run the query whenever she needs an updated list of health and nutrition titles. She returns to the Project Viewer to see that her new query has been added.

8 Click **File** on the menu bar, then click **Close**
The query window closes and you return to the Project Viewer.

9 Click **Queries** in the Project Viewer
Health & Nutrition.qbe appears in the list of query files, as shown in Figure 3-16.

FIGURE 3-15: Save file as dialog box

Query file extension

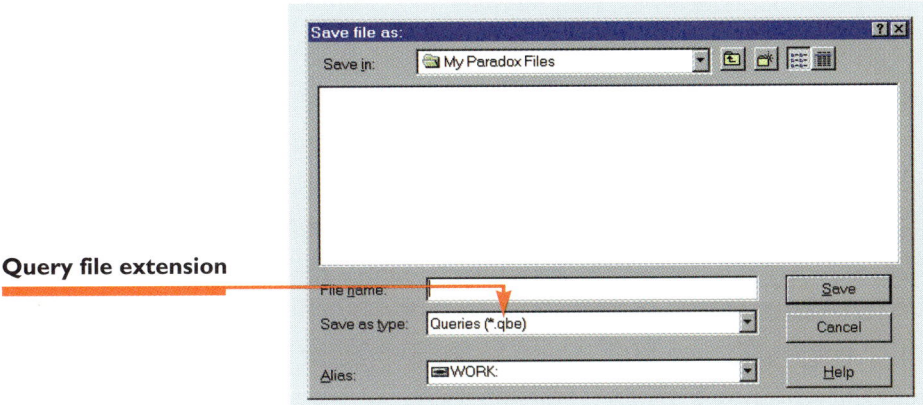

FIGURE 3-16: Project Viewer with new saved query

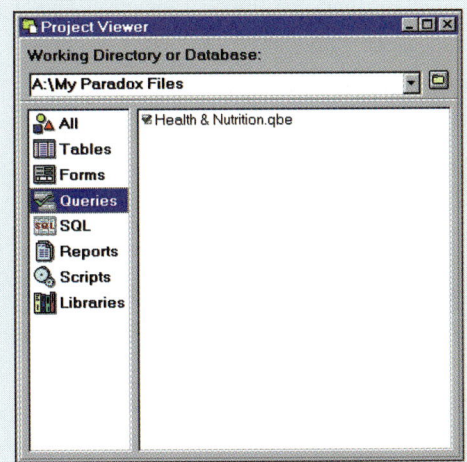

Running an existing query

Once you save a query, its name appears in the Project Viewer list of queries. You can run the query in any of the following ways:

- Double-click the query name in the Project Viewer

- Right-click the query name in the Project Viewer and choose Run Query from the context-sensitive menu

- Click the Open Query button  on the toolbar, then choose the query name from the Open Query dialog box

- Click File on the menu bar, click Open, click Query, then choose the query name from the Select Query dialog box

QUICK **TIP**

If you click Save instead of Save As the first time you save a new file, Paradox opens the Save file as dialog box anyway. You must name the file before Paradox will save it. If you have saved it once already and you click Save, you will overwrite the original file.■

Combining selection conditions

In the previous lesson, you used a selection condition to tell Paradox to display only books in the health and nutrition category. However, if you want to extract records that are both in the health and nutrition category *and* cost at least $10.00, you need to combine the two conditions in an **AND relationship**. If you want to see a list of books that are *either* in the health and nutrition category *or* cost less than $10.00, you must combine the conditions in an **OR relationship**. **case**   Antonio asks Zora for a list of all the health and nutrition books with a price of at least $5.00. To produce this list, Zora needs to create a query using an AND relationship.

1   Start a new query using the **My Books in Stock.DB table** and click the **check boxes** below **Title**, **Cat**, and **Price**

If you need help with this step, refer to the lesson "Creating and running a query" earlier in this unit.

Now that Zora has specified the fields to display in the Answer table, she can add the conditions. The health and nutrition category condition is the same as in the previous query.

2   Click the **Cat field condition box** and type **HN**

Next Zora needs to add a condition to the Price field to indicate that she wants to see only records whose prices are greater than or equal to $5.00. She does this by entering the expression >=5. (Notice that she does not need to type the dollar sign.)

3   Click the **Price field condition box** and type **>=5**

The query image should look like Figure 3-17. The two conditions in different fields make up an AND relationship. They tell Paradox to display only those records that satisfy both conditions.

4   Click the **Run Query button** 🗲 on the toolbar

Figure 3-18 shows the resulting Answer table, which includes only books that are both in the health and nutrition category and that are priced at $5.00 or more. After reviewing the query results on screen, Antonio asks for another query—one that displays all health and nutrition books priced between $9.00 and $12.00. This requires combining the upper and lower price limits into one expression in the same field.

5   Click the **Query window title bar**

Zora returns to the query image, where she can change the selection conditions.

6   Delete the **>=5** expression in the **Price field condition box**, then type **>=9,<=12**

The expression asks Paradox to select records whose Price fields contain values greater than or equal to $9.00 *and* less than or equal to $12.00. The comma separating the two conditions is known as an **AND operator**. Zora must use an AND operator whenever she wants to create an AND relationship between two conditions in the same field. Figure 3-19 shows the completed query image.

7   Click the **Run Query button** 🗲 on the toolbar

The new Answer table includes only records for health and nutrition books in the specified price range, as shown in Figure 3-20. Zora prints this list for Antonio.

8   Print the **Answer table**

FIGURE 3-17: Completed query image

Will extract health & nutrition books priced at $5 or more

FIGURE 3-18:
Answer table showing health and nutrition books costing at least $5

FIGURE 3-19: Query image combining conditions in one field

FIGURE 3-20:
Answer table with health and nutrition books between $9 and $12

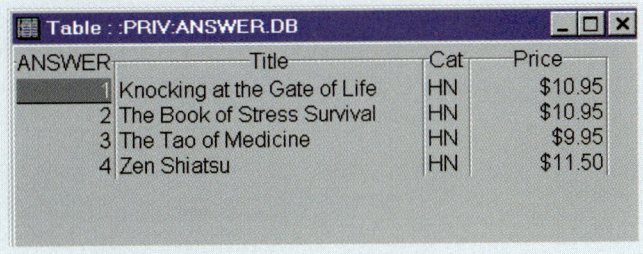

TROUBLE?

A common mistake when performing a query with conditions and operators is not to check any fields. At least one field must be checked before Paradox can run a query. If none are checked, Paradox displays the error message: "Query has no checked fields." Click OK to clear the message box, click check boxes in your query image as necessary, then run the query again. ■

Combining selection conditions, continued

In the previous steps, you combined selection conditions using an AND relationship. The OR relationship combines conditions so that if either condition is met, the record is included in the answer. You used a comma as the operator to indicate the AND relationship of the conditions in the Price field. If you are combining two conditions with an OR relationship, you simply type "OR" (the **OR operator**) between them. For more information on combining selection conditions, see the related topic "Combining conditions in different fields with OR." ▶**case**   While she's working at her computer, a customer asks Zora for help. The customer wants to buy either a science fiction book or a health and nutrition book as a gift for a friend. Zora quickly modifies her last query, using an OR operator to produce a list of possible choices.

9 Click the **Query window title bar**
The Query window becomes active again.

10 Delete the selection conditions in the **Price field condition box**, then click the **Price check mark**
The price conditions are deleted and the field is no longer checked.

11 Click the **Cat field condition box**, then click again to remove the shading
The insertion point appears at the end of the existing HN condition.

12 Press **[Spacebar]**, then type **OR SF**
The condition now reads HN OR SF, as shown in Figure 3-21. This condition tells Paradox to display records with either SF or HN in the category field.

13 Click the **Run Query button** 🗲 on the toolbar
The resulting Answer table is larger because it contains books from both categories, as shown in Figure 3-22. Zora prints the Answer table to give to the customer.

14 Print, then close the **Answer table**
Zora closes the query image without saving it.

15 Click **File** on the menu bar, click **Close,** then click **No,** to close without saving the query
The query image window closes and Zora returns to the Project Viewer.

FIGURE 3-21: Query image with an OR condition

Extracts either health & nutrition OR science fiction books

FIGURE 3-22: Answer table containing both health & nutrition or science fiction books

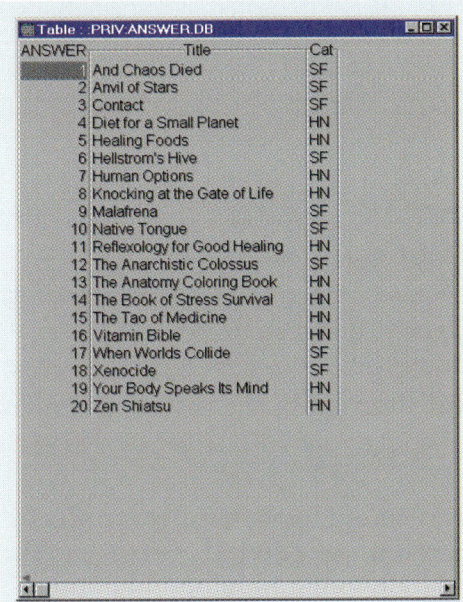

Combining conditions in different fields with OR

When you want to extract records with a specific value in one field as well as those with a specific value in a different field, you can create a two-line query image. For example, suppose you wanted a list of books that either had HN in the category field, or cost at least $5.00. To create this list, enter the HN condition in the category field, as before, press [↓] to add a second line to the image, then enter the price condition in the second line of the Price field. When you combine conditions in different fields, you must also check the same fields in both lines.

QUICK **TIP**

You don't have to check the field in which you have placed a condition. Paradox will still apply the conditions even if you do not include the field in the Answer table.■

Linking tables with a query

The real power of a relational database system like Paradox is the ability to access information in several tables at once. Before you can query multiple tables, you need to make sure the tables share a common field that can serve as the link between the tables. Then you can use a query to tell Paradox which tables you want to link together and which fields they have in common. In this lesson, you'll link the My Books in Stock table to a table that contains the names and addresses of publishers. **case** Zora wants to combine the publisher table with her inventory table in order to create a list showing which books are nearly out of stock, along with their publishers' names and phone numbers. The publisher table's key field is the PUBCODE field, which contains the same codes Zora used in the Publisher field of her inventory table.

STEPS

1 Using the Project Viewer, copy **PD 3-2** and save it to the appropriate directory as **My Publisher.DB**

2 Using the Project Viewer, open the **My Publisher table** and familiarize yourself with its structure and contents
Figure 3-23 shows the My Publisher table in the Table View window.

3 Close the **My Publisher table** and return to the Project Viewer
Now Zora begins building a query that will link the My Publisher table to her original invoice table (My Books in Stock).

4 Start a new query as before, using the **My Books in Stock.DB table**
The query image opens without any fields checked. Next Zora adds the My Publisher table to the query.

5 Click the **Add Table button** 🏢 on the toolbar
The Select File dialog box opens as before.

6 Click **My Publisher** in the file list, then click **Open**
The query image now contains two table skeletons, with My Books in Stock at the top, as shown in Figure 3-24. Next Zora must tell Paradox which is the common field that will link the two tables.

7 Click the **Join Tables button** 🏢 on the toolbar, then move the pointer to the **Publisher field** in the **My Books in Stock table**
The pointer changes to ⬚🏢.

8 Click the **Publisher field**
An example element, "join1," appears in the field. An **example element** is simply a marker that tells Paradox to link this field with the field in another table that has the same marker. Now you can complete the link by placing the companion marker in the PUBCODE field of the My Publisher table.

9 Click the **PUBCODE field** of the **My Publisher table**
The same example element appears in that field, indicating that the publisher code joins the two tables. The status bar shows a message indicating that the join is complete. The My Books in Stock table is now the parent table (the table you begin with), and the My Publisher table is the child table (the table you add, from which you can access additional information). The query image now looks like Figure 3-25.

PARADOX 7 UNIT 3 MANIPULATING DATA

FIGURE 3-23: My Publisher table structure and data

Key field

These are all Alpha fields

Codes in this field match those used in the inventory table's Publisher fields

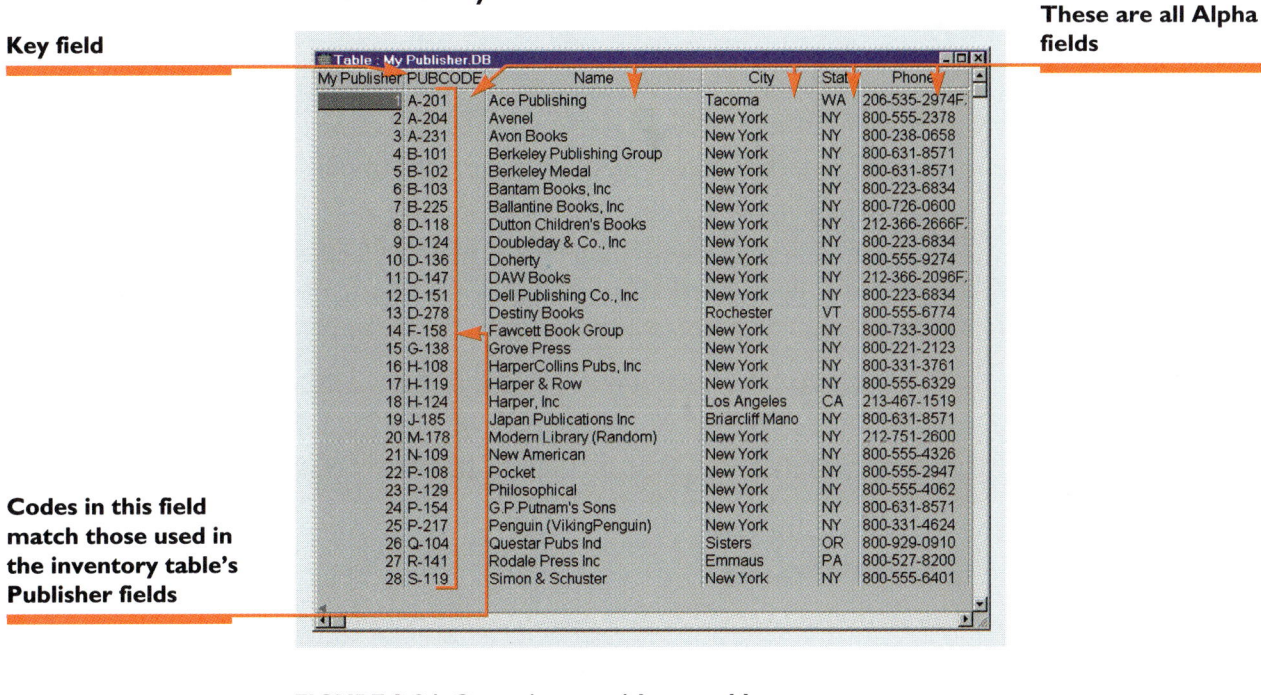

FIGURE 3-24: Query image with two tables

Add Table button

Linking fields

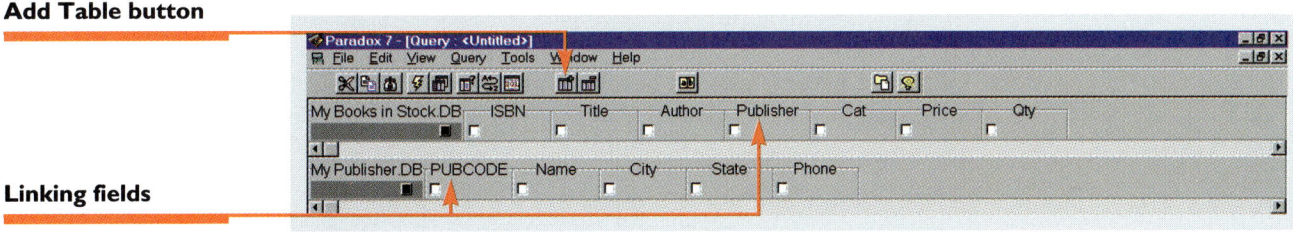

FIGURE 3-25: Two tables joined by publisher code fields

Join Tables button

Example elements

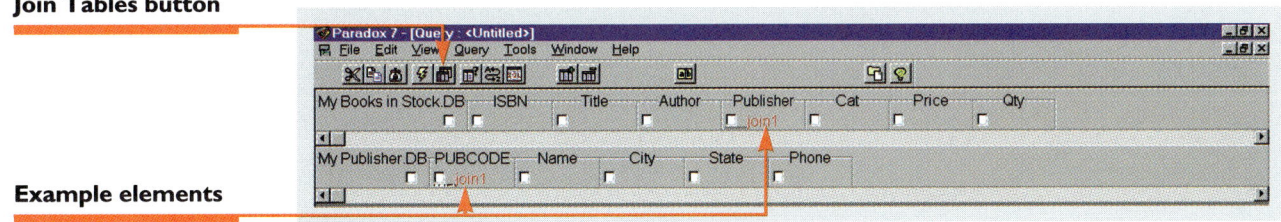

QUICK **TIP**

Linking fields do not have to have the same name in both tables, but they must be compatible types. You cannot, for example, link a Number field with an Alpha field.

Running a multi-table query

After you have joined two tables in a query image, you have access to all the information in both tables. You select the fields and specify the selection conditions just as in a single-table query. You can ask Paradox to save the query results to a permanent table, rearrange the fields in the Answer table, and resize the rows and columns. See the related topic "Types of relationships between tables" for a description of the different ways of relating Paradox tables. ▶**case** Now that Zora has joined her two tables, she can create her query. She wants to find all the books with fewer than two copies in stock, as well as the publisher's name and phone number for each of those books. After printing the resulting Answer table, she can phone in her orders for the books that she thinks will continue to sell well.

STEPS

1 Click the **check boxes** below **Title, Author,** and **Qty** in the **My Books in Stock skeleton**

Three check marks appear. Now Zora adds the condition to the Qty field.

2 Click the **Qty field condition box** and type **<2**

This will extract the information for all books with fewer than two copies in stock. Next, Zora checks the field she wants from the My Publisher table.

3 Click the **check boxes** below **Name** and **Phone** in the **My Publisher skeleton**

The completed query image looks like Figure 3-26. Notice that the field that links the two tables does not have to be checked.

4 Click the **Run Query button** 🔲 on the toolbar

The Answer table, as shown in Figure 3-27, contains titles of books with only one copy left in stock. It also contains the publishers' names and phone numbers that Zora will need to order more copies.

5 Print, then close the **Answer table**

Zora has the information she needs to make her book order.

6 Close the query image

FIGURE 3-26: Query images to extract data from two tables

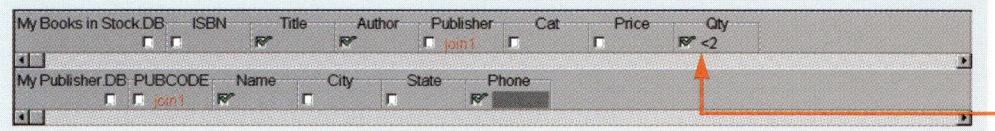

Will extract records for books with fewer than two copies in stock

FIGURE 3-27: Answer table with book and publisher information

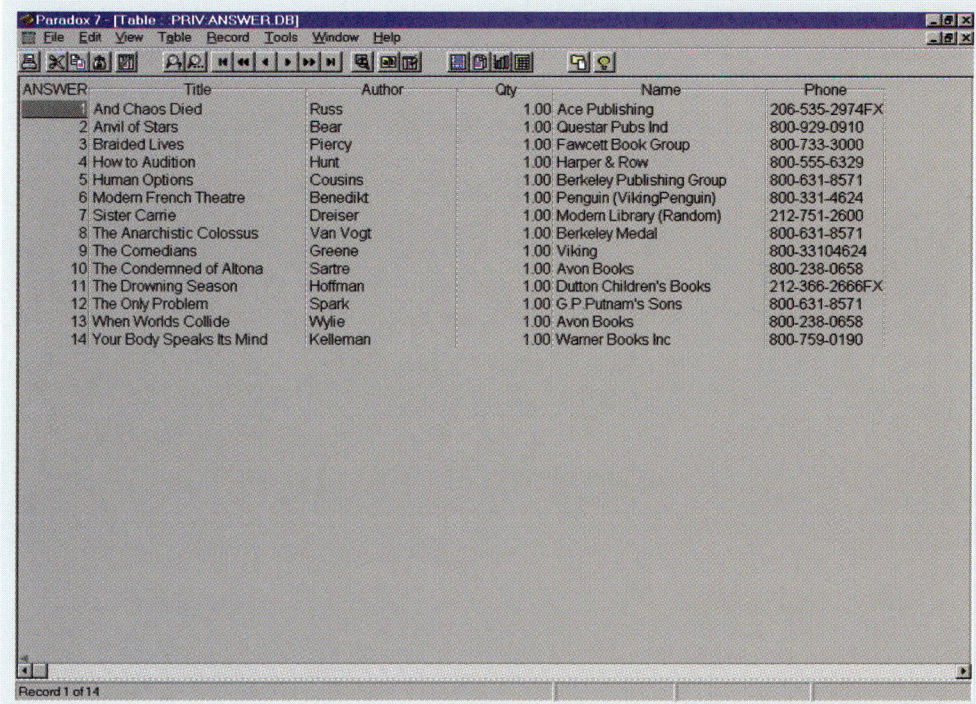

Types of relationships between tables

The relationship you established between the book inventory and publisher tables is a **one-to-one relationship** because each book has only one publisher. In other words, each book record in the parent table (My Books in Stock) is linked to one record in the child table (My Publisher). If you turned it around and made My Publisher the parent table, the relationship would be **one-to-many**, because each publisher might have more than one book in the list. It's also possible to create a **many-to-many** relationship, in which there are many occurrences of a field value in both tables.

QUICK **TIP**

If you want to include the common field in the Answer table, check it in only one skeleton (either the parent table skeleton or the child table skeleton). If you check it in both, the Answer table will contain duplicate values.

TASKREFERENCE

TASK	MOUSE/BUTTON	MENU	KEYBOARD
Add tables	Click , then choose table	Click Edit, click Add Table, then choose tables	
Create a query	Right-click Query in Project Viewer	Click File, click New, then Query	
Link tables	Click , then click in the common fields		
Locate a record	Click	Click Record, Locate, Value	[Ctrl][Z]
Run a query	Click , double-click the query name in the Project Viewer; right-click the query name in the Project Viewer, choose Run Query, click , then choose query name	Click Query, click Run, then click Query	[F8]
Save a query		Click File, click Save	
Save an Answer table	Click , then select Answer tab or Right-click PRIV:ANSWER.DB in list of table files, then rename	Click Query, click Properties, then select Answer tab	

CONCEPTSREVIEW

Label each element of the Query Design window shown in Figure 3-28.

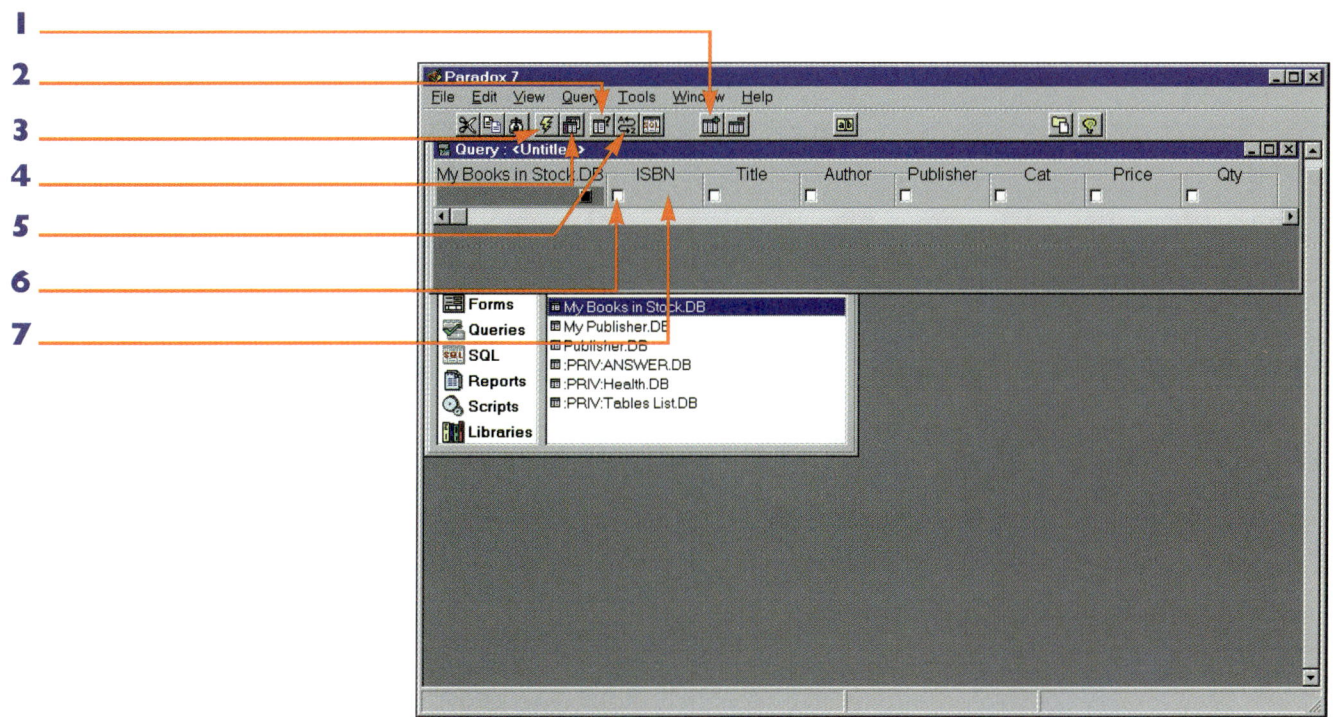

FIGURE 3-28

Match each statement with the term it describes.

8 Use to limit records in the Answer table

9 Combines selection conditions

10 Requires that both conditions be met

11 Requires that either condition be met

12 Query design window

13 Marker that indicates linking field

a. Operator

b. Query image

c. Example element

d. Selection condition

e. AND relationship

f. OR relationship

Select the best answer from the list of choices.

14 The data in the Answer table

   a. Must be deleted before you exit Paradox

   b. Is only temporary unless you rename the Answer table

   c. Cannot be modified or saved

   d. Contains all the fields in the original table but only selected records

15 To extract records with values greater than 2 in a Number field, in the field condition box, type

   a. <2

   b. >2

   c. =2

   d. *2

16 Example elements are used to

a. Create examples of different types of tables

b. Join two tables

c. Change the Answer table name

d. Create new tables for querying

17 The following selection condition finds both reference and theater books

a. RF,TH

b. RF OR TH

c. TH AND RF

d. TH+RF

18 The following selection condition finds books priced in the $3.50 to $6.50 price range

a. >3.50,<6.50

b. >3.50 AND <6.50

c. >3.50 OR <6.50

d. >=3.50,<=6.50

19 You can name an Answer table before you run a query by using the

a. Restructure dialog box

b. Query Properties dialog box

c. Table skeleton

d. Select File dialog box

20 What's the purpose of using the two-dot (..) wildcard in the Locate Value dialog box?

a. To indicate that there's more information to come

b. To locate only words in uppercase characters

c. To indicate that you want to perform the search two times

d. To substitute for any character or characters

SKILLSREVIEW

1 Locate a record.

a. Copy PD 3-3 to a new table named Books Galore.DB.

b. Open Books Galore. Locate books that have authors whose names begin with K.

c. Click the Locate Field Value button.

d. Choose Author in the field box.

e. Type K.. in the Value box and verify that the radio button for wildcards @ and .. is checked.

f. Click OK.

g. Click the Locate Next button to view each occurrence.

h. Close Books Galore.

2 Create and run a query.

a. Open a query image for Books Galore.DB.

b. Instruct Paradox to display the ISBN and Title fields.

c. Run the query.

d. Print the Answer table, then close it.

e. Close the query image window.

3 Select specific records.

a. Return to the query image for Books Galore.DB.

b. Instruct Paradox to display all the fields.

c. Enter the selection condition HN in the Cat field condition box.

d. Uncheck the Publisher and Qty fields.

e. Run the query.

f. Print the Answer table.

4 Sort query results.

a. Return to the query image for Books Galore.DB.

b. Instruct Paradox to display the Title and Category fields.

c. Use the Query Properties dialog box to sort first by category, then by title.

d. Run the query.

e. Print the Answer table, then close it.

f. Close the query image window.

5 Modify the Answer table.

a. Open a new query image for Books Galore.DB.

b. Create a query that displays the ISBN, title, author, and category for all TH and RF books.

c. Rearrange the fields in the Answer table to show title first.

d. Name the Answer table TH-RF.DB.

e. Run the query.

f. Print the TH-RF.DB results.

6 Save a query.

a. Make sure the query image for the calculation query in Step 4 is on the screen; if not, recreate it.

b. Save the query as TH-RF.

c. Close the query, then find the query file in the Project Viewer.

d. Write down the full name of the query file and the directory in which it's located.

7 Combine selection conditions.

a. Open a query image for Books Galore.DB.

b. Create a query to find all books in the LT and HN categories priced less than $8.00, but more than $4.00, displaying fields ISBN, Title, Cat, and Price.

c. Run the query.

d. Print the Answer table, then close it.

e. Close the query image window.

8 Link tables with a query.

a. Copy PD 3-4 to a new table named Book Bin.DB.

b. Copy PD 3-5 to a new table named Publisher Info.DB.

c. Open a query image for Book Bin.DB.

d. Add the Publisher Info.DB table to the query image.

e. Link the tables by the publisher code fields.

9 Run a multi-table query.

a. Check the ISBN, Title, and Author fields in the Book Bin.DB skeleton in the query image you started in Step 8.

b. Check the Name and PUBCODE fields in the Publisher Info.DB skeleton.

c. Run the query.

d. Print the Answer table.

INDEPENDENT
CHALLENGE 1

You decide to catalog your entire music collection and set up the catalog so that you can retrieve various types of information. Use the following fields:

Artist's Name

Name of Recording

Release Date

Cost

Format (Cassette, CD, Vinyl, Reel-to-Reel, or Other)

To complete this independent challenge:

1 Create the table structure and save it as AUDIO.

2 Enter at least 20 records (the data you enter can be real or invented).

3 Open a query image for AUDIO, include all fields to display, and run the following queries (for each query, print the Answer table and be prepared to turn it in):

a. Which recordings are only on CD?

b. Which recordings were released before 1980?

c. Which recordings cost more than $10.00 but less than $23.00?

INDEPENDENT
CHALLENGE 2

You are a database consultant and have just accepted a client whose business is catering. It is growing rapidly and your client wants to be able to ask questions about the recipe file. Based on your interviews with your client, you decide to create a database that includes the recipe name, how many people it serves, whether or not it is vegetarian, how many ingredients it requires, the number of minutes of preparation time, and the total number of calories per serving.

To complete this independent challenge:

1 Create a table of 20 or 30 recipe titles (you can use a cookbook as a guide).

2 After your table is complete, query the data to determine:

   a. The total number of recipes

   b. How many of your recipes take more than 30 minutes to prepare

   c. Which recipes have fewer than 250 calories per serving

   d. Which recipes serve more than 8 people, but take less than an hour to prepare

   e. Which recipes, if any, call for fewer than 5 ingredients, take less than 10 minutes to prepare, and serve 4 or more people.

3 Save query as Short fast for four.

4 Print Short fast for four.

INDEPENDENT
CHALLENGE 3

Your business, Sports Unlimited, employs 3 full-time sales representatives to service customers. You've created a separate table with their names, date of hire, and telephone extension. You've used a Sales Rep Code to link the table to the Client table. Your assistant has added a field for the Sales Rep Code to the Client table and entered the data on which sales rep contacted each client. Begin by making copies of the tables.

To complete this independent challenge:

1 Make a copy of PD 3-6 and name it My Clients & Reps. Make a copy of PD 3-7 and name it My Sales Reps.

2 Open My Clients & Reps, review the data and structure carefully.

3 Open My Sales Reps, review the data and structure carefully.

4 Print a copy of both tables.

5 Create a query that links the two tables using Sales Rep Code as the common element.

6 In the query display only the Company's contacted by Marjorie or Sing-Lee (*Hint*: Put a comma after the common element, join1, and then type in the condition). Include in the Answer table the fields Company, Phone, First Contact date, Sales Rep Name, and Sales Rep extension.

7 Modify the Answer table so that the First Contact date is in the first column and sorted by First Contact date.

8 Save the query and Answer tables as First Contact and print the Answer table.

INDEPENDENT
CHALLENGE 4

Because you have invested in your education and are able to compete in the market place, you are able to purchase a car. You have a vague idea of your needs and have downloaded a database of automobiles in your area from the local newspaper's World Wide Web page. You live in a mountainous area that is treacherous during the winter months, so you would prefer a four-wheel or front-wheel drive vehicle.

To complete this independent challenge:

1 Make a copy of PD 3-8 and name it My Automobiles.

2 Make a copy of PD 3-9 and name it My Dealers.

3 Open My Automobiles, review the data and structure.

4 Open My Dealers, review the data and structure.

5 Print a copy of both tables.

6 Link the two tables using the Dealer Code as the common field. Create a query that lists only those vehicles that are four- or front-wheel drive. List them sorted by year of the vehicle, year, and make at the leftmost.

7 Use Figure 3-29 as your guide for creating the Answer table.

8 Save both the Answer table and query as Mt vehicle. Print the Answer table.

Mt. vehicle	Year	Make	Price	Model	Drive - front, back or 4	Dealer Name	Dealer Phone
1	89	Ford	15,885.00	Bronco	4	Ron's Ford	888-8228
2	90	Honda	10,995.00	Prelude	front	Honda High Mt.	822-8500
3	90	Toyota	13,895.00	4-Runner SR5	4	Lee Girard	897-5689
4	91	Subaru	6,495.00	Station Wagon	front	Lee Girard	897-5689
5	94	Ford	19,995.00	Ranger	4	Ron's Ford	888-8228
6	94	Saturn	10,495.00	SCI	front	Honda High Mt.	822-8500
7	95	Ford	18,885.00	Thunderbirds	front	Ron's Ford	888-8228
8	95	Honda	18,995.00	Odyssey	front	Honda High Mt.	822-8500
9	95	Oldsmobile	18,995.00	Delta 88	front	Lee Girard	897-5689
10	96	Honda	16,895.00	Accord LX	front	Honda High Mt.	822-8500
11	96	Honda	11,995.00	Civic	front	Honda High Mt.	822-8500

FIGURE 3-29

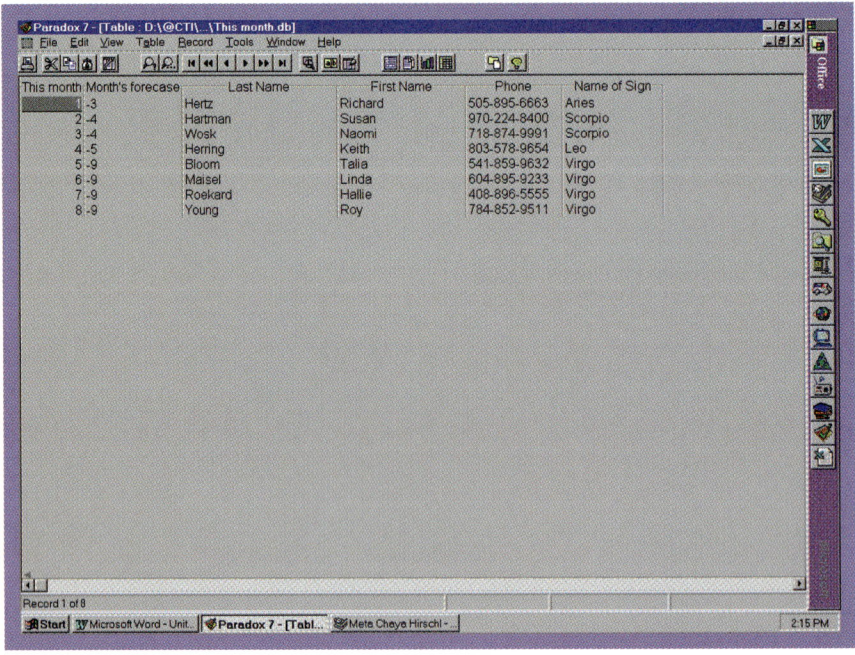

VISUALWORKSHOP

You have a special interest in astrology and have created a table that lists your friends, their addresses, phone numbers, birthdays, and astrology codes. You keep in touch with your friends by sending them notes with information about their sign each month. You also created a table with the astrology code, the name of the sign, the dates of sign, a brief description of the sign, and a forecast number from -10 to +10 (-10 being a month to forget and +10 a month of total joy and perfection) culled from all the reading you do. You haven't finished describing every sign, but you do have the other basic information. You plan on expanding this table in the future. Your Student Disk contains two tables named PD 3-10 and PD 3-11. Begin by making a copy of these tables. Link the two tables by astrology code, then create a query that produces an Answer table, as shown in Figure 3-30. Save the query and Answer table as This Month. Print a copy of the Answer table. (*Hint*: You want to list your friends whose predictions are less than 1, so that you can give them a call and check up on them periodically.)

FIGURE 3-30

Working
WITH TABLES

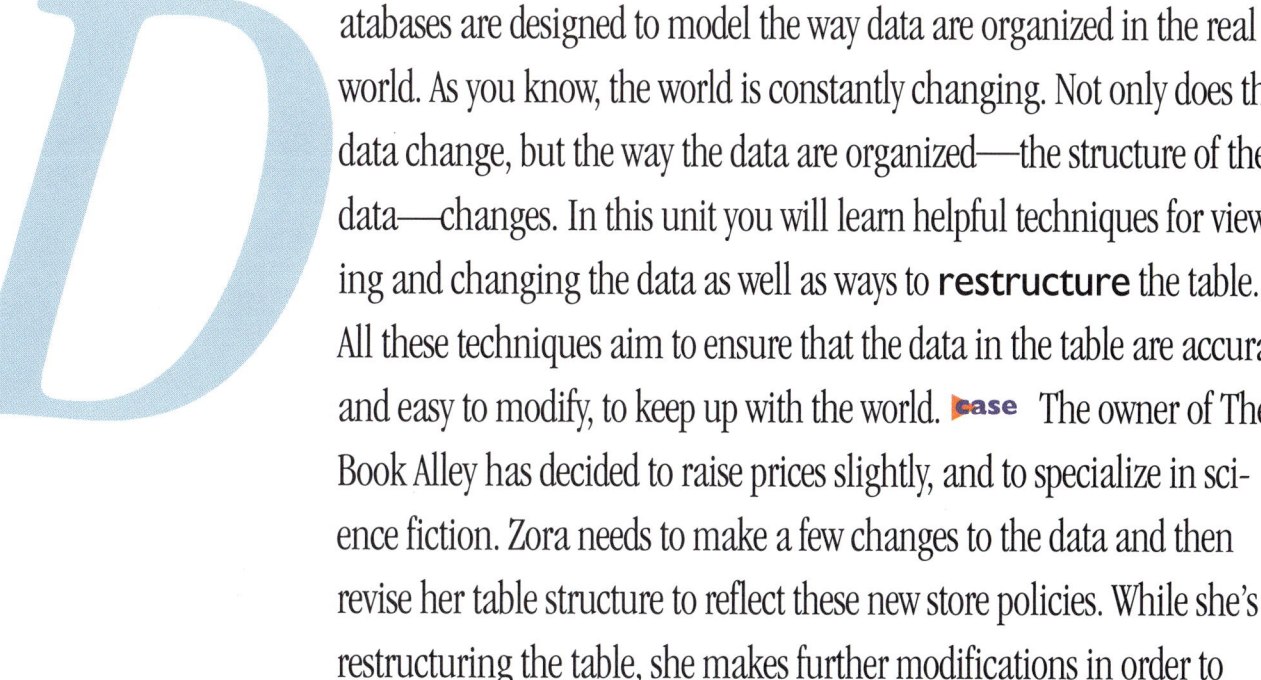

*D*atabases are designed to model the way data are organized in the real world. As you know, the world is constantly changing. Not only does the data change, but the way the data are organized—the structure of the data—changes. In this unit you will learn helpful techniques for viewing and changing the data as well as ways to **restructure** the table. All these techniques aim to ensure that the data in the table are accurate and easy to modify, to keep up with the world. **case** The owner of The Book Alley has decided to raise prices slightly, and to specialize in science fiction. Zora needs to make a few changes to the data and then revise her table structure to reflect these new store policies. While she's restructuring the table, she makes further modifications in order to make her table easier to use. ▶

Using Field view to edit records

In normal Edit mode, whatever you type in a field overwrites the data entered there. To change only part of a field, you can use **Field view**. This extension of Edit mode lets you move through a field character by character. See the related topic "Persistent Field view" to use Field view to edit several fields at once. ▶**case** Zora discovers that the book title *Chaos Died* should be *And Chaos Died*. To avoid retyping the entire entry, she uses Field view to correct the error.

1 Launch Paradox, insert your Student Disk in drive A:\, set the working directory to the appropriate folder, copy the table **PD 4-1** and save it as **My Book List**, then open **My Book List**
   Zora is ready to locate the erroneous record.

2 Maximize the window, click anywhere in the **title field column**, click the **Locate Field button** 🔍, type **..Chaos Died**, then click **OK**
   The entire field is highlighted. If you start typing now, all of the existing data will be deleted and you will have to type it all in again. To avoid retyping the entire entry, you can start Field view.

3 Click the **Field view button** 🔲 on the toolbar
   Paradox is now in Field view, as shown in Figure 4-1. Notice that the highlight in the Title field is replaced by an insertion point at the end of the field. You can now use the arrow keys to move through the field and edit any portion of the data, as described in Table 4-1.

4 Click the **Edit Data button** 🔲, press **[Home]** to move the insertion point to the beginning of the field, then type **And** and press **[Spacebar]**
   The new word is inserted and the existing text moves to the right.

5 Press ⬇ to complete the edit
   The cursor moves to the next record and Paradox exits Field view and the Field view message no longer appears in the status bar. Paradox is still in Edit mode, however.

6 Click 🔲 on the toolbar to exit Edit mode
   Compare your screen to Figure 4-2.

TABLE 4-1: Working in Field view

TO	DO THIS
Move to beginning of field	Press [Home]
Move to end of field	Press [End]
Move left one character	Press [Left Arrow]
Move right one character	Press [Right Arrow]
Delete character to left of insertion point	Press [Backspace]
Delete character to right of insertion point	Press [Delete]

FIGURE 4-1: Book List in Field view

Field view button

Locate button

Indicates record
just located

Indicates Field view

My Book List	ISBN	Title	Author	Category	Price	Qty
21	0-425-03786-6	The Anarchistic Colossus	Van Vogt	SF	$4.95	*********
22	0-425-04647-8	Malafrena	Le Guin	SF	$4.95	*********
23	0-425-07895-0	Hellstrom's Hive	Herbert	SF	$4.99	*********
24	0-425-09210-0	Human Options	Cousins	HN	$3.95	*********
25	0-440-21440-8	Healing Foods	Hausman & Hurley	HN	$6.99	*********
26	0-441-02269-1	Chaos Died	Russ	SF	$3.95	*********
27	0-446-30167-1	Working Smart	LeBoeuf	RF	$4.50	*********
28	0-446-35643-3	Vitamin Bible	Mindell	HN	$5.99	*********
29	0-446-36403-7	Anvil of Stars	Bear	SF	$5.99	*********
30	0-448-62954-3	Emergency Handbook	Arnold	RF	$10.95	*********
31	0-449-20018-3	Braided Lives	Piercy	FN	$3.95	*********
32	0-470-06321-1	The Forgotten Language	Fromm	LT	$4.95	*********
33	0-516-25568-1	Love without Wings	Auchincloss	LT	$5.95	*********
34	0-517-26825-6	Asimov's Guide to Shakesp	Asimov	TH	$25.00	*********
35	0-525-09577-1	The Drowning Season	Hoffman	FN	$8.95	*********
36	0-539-67234-1	The Condemned of Altona	Sartre	TH	$4.95	*********
37	0-553-07245-5	Long Quiet Highway	Goldberg	LT	$19.95	*********
38	0-56657-392-0	My Life in Art	Stanislavski	TH	$3.95	*********
39	0-671-63026-1	The Book of Stress Surviv	Kirsta	HN	$10.95	*********
40	0-671-88448-4	Mama	McMillan	FN	$5.99	*********
41	0-678-54682-1	Fathers and Sons	Turgenev	LT	$5.99	*********
42	0-67835-356-0	Jerusalem the Golden	Drabble	FN	$4.95	*********
43	0-8125-0925-0	Xenocide	Card	SF	$5.99	*********
44	0-87040-439-3	Barefoot Shiatsu	Yamamoto	HN	$11.50	*********
45	0-87857-582-0	Knocking at the Gate of L	Chang	HN	$10.95	*********
46	0-87980-383-5	Reflexology for Good Heal	Kaye & Matchan	HN	$3.50	*********
47	0-87997-945-3	Native Tongue	Haden Elgin	SF	$3.50	*********
48	0-89281-200-1	The Tao of Medicine	Fulder	HN	$9.95	*********
49	0-938190-64-4	Healing with Whole Foods	Pitchford	HN	$24.95	*********
50	0-97040-394-x	Zen Shiatsu	Masunaga	HN	$11.50	*********
51	345-22378-0-1	Diet for a Small Planet	Moore Lappe	HN	$4.95	*********

Record 26 of 51 — Field

FIGURE 4-2: Book List with correction

Corrected title

My Book List	ISBN	Title	Author	Category	Price	Qty
21	0-425-03786-6	The Anarchistic Colossus	Van Vogt	SF	$4.95	*********
22	0-425-04647-8	Malafrena	Le Guin	SF	$4.95	*********
23	0-425-07895-0	Hellstrom's Hive	Herbert	SF	$4.99	*********
24	0-425-09210-0	Human Options	Cousins	HN	$3.95	*********
25	0-440-21440-8	Healing Foods	Hausman & Hurley	HN	$6.99	*********
26	0-441-02269-1	And Chaos Died	Russ	SF	$3.95	*********
27	0-446-30167-1	Working Smart	LeBoeuf	RF	$4.50	*********
28	0-446-35643-3	Vitamin Bible	Mindell	HN	$5.99	*********
29	0-446-36403-7	Anvil of Stars	Bear	SF	$5.99	*********
30	0-448-62954-3	Emergency Handbook	Arnold	RF	$10.95	*********
31	0-449-20018-3	Braided Lives	Piercy	FN	$3.95	*********
32	0-470-06321-1	The Forgotten Language	Fromm	LT	$4.95	*********
33	0-516-25568-1	Love without Wings	Auchincloss	LT	$5.95	*********
34	0-517-26825-6	Asimov's Guide to Shakesp	Asimov	TH	$25.00	*********
35	0-525-09577-1	The Drowning Season	Hoffman	FN	$8.95	*********
36	0-539-67234-1	The Condemned of Altona	Sartre	TH	$4.95	*********

Persistent Field view

Each time you finish editing a field and move to another field or record, Paradox automatically leaves Field view and reverts to standard Edit mode. If you want to remain in Field view in order to make several changes, you can use **Persistent Field view**. To switch to Persistent Field view, press [Ctrl][F2]. You can now move around in the table and remain in Field view. To leave Persistent Field view, click the Field view button 🔲 on the toolbar or press [Ctrl][F2] again.

Tailoring table view

To make a table easier to work with, you can change the way it looks on the screen. You can edit the **table view properties**, characteristics that determine the on-screen appearance of the table. You can move and lock columns for easier viewing, and you can filter data within columns. For information on how Paradox displays data in partially visible columns, see the related topic "Disappearing fields." Keep in mind that changing the way the table looks on the screen has no effect on the data itself, the structure of the table, or the way the table prints. ▶case   Zora wants to modify the appearance of the table to make it easier to use.

1 Move the pointer to the **Qty column heading** until the pointer changes to ⬚, then press the **mouse button** and move the mouse very slightly until the pointer changes again, to ↔
As shown in Figure 4-3, two thick vertical lines appear on either side of the Qty column. The message "Moving column" appears in the status bar. To move a column, you simply drag it to a new location. As you move the pointer, the double vertical lines are replaced by a single line.

2 Drag the **mouse pointer** ↔ to position the single line just to the right of the Category column, then release the **mouse button**
The Qty column is now between the Category and Price columns, as shown in Figure 4-4. Now it's time to decrease the Qty column's width.

3 Move the pointer over the border between the Qty and Price columns until it changes to ⇔
To make the column narrower, you can simply drag the pointer to the left. To increase the width of the column, drag the pointer to the right.

4 Hold down the **mouse button** and drag ⇔ until the column is wide enough to display the longest field value and the heading, then release the **mouse button**
If you see asterisks in any of the fields after you release the mouse button, you have made the column too narrow. To widen it, simply drag the column border to the right until the column is the correct width. Zora wants to center the Category column.

5 Click anywhere in the **Category field**, right-click the mouse, then select **Properties**

6 Click the **Alignment tab** of the Category Properties dialog box, click the **Horizontal Center radio button**, then click **OK**
The Category column is centered.

7 Minimize your screen or resize it, if necessary, so it looks like Figure 4-5
If Zora scrolls to the right to view the complete Price column, she will not be able to see the ISBN and Title columns. To avoid confusion, she decides to lock the first two columns in place, so that they will always appear on the screen, even when she scrolls right.

This column is ready to be moved

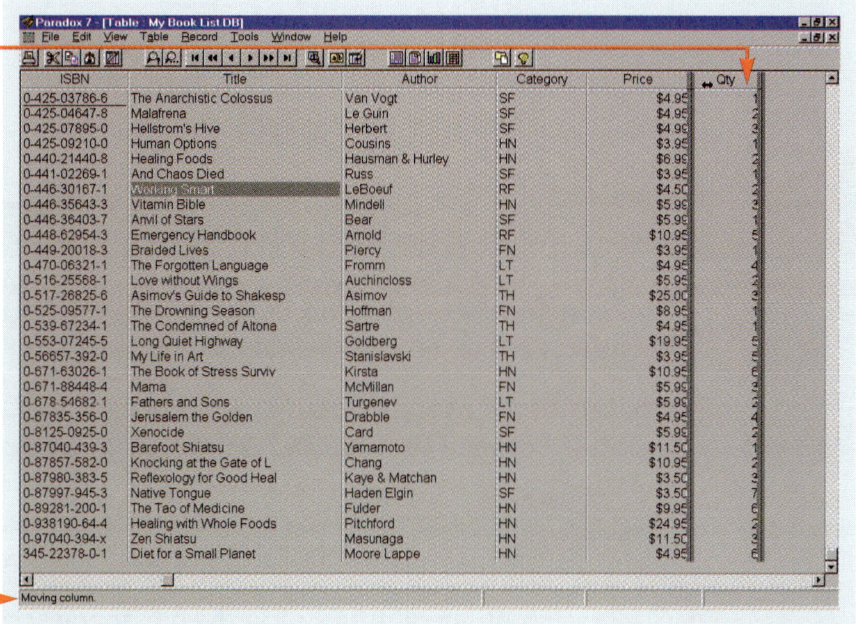

FIGURE 4-3: Moving a column

Current activity

FIGURE 4-4: Qty field in its new position

Qty column has been moved

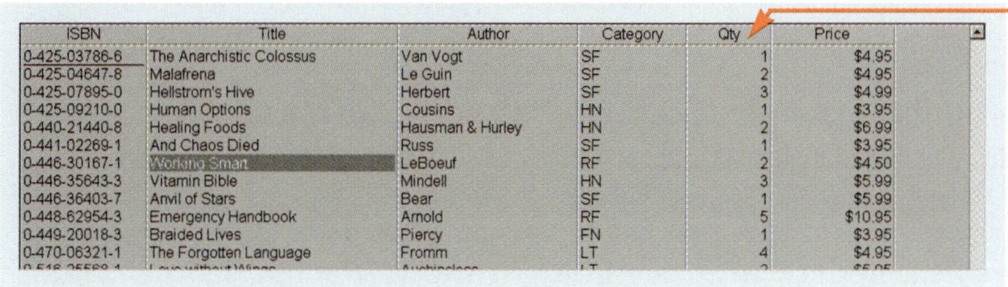

FIGURE 4-5: Column width changed

Aligned center

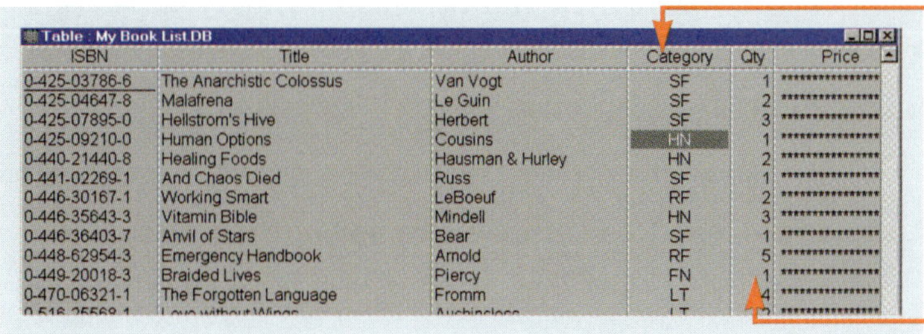

Column width reduced

QUICK **TIP**

Paradox automatically sizes the columns to fit the number of characters you specified for each field. So if you want to see longer titles, you will have to modify the table structure and increase the length of the Title field. Then enter the additional characters for each title.■

Disappearing fields

You might see asterisks in the Price field when only part of that column is visible on the screen. The asterisks tell you that the entire number field will not fit on the screen. For alphanumeric fields (such as the Title and Author fields), Paradox displays as many characters as will fit on the screen.

Tailoring table view, continued

To lock columns in place, you use the **scroll lock**, a small triangle at the left end of the horizontal scroll bar, at the bottom left corner of your screen. You can also filter data by using the right mouse button.

8 Click the **First Rec button** ⏮, hold down the **mouse button** on the left-pointing triangle at the lower left of the screen (just above the horizontal scroll bar) until it changes to ⇔

If you move the pointer slightly it changes to ← →. Next you'll drag the pointer to move a gray rectangle that controls locking to the border between columns.

9 Hold down the **mouse button** and drag the ← → to position the gray rectangle between the Title and Author columns, then release the **mouse button**

The gray rectangle changes to two gray triangles, as shown in Figure 4-6. The ISBN and Title columns are now locked in place. You'll see how this affects the screen display in the next step.

10 Click the **right scroll button** on the horizontal scroll bar to move through the columns

Notice that the ISBN and Title columns don't scroll off the screen along with the rest of the columns. The asterisks in the Price column change to numerals when the entire column is displayed. Zora removes the lock for now.

11 Drag the **double triangle** back to the left corner of the window

The single left-pointing triangle returns. Zora wants to use a **filter** to view only the science fiction books. A filter allows you to view a subset of records.

12 Click anywhere in the **Category field**, right-click the mouse, then click **Filter**

The Field Filter dialog box opens, as shown in Figure 4-7.

13 Type **SF** in the Filter for Category box (make sure the letters are capitalized), then click **OK**

Only the science fiction books are displayed, as shown in Figure 4-8. Zora returns to the complete data view.

14 Repeat step 12 and press **[Delete]** to remove the entry, then click **OK**

All the books are again visible. Zora returns to the beginning of the table before she saves the table view properties.

15 Click ⏮, click **Table** on the menu bar, click **Table View Properties**, then click **Save**

The new table view properties are saved. Compare your screen to Figure 4-9.

FIGURE 4-6: Locking the Title column

Table : My Book List.DB

My Book List	ISBN	Title	Author	Category	Qty
1	0-01-003925-6	Steppenwolf	Hesse	LT	2
2	0-01-004592-1	Studies in Zen	Suziki	RM	5
3	0-01-063490-1	Sister Carrie	Dreiser	LT	1
4	0-01059-342-0	Those Barren Leaves	Huxley	LT	5
5	0-014-46380-1	Training an Actor	Moore	TH	2
6	0-01790-538-0	My Sister in this House	Kesselman	TH	4
7	0-03-293453-0	The Comedians	Graham	LT	1
8	0-03-562912-0	Modern French Theatre	Benedikt	TH	1
9	0-039-25432-1	When Worlds Collide	Wylie	SF	1
10	0-06-012006-1	How to Audition	Hunt	TH	1
11	0-06-080437-0	The Impossible Question	Krishnamurti	RM	3
12	0-06-272027-9	On Writing Well	Zinsser	RF	10
13	0-06-272043-0	Grammar for Grownups	Dumond	RF	8
14	0-07-006421-0	And Never Said a Word	Boll	LT	5
15	0-153216-29-1	The Caine Mutiny	Wouk	LT	3
16	0-2767-1791-1	Jules et Jim	Truffaut	TH	1
17	0-34567-091-1	Your Body Speaks Its Mind	Kelleman	HN	1
18	0-380-45997-3	Uncommon Women and Others	Wasserstein	TH	2
19	0-385-17010-6	Who Dies?	Levine	RM	4
20	0-399-12987-1	The Only Problem	Spark	FN	1
21	0-425-03786-6	The Anarchistic Colossus	Van Vogt	SF	1
22	0-425-04647-8	Malafrena	Le Guin	SF	2
23	0-425-07895-0	Hellstrom's Hive	Herbert	SF	3
24	0-425-09210-0	Human Options	Cousins	HN	1
25	0-440-21440-8	Healing Foods	Hausman & Hurley	HN	2
26	0-441-02269-1	And Chaos Died	Russ	SF	1
27	0-446-30167-1	Working Smart	LeBoeuf	RF	2
28	0-446-35643-3	Vitamin Bible	Mindell	HN	3

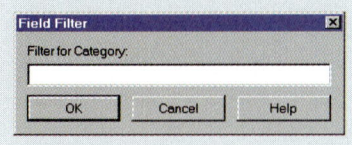

Columns to the left are locked, to the right will scroll

FIGURE 4-7: Field Filter dialog box

FIGURE 4-8: Science fiction filter on

Table : My Book List.DB

My Book List	ISBN	Title	Author	Category	Qty
9	0-039-25432-1	When Worlds Collide	Wylie	SF	1
21	0-425-03786-6	The Anarchistic Colossus	Van Vogt	SF	1
22	0-425-04647-8	Malafrena	Le Guin	SF	2
23	0-425-07895-0	Hellstrom's Hive	Herbert	SF	3
26	0-441-02269-1	And Chaos Died	Russ	SF	1
29	0-446-36403-7	Anvil of Stars	Bear	SF	1
43	0-8125-0925-0	Xenocide	Card	SF	2
47	0-87997-945-3	Native Tongue	Haden Elgin	SF	7

FIGURE 4-9: No filter on

Table : My Book List.DB

My Book List	ISBN	Title	Author	Category	Qty
1	0-01-003925-6	Steppenwolf	Hesse	LT	2
2	0-01-004592-1	Studies in Zen	Suziki	RM	5
3	0-01-063490-1	Sister Carrie	Dreiser	LT	1
4	0-01059-342-0	Those Barren Leaves	Huxley	LT	5
5	0-014-46380-1	Training an Actor	Moore	TH	2
6	0-01790-538-0	My Sister in this House	Kesselman	TH	4
7	0-03-293453-0	The Comedians	Graham	LT	1
8	0-03-562912-0	Modern French Theatre	Benedikt	TH	1
9	0-039-25432-1	When Worlds Collide	Wylie	SF	1
10	0-06-012006-1	How to Audition	Hunt	TH	1
11	0-06-080437-0	The Impossible Question	Krishnamurti	RM	3
12	0-06-272027-9	On Writing Well	Zinsser	RF	10
13	0-06-272043-0	Grammar for Grownups	Dumond	RF	8
14	0-07-006421-0	And Never Said a Word	Boll	LT	5
15	0-153216-29-1	The Caine Mutiny	Wouk	LT	3
16	0-2767-1791-1	Jules et Jim	Truffaut	TH	1
17	0-34567-091-1	Your Body Speaks Its Mind	Kelleman	HN	1
18	0-380-45997-3	Uncommon Women and Others	Wasserstein	TH	2
19	0-385-17010-6	Who Dies?	Levine	RM	4
20	0-399-12987-1	The Only Problem	Spark	FN	1
21	0-425-03786-6	The Anarchistic Colossus	Van Vogt	SF	1
22	0-425-04647-8	Malafrena	Le Guin	SF	2
23	0-425-07895-0	Hellstrom's Hive	Herbert	SF	3
24	0-425-09210-0	Human Options	Cousins	HN	1
25	0-440-21440-8	Healing Foods	Hausman & Hurley	HN	2
26	0-441-02269-1	And Chaos Died	Russ	SF	1
27	0-446-30167-1	Working Smart	LeBoeuf	RF	2
28	0-446-35643-3	Vitamin Bible	Mindell	HN	3

TROUBLE?

If you make a mistake while changing the table properties, you can return the properties to their original settings by clicking Properties on the menu bar, clicking View Properties, then clicking Restore.

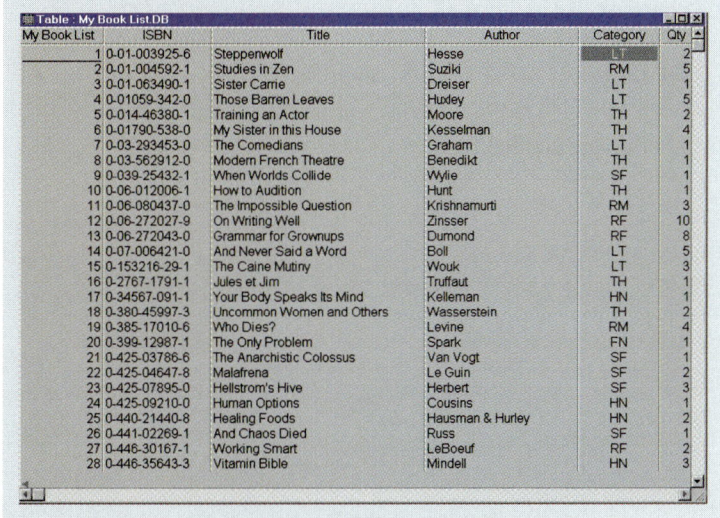

Adding and deleting fields

Before you make any changes to the structure of a table, it's a good idea to review it in a view-only mode first. Once you are certain of the changes you want to make, you can restructure the table in a different window. Remember that when you delete a field, you also delete the data. **case** To help her keep track of book orders, Zora decides to add two new fields—Publisher and Publication Date—to her table structure. First Zora views the structure of her inventory table, then she opens the table and restructures it.

1 Click **Table** on the menu bar, then click **Info Structure**
This opens the Structure Information dialog box, as shown in Figure 4-10. Notice that all the options in the Table properties area are dimmed (unavailable) to prevent you from making changes accidentally. Take a moment to review the structure.

2 Click **Done**
This closes the Structure Information dialog box.

3 Click the **Restructure button** 🖼 on the toolbar
This opens the Restructure dialog box. Zora wants to insert the Publisher and Publication Date fields between the Author and Category fields.

4 Click anywhere in the **Category field row** to select it, then press **[Insert]**
Paradox inserts a blank field row (Row 4) above the Category field. Now Zora can enter the information for the Publisher field, using the Tab key to move from one column to the next.

5 Using **[Tab]** to move between fields, type **Publisher** in the Field Name column, type **A** in the Type column, then type **15** in the Size column
Next, Zora adds a new field row for the Publication Date field between the Publisher and Category fields. She decides to abbreviate "Publication Date" to "Pub Date."

6 Repeat step 4, then type **Pub Date** in the Field Name column, type **A** in the Type column, type **4** in the Size column, then press **[Enter]**
Your table structure should now look like Figure 4-11.

7 Click **Save** to save your changes to the table structure
You return to the table view window, which shows a blank Publisher field. Now Zora starts Edit mode and begins entering data into the new fields.

FIGURE 4-10: Structure Information dialog box

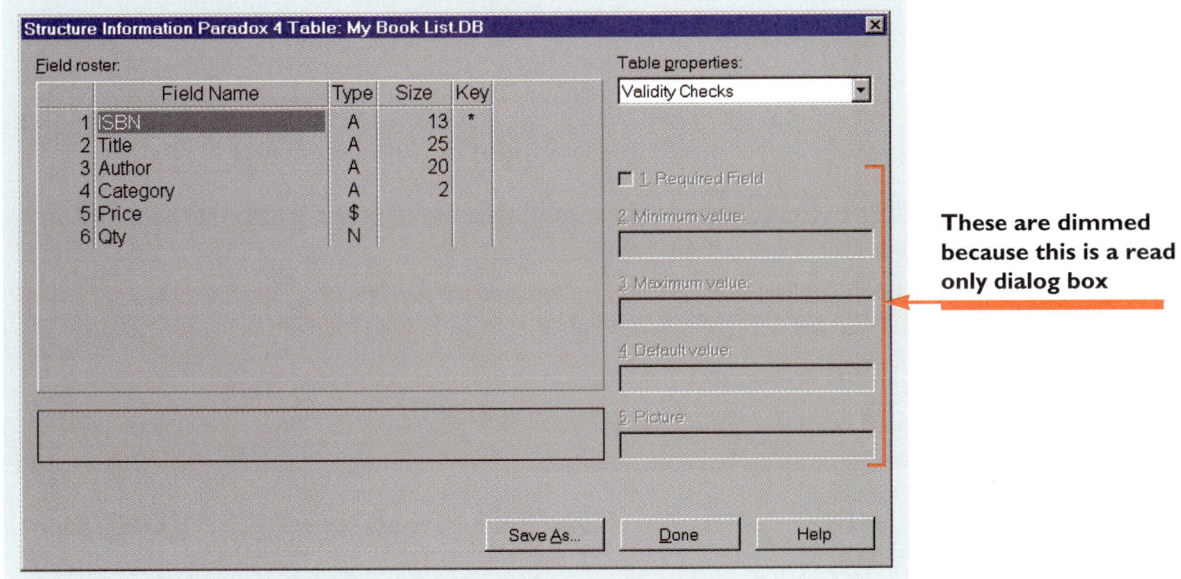

These are dimmed because this is a read only dialog box

FIGURE 4-11: Restructure dialog box with changes

Two new fields

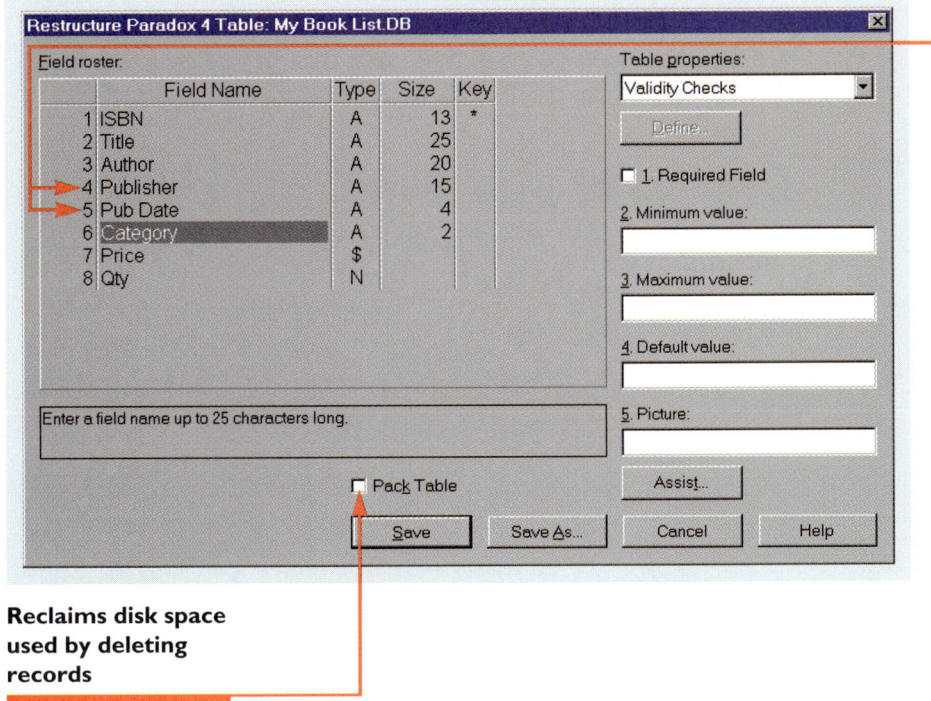

Reclaims disk space used by deleting records

QUICK **TIP**

You might have noticed that, even though you're using Paradox 7, the title bar of the Structure Information dialog box says "Paradox 4 Table." When you created your Paradox 7 table, Paradox automatically saved the table structure in Paradox 4.0 format in order to make it easier to share files between the two versions.■

Adding and deleting fields, continued

Zora returns to the table to enter data and review the table.

8 Click the **Edit Data button** 🖾 on the toolbar and press **[Tab]** until the highlight moves to the **Publisher field** in the first record

9 Type **Modern Library** in the Publisher field, press **[Tab]**, type **1963** in the Pub Date field, then press ⬇

As Zora is entering data, her supervisor stops by to say that he doesn't think the Pub Date field is necessary because it can be part of a Publisher table. So Zora restructures the table again to delete the new field.

10 Click 🖾 to leave Edit mode, then click 🖾

The Restructure dialog box opens as before.

11 Click anywhere in the **Pub Date field row** and press **[Ctrl][Del]**, then click **Save**

The Restructure Warning dialog box shown in Figure 4-12 opens. Whenever you make a structure change that could affect your data, this dialog box gives you a chance to change your mind. In this case, it's asking if you're sure you want to delete the Pub Date field.

12 Click **OK** and when the My Book List table reappears, scroll right to verify that the Pub Date field has been deleted, then click the **First Rec button** 🖼

Figure 4-13 shows My Book List with the new Publisher field added and the Pub Date field deleted.

FIGURE 4-12: Restructure Warning dialog box asks you to confirm deletion

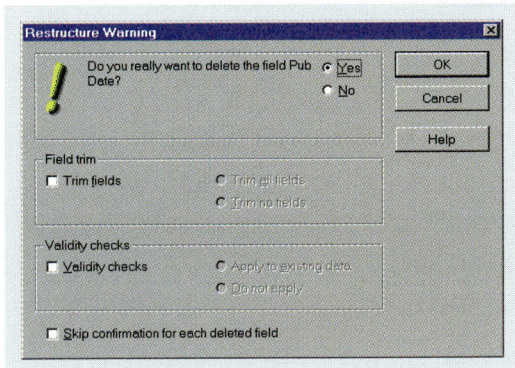

FIGURE 4-13: My Book List with the new Publisher field added and the Pub Date field deleted

New field

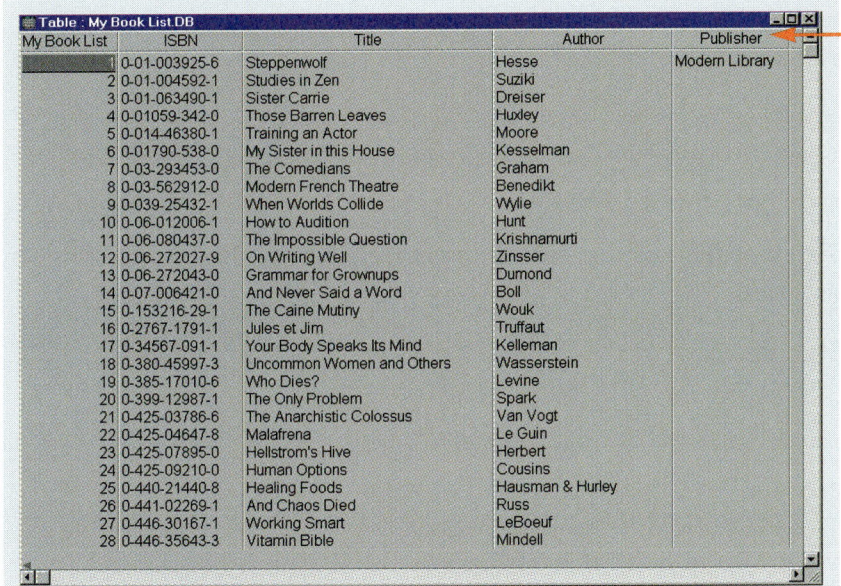

TROUBLE?

If you accidentally delete a field you need, or make other changes you don't want, click Cancel to leave the Restructure Warning dialog box without saving the changes.■

QUICK TIP

Zora made Pub Date an Alpha field because she plans to enter only the year in this field (for example, 1996). If she had made Pub Date a Date field, Paradox would require a complete date, with the day, month, and year (for example, 1/6/96).■

Changing a field name or size

When you view a table, Paradox widens the field columns to accommodate the width of the field names (at the top of the columns), not the size of the field itself. So you might find that you are wasting viewing screen space with overly long field names. Fortunately, Paradox makes it easy to change the size of any field name as well as the size of the field itself. When shortening fields, keep in mind that you risk losing any existing data that exceeds the new field length. **case** Zora wants to abbreviate the name for the Category field so it doesn't have to take up so much space on the screen. She's also discovered that she needs to make some field size changes.

1 Click the **Restructure button** 📧 on the toolbar to open the Restructure dialog box again
Zora begins by shortening the Category field name to "Cat."

2 Click **Category** in the Field Name column
Paradox highlights the entire word.

3 Type **Cat**
The word "Category" is replaced by "Cat." Next, Zora increases the size of the Title field to 30 characters to accommodate longer book titles.

4 Click the **Size column** of the Title field row, then type **30**
Finally, Zora reduces the size of the Publisher field to six characters.

5 Click the **Size column** of the Publisher field row, type **6**, then press **[Enter]**
Your Restructure dialog box should look like Figure 4-14.

6 Click **Save**
The Restructure Warning dialog box opens again, as shown in Figure 4-15. In this case, it's letting you know that reducing the size of the Publisher field could result in the loss of any publisher data that is longer than six characters. If you click OK, Paradox will shorten (or trim) the existing data to six characters. Because Zora intends to abbreviate the publishers' names anyway, this isn't a problem.

7 Click **OK**
The dialog box closes, and you return to the restructured My Book List table. The publisher name you entered has been trimmed to six characters, as shown in Figure 4-16.

FIGURE 4-14:
Your Restructure dialog box should look like this

Longer field size

New name

Shorter field size

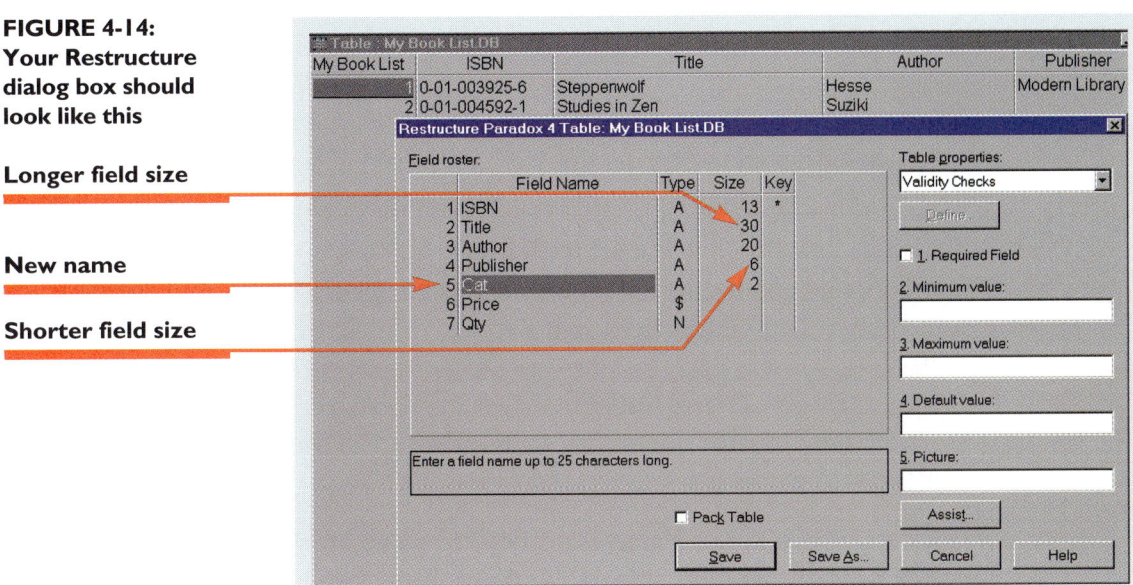

FIGURE 4-15:
Paradox is about to trim data from the Publisher field

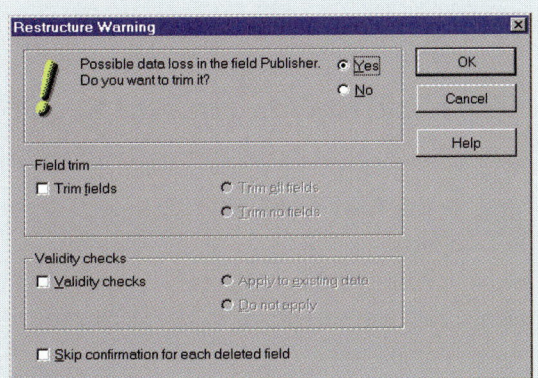

FIGURE 4-16: Table with changes to field name and size

Larger field

New name

Trimmed Publisher data

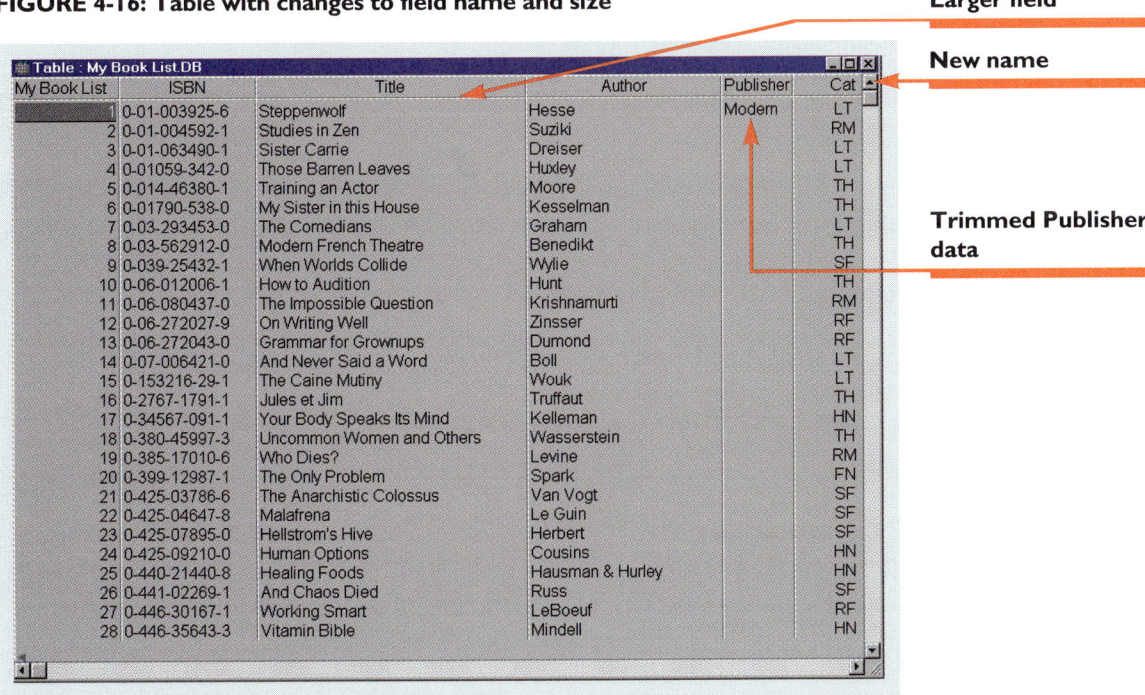

Adding validity checks

To ensure that data are entered correctly into a table, you can place restrictions, called **validity checks**, on the data in any field. When you enter data in a field for which you have specified a validity check, Paradox checks the data to make sure they are valid. See the related topic "Controlling entered characters" for information on restrictions on individual characters. **case** Zora decides to add several validity checks to her table.

1 Click the **Restructure button** 🖫 on the toolbar
The Restructure dialog box appears. Zora wants to place a minimum value validity check on the Price field to prevent her from entering a price less than $3.00.

2 Click anywhere in the **Price field row** to select it, click the **Minimum value box** on the right side of the dialog box, then type **3**
Note that you don't have to type a dollar sign or decimal places because the Price field is already specified as a Money field. Next, Zora wants to make sure every book record has an ISBN, so she designates the ISBN field as a required field.

3 Click in the **ISBN field row**, then click the **Required Field check box**
Next, Zora wants to specify SF as the default entry in the Cat field.

4 Click anywhere in the **Cat field row** to select it, then type **SF** in the Default value text box
Figure 4-17 shows your Restructure dialog box with the default value for the Cat field. Now, Paradox will automatically enter the default value "SF" in the Category field. To enter a different category code, you can simply type over the default value.

5 Click anywhere in the **Price field row**
Note the 3 in the Minimum value box. The validity check for each field appears when that field row is highlighted.

6 Click **Save** to save the structure changes
A Restructure Warning dialog box opens, as shown in Figure 4-18, asking if you want the new validity checks enforced on data already in the table. If you respond "Yes," any records that do not conform to the new restrictions will be removed from the table and placed in a temporary table where you can correct the validity failures. Then you can return the records to the original table. Because you specified three validity checks, you will see three Restructure Warning dialog boxes.

7 Click **OK** in all three Restructure Warning dialog boxes to enforce the validity checks on the existing data
When you close the third warning dialog box, a temporary table named KEYVIOL.DB opens, containing records that do not conform to the new restrictions (records that failed the validity check).

8 Scroll right to display the **Price field** containing a value of **$2.95**
Your screen should look like Figure 4-19. The record in this table is known as a **key violation** because it violates (or does not conform to) the minimum value of $3.00 you specified for the Price field.

FIGURE 4-17:
Restructure dialog box with validity check

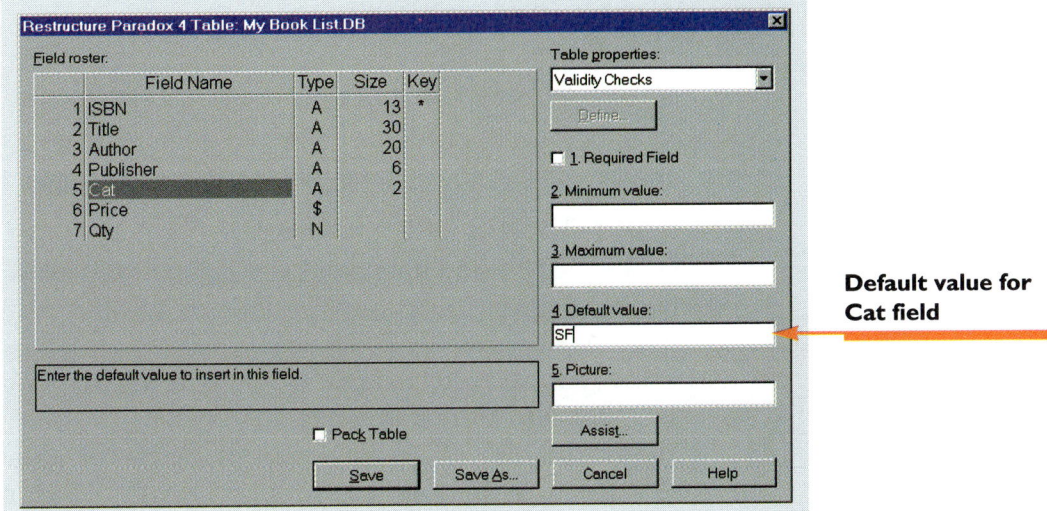

Default value for
Cat field

FIGURE 4-18:
Restructure Warning dialog box after adding validity checks

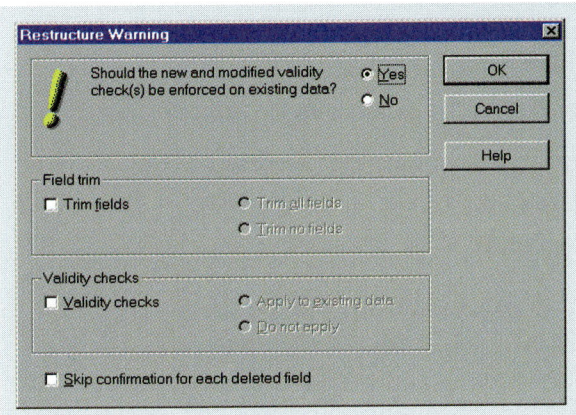

FIGURE 4-19: KEYVIOL table

Only 1 record failed the validity checks

Price below the minimum value of $3.00

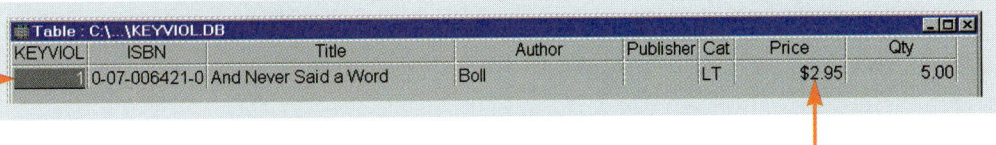

Controlling entered characters

Besides being able to control values entered into a field using validity checks, you can also control individual characters. A **picture template** uses characters and symbols to specify valid characters for each position in a field. For example, the pound sign (#) indicates that only numbers can be entered in that position. The picture template for a phone number is (###) ###-####. You can create a picture template for a field with the Structure (or Restructure) Table dialog box. For more detail, see the User Guide Index under "picture strings."

Correcting key violations

You edit the records in a KEYVIOL table just as you would records in any other Paradox table. After editing the records to make them conform to the validity checks, you can return the records to the original table. This process is known as **correcting key violations**. ▶case Zora increases the price of the book to comply with the validity check and then returns the record to the My Book List table.

1 Press **[F9]** to switch to Edit mode, type **3** in the Price field, then press **[F9]** again to leave Edit mode
The status bar briefly displays the message, "Record has been posted," which means that the correction has been saved in the KEYVIOL table. Now that the data conforms to the validity check, you can add the record to the My Book List.DB table.

2 Click **Tools** on the menu bar, click **Utilities**, click **Add**, click the **Alias list arrow**, then click **PRIV:**
The Add records in dialog box lists the files in the Private folder shown in Figure 4-20. You can now tell Paradox which table contains the records you want to add.

3 Click **Keyviol** in the file list, then click **OK**
Add records in Keyviol.DB appears in the upper text box. Now you can tell Paradox which table to add the records to.

4 Click **My Book List** from the file list
My Book List.DB appears in the File name text box.

5 Click **Add**
"Records successfully appended" appears in the status bar indicating that the new, corrected data is back in the My Book List table. You have corrected the key violation. To verify this, Zora closes the KEYVIOL table.

6 Click **File** on the menu bar, then click **Close**
The KEYVIOL table closes and the My Book List table opens in the table view window.

7 Locate the Author **Boll**, then tab to display the Price field
Figure 4-21 shows the record that violated the validity check with a new price. Zora doesn't need the My Book List.DB table now, so she closes it.

8 Click **File** on the menu bar, then click **Close**
The My Book List.DB table closes and you return to the Project Viewer window

FIGURE 4-20: Add dialog box

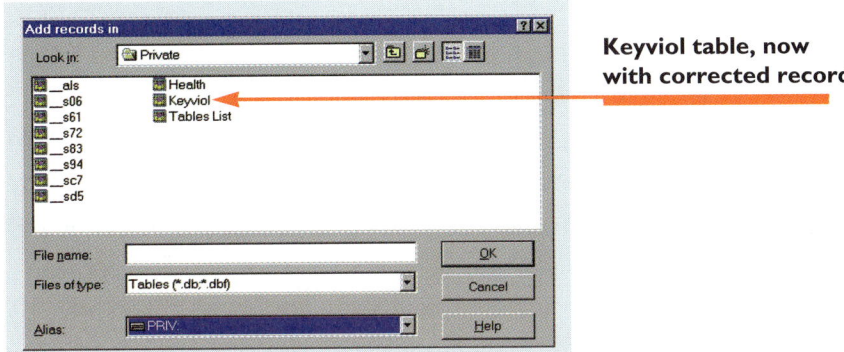

Keyviol table, now
with corrected record

FIGURE 4-21: My Book List table with the corrected record

Corrected record with
valid price

Title	Author	Publisher	Cat	Price	Qty
Steppenwolf	Hesse	Modern	LT	$4.99	2
Studies in Zen	Suziki		RM	$4.95	5
Sister Carrie	Dreiser		LT	$5.95	1
Those Barren Leaves	Huxley		LT	$4.50	5
Training an Actor	Moore		TH	$4.95	2
My Sister in this House	Kesselman		TH	$5.95	4
The Comedians	Graham		LT	$4.99	1
Modern French Theatre	Benedikt		TH	$3.75	1
When Worlds Collide	Wylie		SF	$4.99	1
How to Audition	Hunt		TH	$4.95	1
The Impossible Question	Krishnamurti		RM	$3.50	3
On Writing Well	Zinsser		RF	$11.00	10
Grammar for Grownups	Dumond		RF	$8.00	8
And Never Said a Word	Boll		LT	$3.00	5
The Caine Mutiny	Wouk		LT	$7.95	3
Jules et Jim	Truffaut		TH	$10.95	1
Your Body Speaks Its Mind	Kelleman		HN	$7.95	1
Uncommon Women and Others	Wasserstein		TH	$4.95	2
Who Dies?	Levine		RM	$9.95	4
The Only Problem	Spark		FN	$14.95	1
The Anarchistic Colossus	Van Vogt		SF	$4.95	1
Malafrena	Le Guin		SF	$4.95	2
Hellstrom's Hive	Herbert		SF	$4.99	3
Human Options	Cousins		HN	$3.95	1
Healing Foods	Hausman & Hurley		HN	$6.99	2
And Chaos Died	Russ		SF	$3.95	1
Working Smart	LeBoeuf		RF	$4.50	2
Vitamin Bible	Mindell		HN	$5.99	3

QUICK **TIP**

The KEYVIOL table is a temporary table that is deleted when you exit Paradox. However, if you prefer, you can delete it after you have successfully returned the records to the original table. To delete the KEYVIOL table using the Project Viewer, right-click the file-name, then click Delete. If more than one KEYVIOL table is created while you are in Paradox, each additional table will be named with a number (KEYVIOL1, KEYVIOL2), the highest number being the most recently created table. ■

Creating a lookup table

In this lesson, you'll learn yet another restructuring technique—defining a link to a lookup table—that will help ensure that data is entered correctly. A **lookup table** is a list of valid field entries. There are two steps to adding a lookup table to your database: first create the lookup table, just as you would any other table; then restructure the original table (in this case, the My Book List.DB table) to define a **link** between the two tables. A link is simply identifying a common field between tables. ▶**case**   Zora wants to make sure all the values in the Category field are taken from a list of accepted codes that can be displayed when entering records. So Zora decides to create a lookup table of book category codes.

STEPS

1 Right-click **Tables** in the Project Viewer window, then click **New** from the context-sensitive menu
The Create Table dialog box opens.

2 Click **OK** to instruct Paradox to create a Paradox 7 for Windows table
The Create Paradox 7 Table dialog box opens, with an empty Field roster.

3 Use the specifications shown in Table 4-2 to create the lookup table structure
Now that the table structure is complete, Zora must save the table before she can enter data in it.

4 Click **Save As**
The Save Table As dialog box opens. Zora wants to enter data right away, so she asks Paradox to display the table immediately after saving the structure.

5 Click **Display table** in the Save As dialog box
Because the table will contain a list of book category codes, Zora uses the table name Book Categories.

6 Type **Book Categories** in the New File Name text box, then click **Save**
The empty Book Categories table appears in the table view window. Now Zora enters the list of book category codes.

7 Click the **Edit Data button** 🖉 on the toolbar, then enter the data shown in Table 4-3
As you complete each record, notice that Paradox automatically places the record in its proper alphabetical order, by Code (the key field). If you pressed ⬇ or [Enter] and end up with eight rows, just press ⬆ to delete the blank row. The new Book Categories lookup table is shown in Figure 4-22.

8 Close the **Book Categories table**
Now that she has created the Book Categories lookup table, Zora needs to restructure the My Book List.DB table to link it to the lookup table. The link she'll create will tell Paradox to look in the Book Categories.DB table for valid entries for the Category field. If a clerk attempts to enter a code in the My Book List.DB table that is not in the lookup table, Paradox will display a warning message.

FIGURE 4-22: Book Categories table

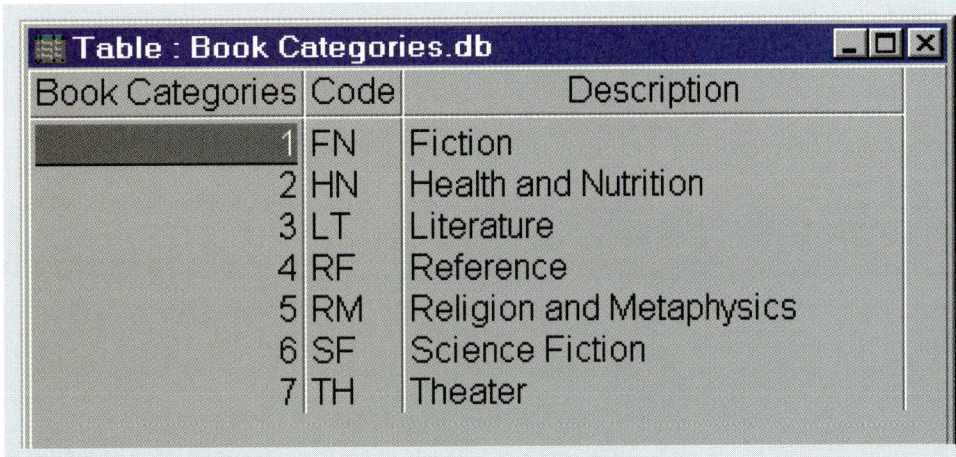

TABLE 4-2: Book Categories.DB table structure

FIELD NAME	TYPE	SIZE	KEY
Code	A	2	*
Description	A	30	

TABLE 4-3: Data for Book Categories.DB

CODE	DESCRIPTION
TH	Theater
LT	Literature
SF	Science Fiction
HN	Health and Nutrition
FN	Fiction
RM	Religion and Metaphysics
RF	Reference

QUICK **TIP**

The first field in the lookup table roster must be the field you want to link to the original table (in this case, the My Book List.DB table). This field in the lookup table must be the same type and size as the corresponding field in the original table.■

Creating a lookup table, continued

To create a link between two tables, you simply need to tell Paradox which two fields contain the same data. In this case, Zora links the Cat field in the My Book List table to the Code field in the lookup table.

9 Double-click **My Book List.DB** in the Project Viewer window, then maximize the table if necessary
The My Book List table opens in table view.

10 Click the **Restructure button** 📇 on the toolbar
The Restructure dialog box opens.

11 Click the **Table properties list arrow**
The Table properties appear, as shown in Figure 4-23. A table link is only one of a number of properties you can define for a table. Don't worry about the other properties in this menu. For now, you're only concerned with defining the Table Lookup property.

12 Click **Table Lookup**, then click **Define**
The Table Lookup dialog box opens, as shown in Figure 4-24. The Fields list displays all the fields from My Book List.DB. The Lookup table list shows all the tables in your working directory. Zora wants to link the Cat field in My Book List.DB to the Book Categories.DB table.

13 Click **Cat [A2]** in the Fields list to select it, then click the **right arrow button** pointing to the Field name box
This places the Cat[A2] field in the Field name box. Next you need to choose the lookup table name from the Lookup table list.

14 Click **Book Categories.db** in the Lookup table list, then click the **left arrow button** pointing to the Lookup field box
Paradox automatically places the first field in the Book Categories.db table (Code) in the Lookup field box. Zora wants her clerks to be able to display the lookup table for reference while they are entering data, so she decides to use the Help and fill option.

15 Click **Help and fill** in the Lookup access radio button, if it's not already checked
Your Table Lookup dialog box should look like Figure 4-25.

16 Click **OK**
The Table Lookup dialog box closes and you return to the Restructure dialog box, which shows Book Categories.db (the lookup table) listed in the Table properties list. This confirms the link between the Cat field (highlighted in the Field roster) in the My Book List table and the Book Categories lookup table.

17 Click **Save**
A Restructure Warning dialog box opens, asking if you want the table lookup restriction enforced on existing data.

18 Click **OK**
The Restructure dialog box closes and you return to the table view window displaying the My Book List table. No KEYVIOL table appears, indicating that all entries in the Cat field are valid—in other words, there is nothing in the Cat field that isn't listed in the Book Categories lookup table.

FIGURE 4-23: Table properties list

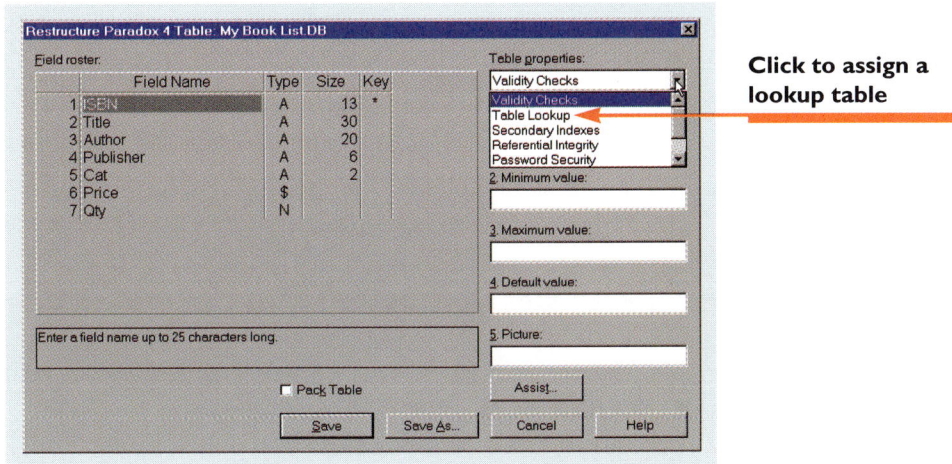

Click to assign a lookup table

FIGURE 4-24: Table Lookup dialog box

ISBN is an Alpha field with 13 characters

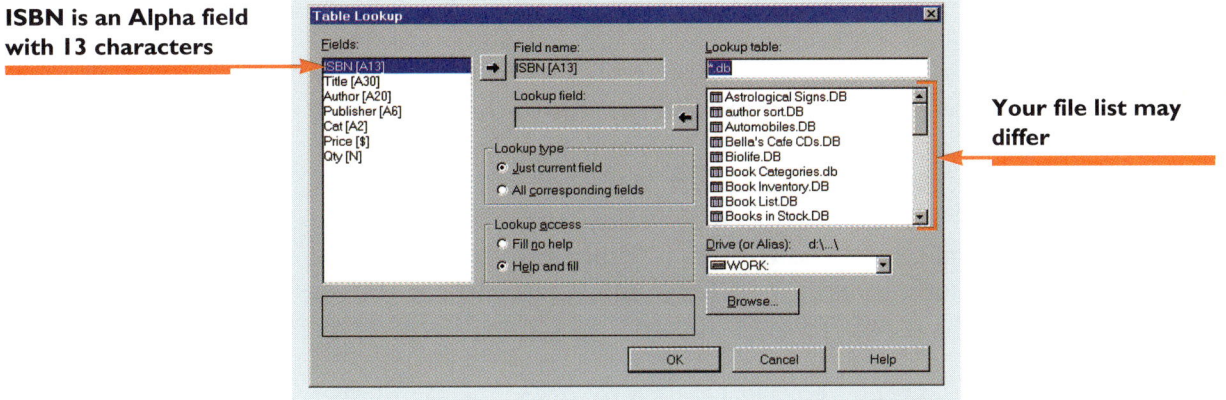

Your file list may differ

FIGURE 4-25: Completed Table Lookup dialog box

Linked fields

Click to make it possible to view the lookup table during data entry

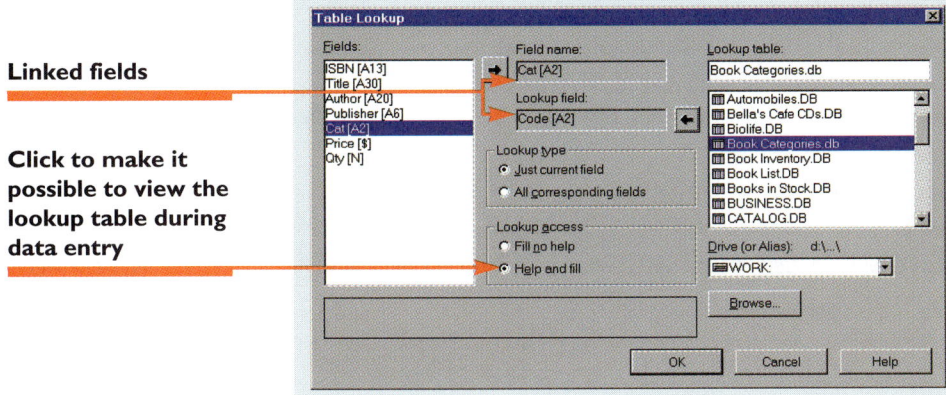

Testing the new lookup table

In this lesson you will see how structure changes you made in earlier lessons prevent you from entering invalid data. **case**   The Book Alley has received a new shipment of books, and Zora wants to enter the new titles into the inventory table and test the lookup table. She expects them to speed up data entry and prevent her from making any serious mistakes.

1 Click the **Edit Data button** 📖 on the toolbar, click the **Last Rec button** ▶️, then press ⬇️

The cursor moves to a new, blank row, record number 52. First, Zora tests the required field validity check by leaving the ISBN field blank.

2 Pressing **[Tab]** to move between fields, leave the ISBN field blank, type **Contact** in the Title field, type **Sagan** in the Author field, type **Pocket** in the Publisher field, then press **[Tab]** to move the cursor to the Cat field

Paradox enters the default value SF in the Cat field.

3 Press [Tab], type **14.95** in the Price field, type **4** in the Qty field, then press ⬇️ to add another record

Paradox beeps and displays the message, "Field Value Required. Field: ISBN" in the status bar. An ISBN must be entered before leaving the record.

4 Press **[Shift][Tab]** until you move the cursor to the blank ISBN field, then type **0-671-43422-5** and press ⬇️

A new, blank row appears. Now Zora tests the lookup table link.

5 Pressing **[Tab]** to move between fields, type **0-671-22604-5** in the ISBN field, type **Economics in Plain English** in the Title field, type **Silk** in the Author field, type **S&S** in the Publisher field, then press **[Tab]** to move the cursor to the Cat field

When you reach the Cat field, the status bar advises you to press Ctrl+Space to view the lookup table. In the next step Zora attempts to enter a code that is not listed in the lookup table.

6 Type **EC** in the Cat field, then press **[Tab]**

Paradox displays the message "Unable to find lookup value" in the status bar. This means that the code you entered is not one of the codes listed in the lookup table and is therefore invalid. Now Zora displays the lookup table to display the list of valid codes.

7 Press **[Ctrl][Spacebar]**

The Lookup Help dialog box opens with the Book Categories lookup table data, as shown in Figure 4-26. The code for Reference, RF, appears in the lookup table as a valid code.

8 Click **RF** in the lookup table, then click **OK**

The Lookup Help window closes and RF appears in the Cat field. Finally, you'll test the minimum price validity check.

9 Press **[Tab]**, type **2** in the Price field, then press **[Tab]** to move to the Qty field

Paradox won't accept that price. The status bar displays the message, "A value no less than $3.00 is expected," as shown in Figure 4-27.

10 Delete **2** and type **18.95**, press **[Tab]**, enter **3** in the Qty field, then click 📖 to exit Edit mode

Zora has tested all the features she added to the table structure and found them helpful in keeping the data accurate and complete.

FIGURE 4-26: Lookup Help dialog box

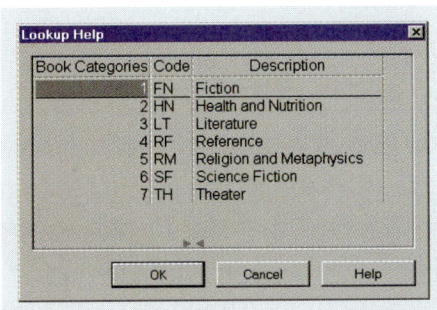

FIGURE 4-27: Message in status bar indicates a minimum value violation

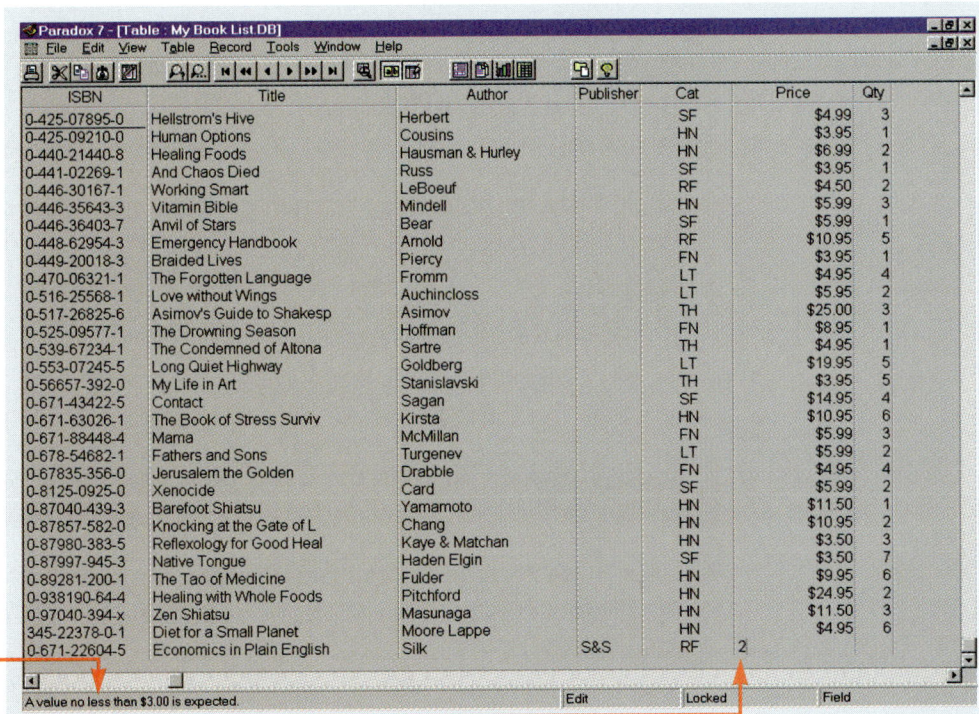

Error message

Invalid entry

Adding secondary indexes

In this lesson you'll learn how to make one more change to the table view. As you know, the records in a table are sorted either alphabetically or numerically based on the values in the key field. If you want to view the records in a different order, for example, alphabetically by author, you can create a **secondary index**. Unlike the values in the key field, the values in the secondary index need not be unique. ▶**case**   The Book Alley customers usually request books by title or category, not by the ISBN. For this reason, Zora wants to be able to view the book inventory arranged in alphabetical order by title and category. She decides to define a secondary index.

1 Click the **Restructure button** 🖾 on the toolbar
The Restructure dialog box opens, as in the previous lessons.

2 Click the **Table properties list arrow**
The Table properties options appear.

3 Click **Secondary Indexes** from the Table properties menu, then click **Define**
The Define Secondary Index dialog box opens, as shown in Figure 4-28. Zora wants to display the book data in alphabetical order by title, so she chooses Title as the indexed field.

4 Click **Title** in the Fields list, then click the **right arrow button**
Title moves to the Indexed fields list.

5 Click **OK**
The Define Secondary Index dialog box closes and the Save Index As dialog box opens. The next step is to name and save the index. Zora decides to name the index "Alpha by Title," to remind herself that this secondary index will arrange the records alphabetically by title.

6 Type **Alpha by Title** in the Index Name text box, then click **OK**
You return to the Restructure dialog box where you see the new secondary index name.

7 Click **Save** to save the table structure
The Restructure dialog box closes and you return to table view. The records are still arranged numerically by ISBN. Next, Zora uses a filter to arrange the records according to the newly defined secondary index—that is, alphabetically by title. Another use of a **filter** is to view records in a different order than the one specified by the primary key.

8 Click the **Filter button** 🖾 on the toolbar
This opens the Filter Tables dialog box shown in Figure 4-29. Zora has a choice of the primary key ISBN (the * in the Order by list identifies the key field), or the new secondary index, Alpha by Title.

9 Click **Alpha by Title** in the Order by list, then click **OK**
As shown in Figure 4-30, the books are now listed in alphabetic order by title.

FIGURE 4-28:
Define Secondary
Index dialog box

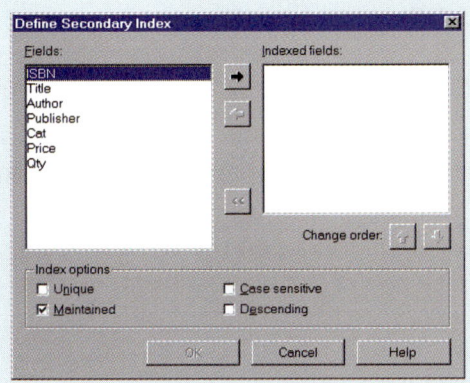

FIGURE 4-29:
Filter Tables
dialog box

Filter button

Primary key

Secondary index

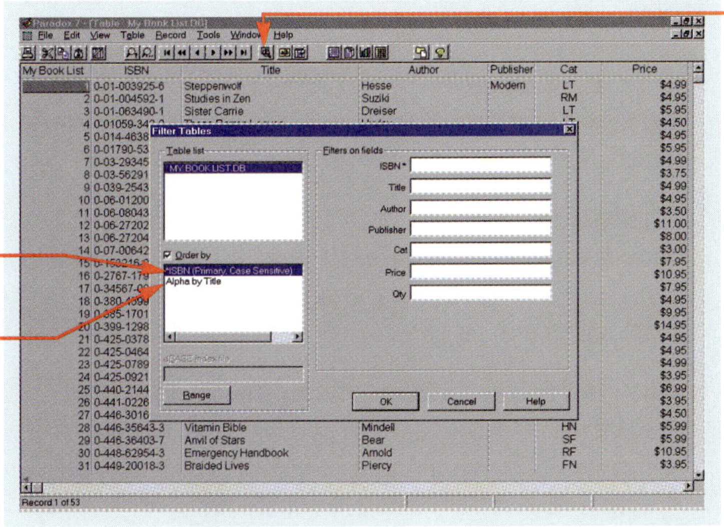

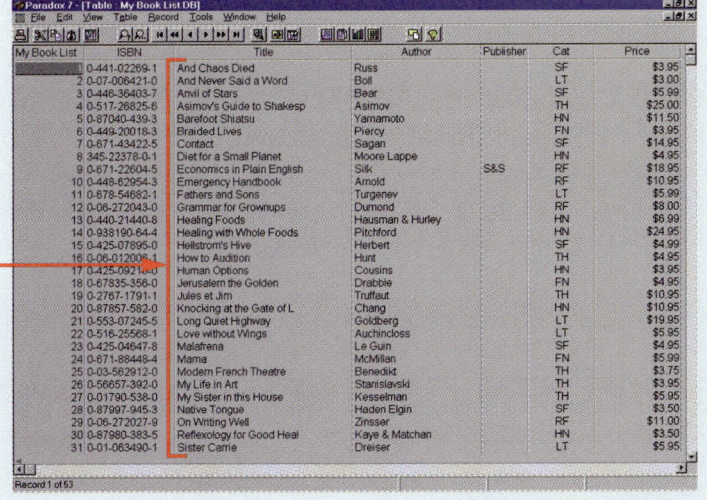

FIGURE 4-30:
My Book List.DB
ordered by the
secondary index

Records arranged in
alphabetical order
by title

TROUBLE?

If you move the
wrong field name
into the Indexed
fields list in the
Define Secondary
Index dialog box,
just select the field
and click the left
arrow button to
remove it. If you
want to redefine the
index, click Clear All
to place all your field
names back in the
Fields list.■

QUICK TIP

Remember that
changes to the Table
view have no effect
on the way the table
prints.■

Adding secondary indexes, continued

Now Zora wants to define another index that will arrange the records by category first, then in alphabetic order by title within each category. An index containing two or more fields is called a **composite secondary index**.

10 Repeat Steps 1 through 3 to open the Define Secondary Index dialog box, click **Cat**, then click the **right arrow button**
The Cat field name moves to the Indexed fields list. Now you'll make the Title field the second field in the index.

11 Click **Title,** click the **right arrow button**, then click **OK**
The Title field name moves to the Indexed fields list and the dialog box closes. The Save Index As dialog box opens, as before. Again, Zora chooses a name that will help her remember the purpose of the index.

12 Type **By Category and Title** in the text box, then click **OK**
You return to the Restructure dialog box, which now looks like Figure 4-31, with the two new secondary indexes.

13 Click **Save**
Paradox saves the changes to the My Book List table structure and you return to table view. Now Zora can arrange the records alphabetically by category, with the records arranged alphabetically by title within each category.

14 Click the **Filter button** ▣ on the toolbar
The Filter Tables dialog box opens as before, but now it shows both new secondary indexes as well as the ISBN key field. The Alpha by Title index is highlighted in the Order by list, indicating that the table is currently arranged in that order.

15 Click **By Category and Title** in the Order by list, then click **OK**
The My Book List records now appear in order by category, then in alphabetic order by title within each category, as shown in Figure 4-32. Now Zora arranges the records again in their original ISBN order.

16 Click ▣ again, click ***ISBN** in the Order by list, then click **OK**
The book inventory records appear once again in the original order, by ISBN, as shown in Figure 4-33. Zora is pleased with her newly structured inventory table. She's certain the new features will ensure quick and accurate data entry. The new indexes will also allow her to quickly identify books in stock for her customers.

FIGURE 4-31: Restructure dialog box showing two secondary indexes

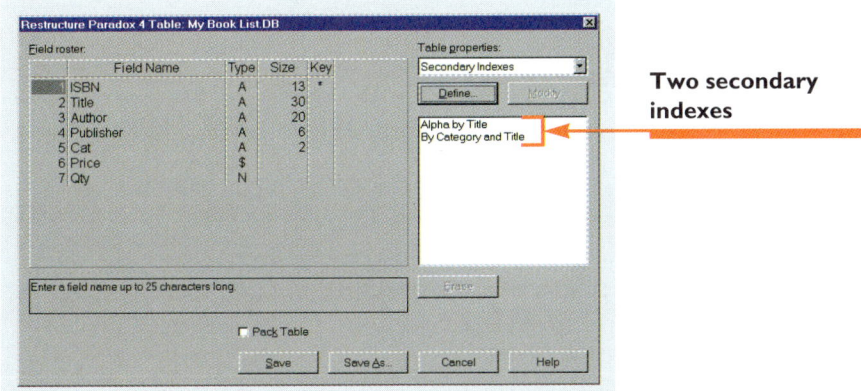

Two secondary indexes

FIGURE 4-32: My Book List ordered by category then title

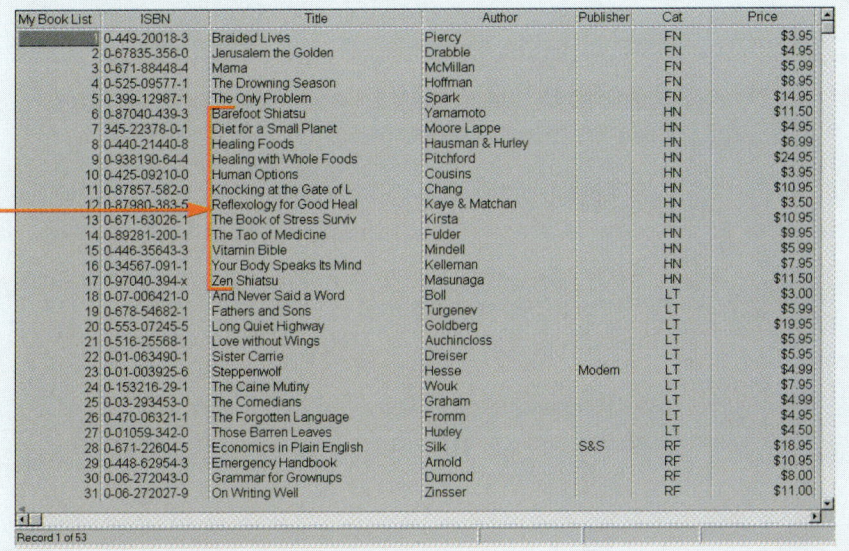

Ordered by title within category

My Book List	ISBN	Title	Author	Publisher	Cat	Price
1	0-449-20018-3	Braided Lives	Piercy		FN	$3.95
2	0-67835-356-0	Jerusalem the Golden	Drabble		FN	$4.95
3	0-671-88448-4	Mama	McMillan		FN	$5.99
4	0-525-09577-1	The Drowning Season	Hoffman		FN	$8.95
5	0-399-12987-1	The Only Problem	Spark		FN	$14.95
6	0-87040-439-3	Barefoot Shiatsu	Yamamoto		HN	$11.50
7	345-22378-0-1	Diet for a Small Planet	Moore Lappe		HN	$4.95
8	0-440-21440-8	Healing Foods	Hausman & Hurley		HN	$6.99
9	0-938190-64-4	Healing with Whole Foods	Pitchford		HN	$24.95
10	0-425-09210-0	Human Options	Cousins		HN	$3.95
11	0-87857-582-0	Knocking at the Gate of L	Chang		HN	$10.95
12	0-87980-383-5	Reflexology for Good Heal	Kaye & Matchan		HN	$3.50
13	0-671-63026-1	The Book of Stress Surviv	Kirsta		HN	$10.95
14	0-89281-200-1	The Tao of Medicine	Fulder		HN	$9.95
15	0-446-35643-3	Vitamin Bible	Mindell		HN	$5.99
16	0-34567-091-1	Your Body Speaks Its Mind	Kelleman		HN	$7.95
17	0-97040-394-x	Zen Shiatsu	Masunaga		HN	$11.50
18	0-07-006421-0	And Never Said a Word	Boll		LT	$3.00
19	0-678-54682-1	Fathers and Sons	Turgenev		LT	$5.99
20	0-553-07245-5	Long Quiet Highway	Goldberg		LT	$19.95
21	0-516-25568-1	Love without Wings	Auchincloss		LT	$5.95
22	0-01-063490-1	Sister Carrie	Dreiser		LT	$5.95
23	0-01-003925-6	Steppenwolf	Hesse	Modern	LT	$4.99
24	0-153216-29-1	The Caine Mutiny	Wouk		LT	$7.95
25	0-03-293453-0	The Comedians	Graham		LT	$4.99
26	0-470-06321-1	The Forgotten Language	Fromm		LT	$4.95
27	0-01059-342-0	Those Barren Leaves	Huxley		LT	$4.50
28	0-671-22604-5	Economics in Plain English	Silk	S&S	RF	$18.95
29	0-448-62954-3	Emergency Handbook	Arnold		RF	$10.95
30	0-06-272043-0	Grammar for Grownups	Dumond		RF	$8.00
31	0-06-272027-9	On Writing Well	Zinsser		RF	$11.00

Record 1 of 53

FIGURE 4-33: My Book List ordered by ISBN

My Book List	ISBN	Title	Author	Publisher	Cat	Price
1	0-01-003925-6	Steppenwolf	Hesse	Modern	LT	$4.99
2	0-01-004592-1	Studies in Zen	Suziki		RM	$4.95
3	0-01-063490-1	Sister Carrie	Dreiser		LT	$5.95
4	0-01059-342-0	Those Barren Leaves	Huxley		LT	$4.50
5	0-014-46380-1	Training an Actor	Moore		TH	$4.95
6	0-01790-538-0	My Sister in this House	Kesselman		TH	$5.95
7	0-03-293453-0	The Comedians	Graham		LT	$4.99
8	0-03-562912-0	Modern French Theatre	Benedikt		TH	$3.75
9	0-039-25432-1	When Worlds Collide	Wylie		SF	$4.99
10	0-06-012006-1	How to Audition	Hunt		TH	$4.95
11	0-06-080437-0	The Impossible Question	Krishnamurti		RM	$3.50
12	0-06-272027-9	On Writing Well	Zinsser		RF	$11.00
13	0-06-272043-0	Grammar for Grownups	Dumond		RF	$8.00
14	0-07-006421-0	And Never Said a Word	Boll		LT	$3.00
15	0-153216-29-1	The Caine Mutiny	Wouk		LT	$7.95
16	0-2767-1791-1	Jules et Jim	Truffaut		TH	$10.95
17	0-34567-091-1	Your Body Speaks Its Mind	Kelleman		HN	$7.95
18	0-380-45997-3	Uncommon Women and Others	Wasserstein		TH	$4.95
19	0-385-17010-6	Who Dies?	Levine		RM	$9.95
20	0-399-12987-1	The Only Problem	Spark		FN	$14.95
21	0-425-03786-6	The Anarchistic Colossus	Van Vogt		SF	$4.95
22	0-425-04647-8	Malafrena	Le Guin		SF	$4.95
23	0-425-07895-0	Hellstrom's Hive	Herbert		SF	$4.99
24	0-425-09210-0	Human Options	Cousins		HN	$3.95
25	0-440-21440-8	Healing Foods	Hausman & Hurley		HN	$6.99
26	0-441-02269-1	And Chaos Died	Russ		SF	$3.95
27	0-446-30167-1	Working Smart	LeBoeuf		RF	$4.50
28	0-446-35643-3	Vitamin Bible	Mindell		HN	$5.99
29	0-446-36403-7	Anvil of Stars	Bear		SF	$5.99
30	0-448-62954-3	Emergency Handbook	Arnold		RF	$10.95
31	0-449-20018-3	Braided Lives	Piercy		FN	$3.95

Record 1 of 53

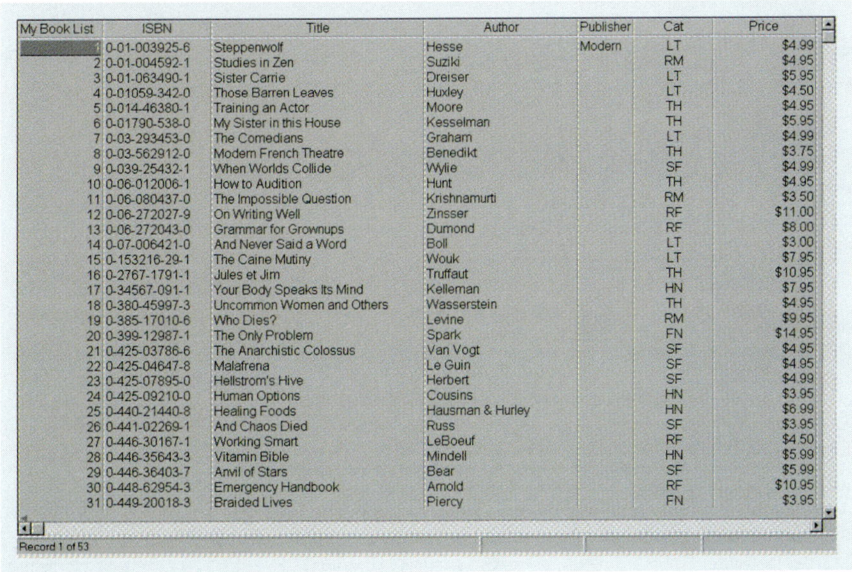

TASKREFERENCE

TASK	MOUSE/BUTTON	MENU	KEYBOARD
Add a field			[Insert]
Add records from one table to another table	Right-click a table in Project Viewer, select Add	Click Tools, then Utilities, then Add	
Change Field view properties	Right-click on data in field, select Properties, click tab of choice	Click Table, then Table View Properties, then choose tab of choice	[Ctrl][M]
Delete a field			[Ctrl] [Del]
Display lookup table		Click Record, click Lookup Help	Press [Ctrl][Spacebar]
Filter field	Right-click on data in field, select Filter, enter restriction of choice or Click 🔳	Click Table, then Filter	
Move a column	Move pointer to heading, press and hold until it changes to ↔ then drag to desired location		
Resize a column	Move the pointer to the gridline between columns until it changes to ↔ then drag to desired size		
Restructure table	Click 🔳 or Right-click a table in Project Viewer, select Restructure	Click Table, Restructure	In Restructure dialog box, move to the location, press [Insert]
Turn on secondary index	Click 🔳, click Order by box, select index or Click in Order by box, select index	Click Table, then Filter, Click Order by box, select index	
View table structure	Right-click table in Project Viewer, select Info Structure	Click Table, Info Structure	
Use Field view	Click 🔳		[F2]
Use Persistent Field view			[Ctrl] [F2]

CONCEPTSREVIEW

Label each element in the Restructure dialog box shown in Figure 4-34.

1
2
3
4
5
6

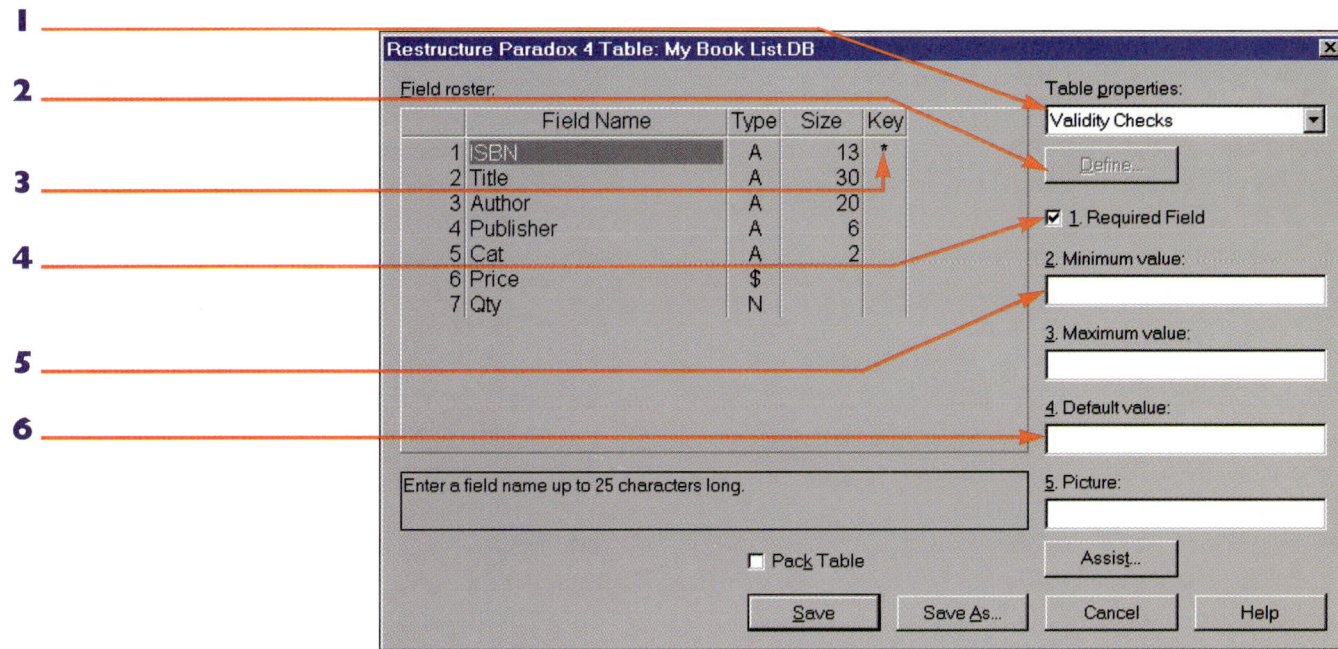

FIGURE 4-34

Match each statement with the term it describes.

7 A value that Paradox automatically enters into a field

8 A table that contains records that failed a newly enforced validity check

9 A table that contains valid values for a specific field in a data-entry table

10 A message that appears when a structure change might result in loss of data

11 A restriction on field data

12 A field that must contain a value

a. Lookup table

b. Required field

c. Validity check

d. Default value

e. Restructure warning

f. KEYVIOL table

Select the best answer from the list of choices.

13 The Structure Information dialog box

a. Allows you to change the structure of a table

b. Allows you to view the structure of a table but not change it

c. Allows you to add records from another table

d. Allows you to view the data in a lookup table

14 After the table structure is complete

a. You cannot add or delete fields.

b. You can only delete existing fields.

c. You can add and delete fields.

d. You can only add fields from other tables.

SKILLSREVIEW

1 Use Field view.

a. Make a copy of PD 4-2, name it My Books4, and save it to the appropriate directory.

b. Open My Books4, and click the Edit Data button.

c. Locate *Dieting Small Planet*. Click the Field view button.

d. Click at the end of *Dieting*, delete "ing," press [spacebar], type **for a**. The book title is now, *Diet for a Small Planet*.

e. Press the [Up Arrow] to complete the edit.

f. Click the Edit Data button to exit Edit mode.

2 Tailor Table view.

a. Move the cursor to the line between Price and Qty until it changes to a white double-headed arrow.

b. Drag the mouse pointer until the Price column is just large enough to display all the data and the field heading. Release the mouse button.

c. Move the pointer to the Qty column heading and move it slightly until the pointer changes to a black doubleheaded arrow, and two thick vertical lines appear on either side of the Qty column.

d. Drag the mouse pointer to position the line just to the right of the Cat column, then release the mouse button. The Qty column is now between Cat and Price.

e. Click Table on the menu bar, click Table View Properties, then click Save.

3 Add and delete fields.

a. Click the Restructure button. Select each field name and view any validity checks.

b. Make a list of the validity checks you found.

c. Close the Structure Information dialog box.

d. Make a copy of My Books4.DB, name it Abbreviations.DB, and save it to the appropriate directory.

e. Open the Restructure dialog box for Abbreviations.DB, add two new fields between the Price and Qty fields, using the following specifications:

Field Name	Type	Size	Key
Binding	A	2	
Pages	N		

f. Save the structure, open the Abbreviations.DB table, click the Restructure button then delete the Pages field.

g. Save the structure, accepting the Restructuring Warning.

4 Change a field name and size.

a. Click the Restructure button. Change the name of the Binding field to "Cover."

b. Change the size of the Author field to 10 and the size of the Title field to 20.

c. Save the table structure accepting the two Restructure Warnings, then print the table.

5 Add validity checks.

a. Click the Restructure button. Make "2" the minimum entry for the Qty field.

b. Make "PB" (for Paperback) the default value for the Cover field.

c. Save the structure and enforce the validity checks on existing data.

6 Correct key violations.

a. Change all quantities in the KEYVIOL table that are less than 2 to "2."

b. Add the now-valid records to the Abbreviations.DB table by clicking Tools on the menu bar, click Utilities, then click Add.

c. Click the Alias list arrow, select PRIV:, then double-click the KEYVIOL table in the file list.

d. In the Add records in KEYVIOL.db dialog box select Abbreviations.DB, click Add, then close it.

e. Print the Abbreviations.DB table with the corrections.

7 Create a lookup table.

a. Create a table called Publisher4 that uses the following structure:

Field Name	Type	Size	Key
Pub Code	A	6	*
Publisher	A	25	

b. Enter the following data in the table:

Pub Code	Publisher	Pub Code	Publisher
Modern	Modern Library	H&R	Harper & Row
Philos	Philosophical	Bantam	Bantam
Pengui	Penguin	New Am	New American
Dblday	Doubleday	S&S	Simon & Schuster

c. Print the Publisher4.DB table.

d. Restructure the Abbreviations.DB table to include the Publisher4 lookup table for the Publisher field so that you can view the table when entering data.

e. Save the structure enforcing the lookup table on existing data.

8 Test the new lookup table.

a. Edit the Abbreviations.DB table and enter the following data in a new record:

ISBN:	0-449-20618-1
Title:	Murder at the FBI
Author:	Truman
Cover	PB

b. Press [Ctrl][Spacebar] to open the lookup table for the Publisher field and choose "Bantam."

c. Accept SF as the category, then try to enter "12.95" in the Price field.

d. Change the price to "15.99" to comply with the minimum allowed, then enter "4" in the Qty field.

e. Leave Edit mode and print the table data.

9 Add secondary indexes.

a. Open the Define Secondary Index dialog box.

b. Create a secondary index that will arrange records in ascending order by price, then name it "By Price."

c. Save the structure. Use a filter to display the abbreviations records in the new index order.

d. Print the table and indicate on the printout how it differs from the screen display.

INDEPENDENT
CHALLENGE 1

Antonio Martinez, personnel director of the StyleLine men's clothing store, needs a database to keep track of his employees.

Antonio wants to be able to look up the employee ID, first and last names, current salary, and date of last review. He asks you to help.

To complete this independent challenge:

1 Create a new table structure with the appropriate fields, using the proper field type and a useful field size.
2 Enter records for at least six employees.
3 Add validity checks to the table structure that will ensure that every employee has an ID number and that no salary is less than $6 per hour.
4 Create a composite secondary index that will let the manager view the records in order of last name, then by first name within last name.
5 View the table data and print the table with the composite secondary index on.

INDEPENDENT
CHALLENGE 2

Keri Farr, owner of the Aloha Sports Emporium, has asked you to make some changes to her customer database. Some of the fields are no longer required. She also wants to add a new field.

To complete this independent challenge:

1 Copy the PD 4-3.DB table file to the appropriate directory and name the copy Aloha.DB.
2 The Street field data are shorter than the field size, so decrease the field size to match.
3 Delete the First Contact field.
4 Add a new field at the end of the Field roster, named Contact.
5 Save the structure and enter data in the new field in the first five records.
6 Print the table data.

INDEPENDENT
CHALLENGE 3

You have been working with a list of CDs and realize that a few additional structural changes need to be made. Additionally, you need to correct a spelling error. Because you want to speed up data entry as you expect a list of hundreds of CDs to arrive soon that need to be entered in the table, you want to create a lookup table. You want to balance the collection by category, so you think it would be helpful to be able to view the table in order by Category.

To complete this independent challenge:

1 Begin by making a copy of the table PD 4-4, name it My CDs, and save it to the appropriate directory.
2 Using Field view, correct the spelling of Mozart's name.
3 Delete the field, Last Played.
4 Create a lookup table for Category, name it Music Categories, create one field: Category, A, 7.
5 Add the categories based on the records in My CDs. Add at least one additional record, using the lookup table. Fill in any missing data.
6 Print a copy of the Music Categories table.
7 Create a secondary index on Category.
8 Turn the secondary index on, print the table.
9 Close all tables, exit Paradox.

INDEPENDENT
CHALLENGE 4

You need to update the food table used by Gallery Receptions to make it more helpful to your staff. The table needs to reflect whether a given recipe requires utensils, so that the staff can order and bring them along with the food. Also you want to make the table easier to view and add correct data to, as your staff begins to use it.

To complete this independent challenge:

1 Begin by making a copy of the table PD 4-5, name it My and save it to the appropriate directory.
2 Change the table properties so quantity is displayed as an integer.
3 Reduce the column width of quantity so that it is just big enough to display the data.
4 Move the price column next to the description column.
5 Restructure the My Food List table to add a field called, meal type. Then change the name to "utensils required." Shorten the name to "utensil req."
6 Add data for the utensil req field for each recipe choosing from: finger food, fork, spoon, or toothpick.
7 Create the following validity checks: price required, minimum price of $5.00, default value of utensil req of finger food. Apply the validity checks to the existing data.
8 Print the KEYVIOL table. Make necessary corrections and add the records back to the My Food List table. Close the KEYVIOL table.
9 Create a secondary index to order by utensil req.
10 Apply the secondary index and print the table.

VISUALWORKSHOP

You have been hired to create a table of automobile information for a client setting up a Web page to sell cars. A table has been started, but you must enhance it, both to make it easier for clerks to enter data, and to display the data ordered as specified by your client. Begin by making a copy of the table PD 4-6, name it My Food list Autos Avail and save it to the appropriate directory. Review the structure of the table as well as the data itself. You will want to restructure the table, add a lookup table for ease of data entry, and add a secondary composite index so that the data can be viewed in order by price then by year. Using Figure 4-35 as your guide, make the appropriate changes. Increase the width of the Color column so the entries are visible. Create a lookup table for the three dealer codes, name it Dealer Codes, enter the data based on the records in My Autos Avail table, and print the Dealer Codes table. Add a new record for an Oldsmobile as seen in the figure. Create the composite secondary index. Print a copy of the My Autos Avail table with the composite secondary index filter on.

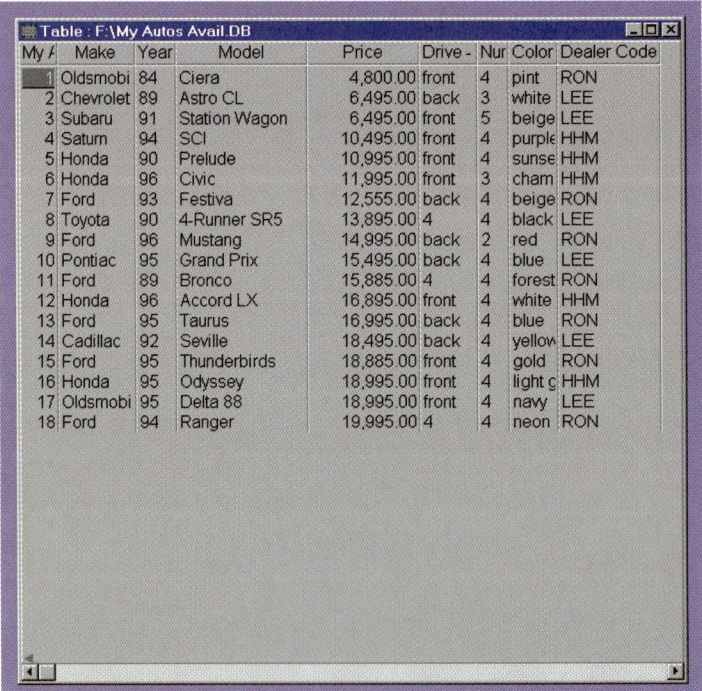

FIGURE 4-35

UNIT 5

Working
WITH FORMS

*T*able view is useful when you need to look at a number of your records at once. But when entering data, it's usually easier and more efficient to use a form. A **form** is a special window that allows you to display only one record at a time, eliminating the need to scroll across the table to see all the fields. You can customize the form to display specific fields and match familiar paper forms. ▶case With every new shipment of books, Zora receives a packing list (on paper) containing most of the information she needs to create a new record for each book—price, author, publisher, etc. To make the data entry job easier for her clerks, she decides to create a Paradox form to match the paper form. ▶

Creating a Quick Form

A Quick Form is the simplest kind of form you can create with Paradox. It displays one record at a time and includes all the fields in the record. You can use a Quick Form for basic data entry and editing tasks. ▶case Figure 5-1 shows a typical packing list that The Book Alley receives with a shipment of books. Notice that this paper form contains only some of the fields in Zora's inventory table. Zora creates a Quick Form first to see how closely it resembles the paper form.

1 Launch Paradox 7, use the Project Viewer to copy **PD 5-1** and save it to the appropriate directory as **My Book Forms.DB**, then copy **PD 1-5A** and **PD 5-1B** to the same directory, saving them as **Publist** and **Ctgory**

2 Set the correct working directory, double-click **My Book Forms.DB** to open it, then click the **Maximize button**, if necessary
Zora is accustomed to viewing data organized in table view. Now she'll display the data in a form.

3 Click the **Quick Form button** 🖼 on the Table toolbar
The Quick Form button creates a standard form named "Form: New," shown in Figure 5-2. The Form toolbar contains buttons relevant to working with forms. Zora sees that the form contains some fields that are different from the packing list. As she's working at her computer, a customer asks for information about the book titled *Emergency Handbook*. Zora locates the record and displays it in the Quick Form.

4 Click the **Locate Field Value button** 🔍 on the toolbar
The Locate Value dialog box opens.

5 Type **Emergency..** in the Value text box, click **Title** in the Fields list, then click **OK**
Emergency Handbook is now the current record in the Quick Form. Zora prints the data for the customer.

6 Click the **Print button** 🖨 on the toolbar, then click **OK**
Now Zora wants to return to table view to see how she previously viewed her data.

7 Click the **Table View button** 🖽 on the Form toolbar
This displays the inventory table in table view, with the *Emergency Handbook* record highlighted. The Quick Form window is now hidden behind the Table View window. To return to the Quick Form, Zora uses the Window menu, which displays a list of all open Paradox windows.

8 Click **Window** on the menu bar, then click **Form: New**
Zora returns to the Form window, as shown in Figure 5-3.

FIGURE 5-1: Typical packing list

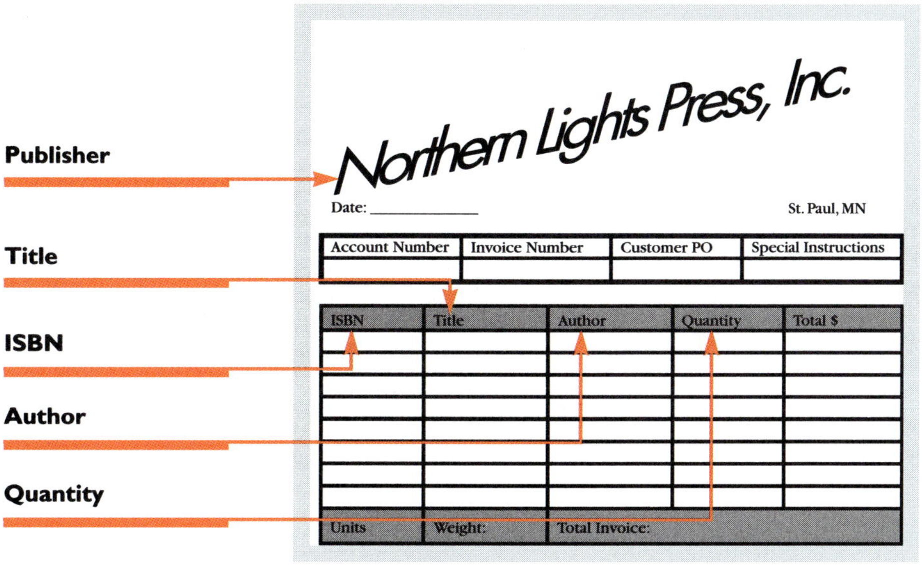

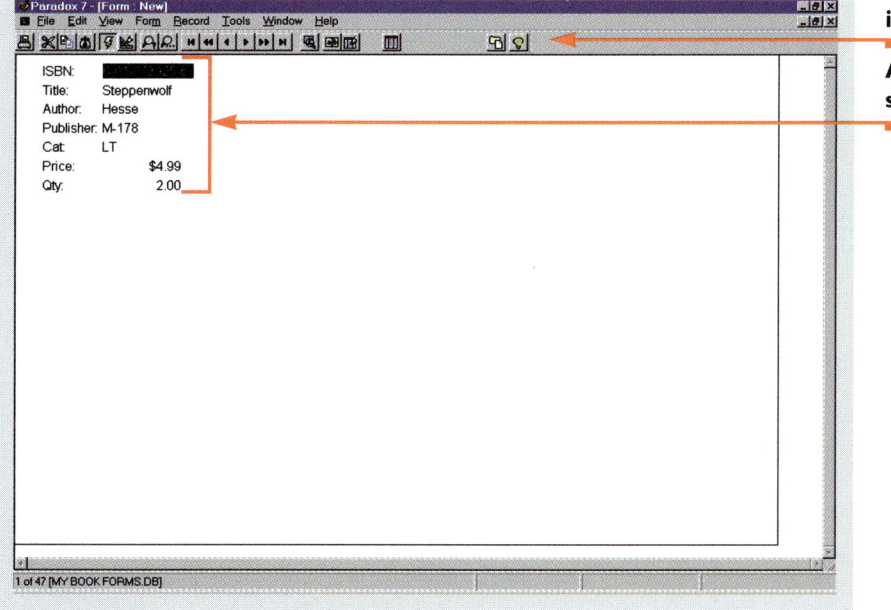

Publisher

Title

ISBN

Author

Quantity

FIGURE 5-2: First book record in a Quick Form

Toolbar contains buttons relevant to working with forms

All fields are on one screen

FIGURE 5-3: Found record in a Quick Form

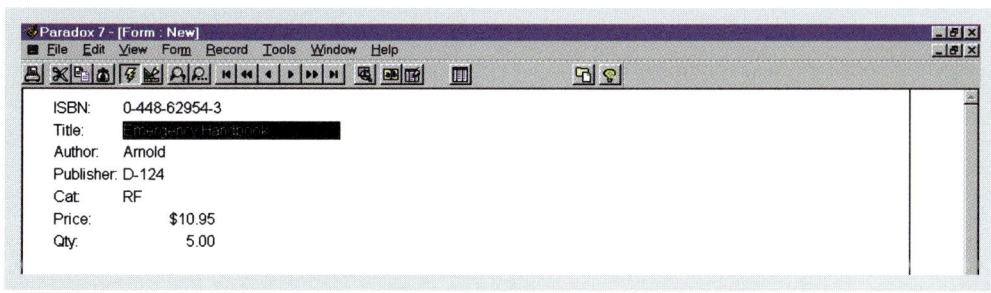

TROUBLE?

If someone using the computer before you created a Quick Form, then modified it, your Quick Form might not match Figure 5-2. For example, the field values in your form might be displayed in three-dimensional boxes. Just make sure your Quick Form displays all the fields in one record. ■

Entering data into the form

In this lesson, you will learn how to enter data into a form. Remember that data you enter is automatically saved in your table, just as it is in table view. Entering data into a form is similar to entering data in table view—you still need to use Edit mode and the various navigation buttons. Press [Tab] to move among fields, or simply click in the field in which you want to enter data. ▶case Zora just received a new shipment of books. She uses the Quick Form to enter the new data into the inventory table. To streamline her data entry chores, Zora plans to use the PUBLIST table as a lookup table, to provide the code for each publisher.

1   Click the **Edit Data button** 🖹 on the toolbar to switch to Edit mode
    Zora knows that the new books have never been entered into the inventory database, so she can simply create new records for them. As in table view, to add a new record in form view, you must add a blank record after the last record in the table.

2   Click the **Last Record button** ▶ on the toolbar, then click the **Next Record button** ▶
    A blank record appears in the form. No data appear in any fields, but the field labels are still visible, as shown in Figure 5-4. The status bar indicates that this is an empty record in the MY BOOK FORMS.DB table. The title bar displays "Form:New [Data Entry]," indicating that this blank form is ready for data entry.

3   Click in the space to the right of the **ISBN field label**, then enter the ISBN, title, and author data shown below, pressing **[Tab]** to move between fields

ISBN	Title	Author
0-425-10485-0	**Phone Power**	**Walther**

4   Press **[Tab]** to move to the **Publisher field**, then press **[Ctrl][Spacebar]**
    The Lookup Help dialog box opens, as shown in Figure 5-5, with the list of publishers and their codes.

5   Click **B-101**, the code for the Berkeley Publishing Group, then click **OK**
    The code B-101 appears in the Publisher field. Notice that the default value for Cat is SF. To override a default, simply type in the desired value.

6   Enter the remaining data as shown below, then press **[Enter]**

Cat	Price	Qty
RF	**4.95**	**1**

Compare your screen to Figure 5-6.

FIGURE 5-4: Blank Quick Form

Title bar indicates form is ready for data entry

Empty record

You are in Edit mode

Table name

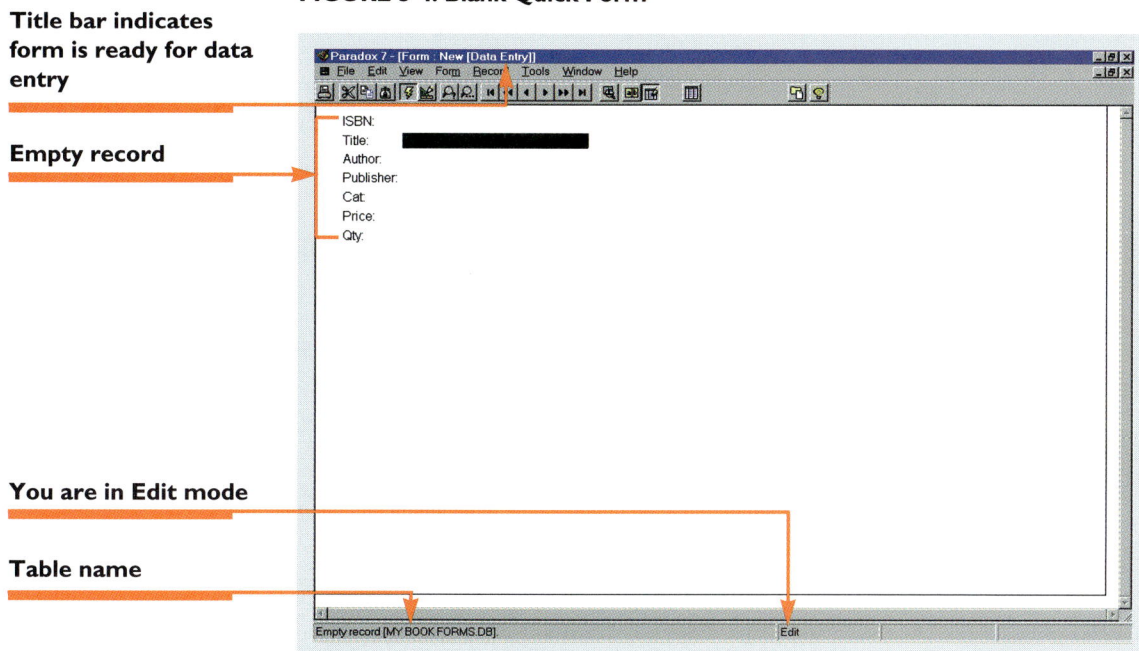

FIGURE 5-5: PUBLIST Lookup Help dialog box

Publisher codes

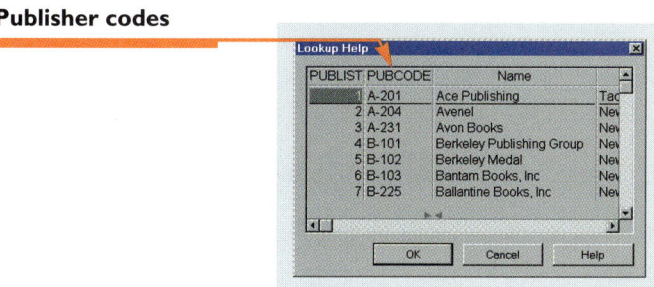

FIGURE 5-6: New record in Quick Form

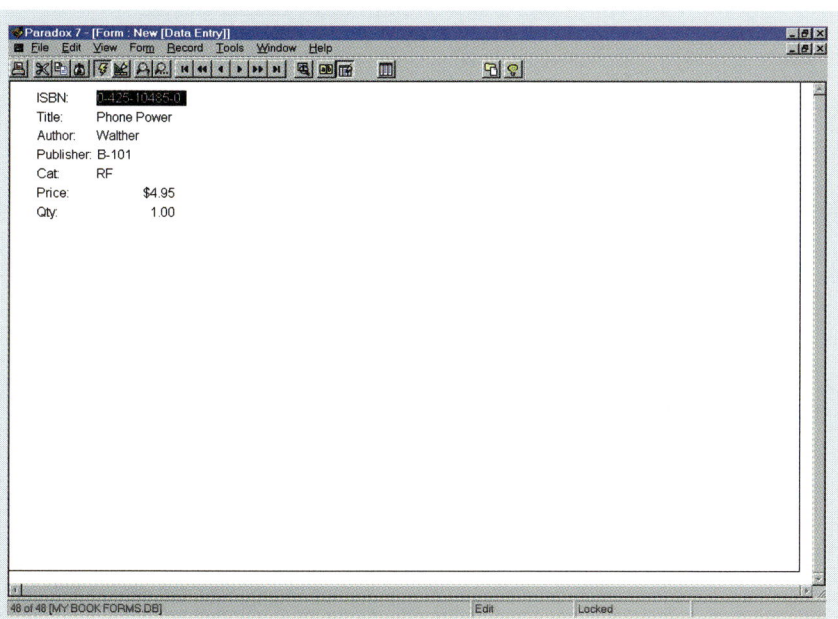

Entering data into the form, continued

Zora knows she doesn't need to save the Quick Form when she is through entering data because she can open it at any time by clicking the Quick Form button. She leaves Edit mode and closes the Form window.

7   Click the **Next Record button** ▶ on the Form toolbar
A new, blank form appears.

8   Repeat Steps 3 through 7 to enter the following data:

ISBN	Title	Author	Publisher	Cat	Price	Qty
0-670-85503-0	**Insomnia**	**King**	**Code for Penguin**	**FN**	**27.95**	**10**
0-394-71366-4	**Bio-Futures**	**Sargent**	**Code for Vintage**	**SF**	**5.95**	**5**

9   Click the **Edit Data button** 📝 on the toolbar
The status bar shows that Paradox is no longer in Edit mode.

10   Click **File** on the menu bar, then click **Close**
Paradox asks Zora if she wants to save the form.

11   Click **No**
The Form window closes and the My Book Forms.DB table reappears in table view. Zora looks to see if the new data she entered appears in the Table View window.

12   Click the **Locate Field Value button** 🔍 on the toolbar

13   Type **Bio..** in the Value text box, click **Title** in the Fields list, then click **OK**
Figure 5-7 shows the table with the three new records.

14   Click **File** on the menu bar, then click **Close**
The table closes and you return to the Project Viewer.

FIGURE 5-7:
Table view showing
new records

New records

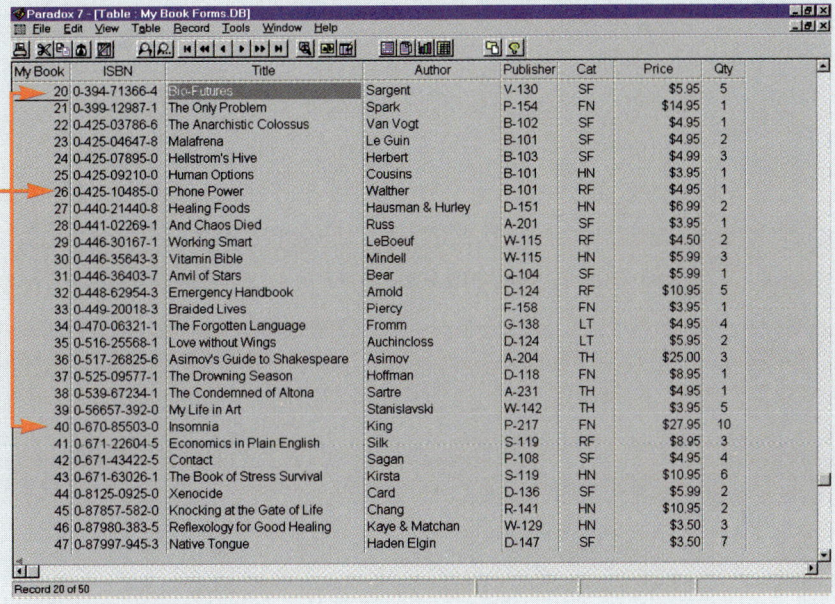

TROUBLE?

If you clicked the Next Record button on the Form toolbar and you didn't see a blank record, you probably were not in Edit mode. Remember, you need to be in Edit mode before you can add or edit records in form view.■

QUICK TIP

As in table view, when you enter a new record in form view, Paradox automatically moves the record to its proper location based on the key field.■

Using the Form Expert

Although Quick Form creates a form quickly and easily, it doesn't allow you to tailor the form. The **Form Expert** allows you to define how you want to view the fields on your screen and encourages you to arrange the data to suit your needs. Once you activate the Form Expert, Paradox displays a series of dialog boxes that lead you through the process of creating a form. ▶**case** Zora doesn't want her data entry clerks to be able to enter category information or retail prices for new books. She prefers to enter this information herself, based on her years of experience in the book trade. So she decides to create a data entry form using Form Expert that limits the fields and more closely matches the packing lists that arrive with book shipments.

1 Click the **Expert button** 🖳 on the toolbar
The Paradox Experts dialog box opens, as shown in Figure 5-8. The Form Expert is one of three Paradox experts that guide you through a design process. You can also use an expert to help design mailing labels or design a report.

2 Click **Form**, then click **Run Expert**
The Paradox Form Expert – Step 1 of 7 dialog box allows you to use data from one table or two. Zora uses just one table, which is the default.

3 Click **Next**
The Paradox Form Expert – Step 2 of 7 dialog box opens, as shown in Figure 5-9. In this dialog box you choose form layout. The **form layout** determines how many records are displayed on the screen at once and how the fields are arranged. To choose a layout, you can click either the picture of the layout you want or the radio button next to the numbered description. Zora accepts the default layout.

4 Click the **top radio button**, if necessary, click **Next**, click **My Book Forms.DB** from the Table list, then click **Next**
The fields from My Book Forms are displayed, as shown in Figure 5-10. Zora can select which fields to include in the form.

FIGURE 5-8: Paradox Experts dialog box

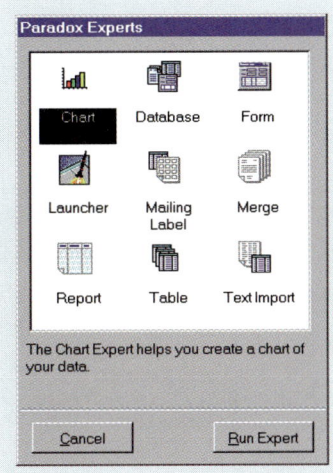

FIGURE 5-9: Step 2 of the Form Expert

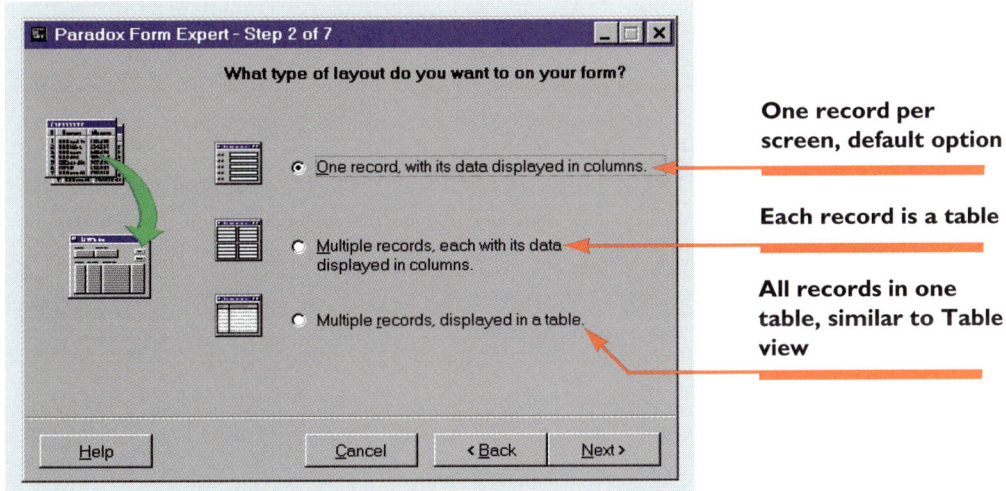

One record per screen, default option

Each record is a table

All records in one table, similar to Table view

FIGURE 5-10: Step 4 of the Form Expert

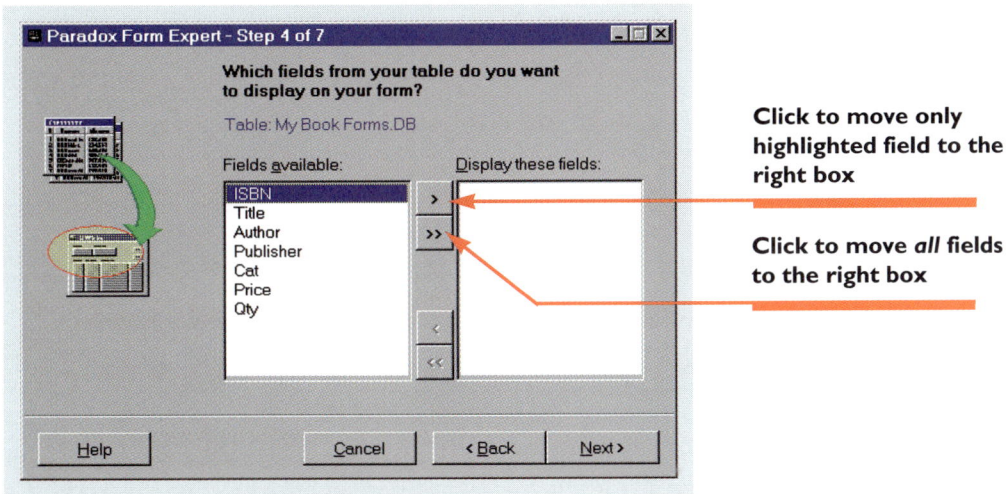

Click to move only highlighted field to the right box

Click to move *all* fields to the right box

TROUBLE?

If you don't see the table you want for the form in the Paradox Form Expert - Step 3 of 7 dialog box, you can click the Browse button and use the Directory Browser to switch to the directory that contains your table.■

QUICK TIP

If you want to return to a previous Form Expert dialog box to change a setting, you can click Back.■

Using the Form Expert, continued

Now Zora can specify which fields she wants displayed in her form. By default, all the fields in the table appear in the Fields available box, indicating that they can all be included in the form. By selecting fields from that list, Zora can add them to the form. See the related topic "A form for each purpose" for an explanation of why this feature is so useful.

5 Click ⟩⟩ to move all the fields to the **Display these fields box**
Zora wants to remove Cat and Price from the form.

6 Double-click **Price**, then double-click **Cat** to move it back to the **Fields available box**
Your screen should look like Figure 5-11.

7 Click **Next**
In this step, you specify the destination of your form. Usually a form is displayed on the screen, but you have the option of printing it instead. If you choose the screen, you have a choice of display types (check with your instructor or technical support person for your display type). If you choose the printer, you can choose from available printers and select a page orientation and size.

8 Click the **video screen radio button** if necessary, then click **Next**
The Form Expert asks you to select a style sheet in this last step. The **style sheet** determines the appearance of the form, including the frames around the data entry areas, colors, three-dimensional effects, and other visual characteristics.

9 Click **Control 3D style** in the Style sheets list box
Notice the Sample area on the right that previews the style. Control 3D style gives a recessed, three-dimensional look to the data entry areas. Verify that your screen looks like Figure 5-12.

10 Click **Next**
The Paradox Form Expert - Step 7 of 7 dialog box allows you to name the form and choose whether you run the form or modify it in the design window.

11 Type **Form for Clerks** in the text box, click the **top radio button**, if necessary, then click **Do it!**
After a moment, a dialog box opens, informing you that the form is complete.

12 Click **OK**
The new form appears containing data, as shown in Figure 5-13. Notice that the file extension for forms is fsl.

FIGURE 5-11: Field selection

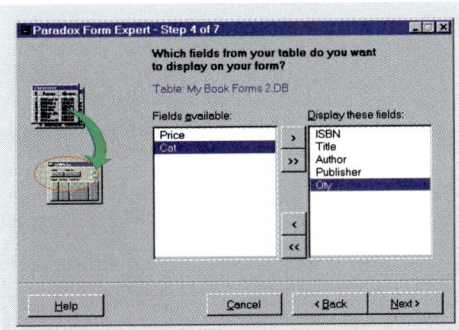

FIGURE 5-12: Style sheet selection

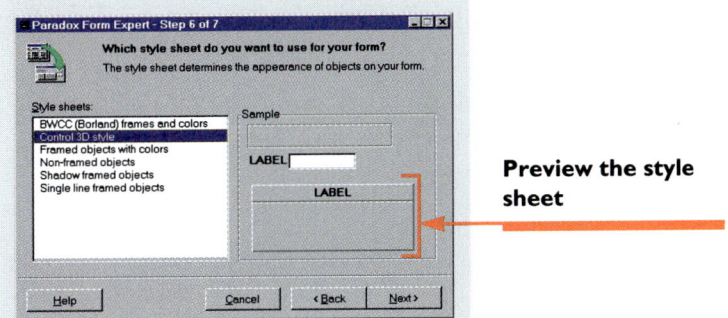

Preview the style sheet

FIGURE 5-13: Form for clerks

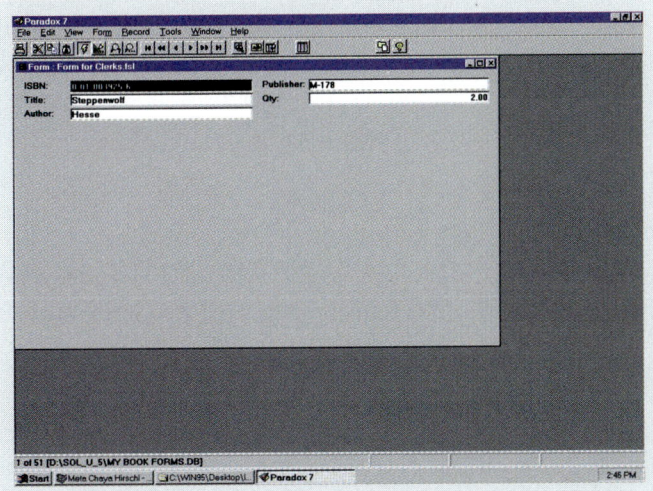

A form for each purpose

If different people are using a database for different purposes, you might want to design a form specifically for each purpose. For example, you might not want the data entry clerks in the personnel department to see the salaries of other employees or to have access to current job evaluations. You could design a simple form and exclude those fields, then you could create another form in which another person would enter the additional information.

TROUBLE?

If you move the wrong field into the Display these fields box by mistake, simply double-click the field again to move it back into the Fields available box, or use the arrow buttons. ■

QUICK TIP

Removing a field from the form has no effect on the data in the table. ■

Using the Form Designer

Now that you've created a form that includes only the fields you want, you can modify the form's design using the Form Design window. A form design contains **objects**, a general term used to refer to all the elements of a design, from the data entry fields to added text, graphic images, lines, and boxes. To move, resize, or make other changes to an object, you must first select the object by clicking it with the left mouse button. When you first click a data field, small gray squares called **handles** appear around the **container** (the field name and data entry area together). Clicking the **field label** selects that text and clicking the empty box next to the field label selects the **edit region**, the area where you enter data. See the related topic "Customizing a Quick Form" for the way to start the Form Designer from a Quick Form. ▶**case** Zora wants to make a few changes to the design of her new form, such as moving the fields around to resemble the paper packing list form. Before she makes the changes, however, she decides to practice using the tools in the Form Design window.

1 Click the **Design Form button** 🖼 on the toolbar, and when the Form Design window opens, click the **Maximize button**
The Form Design window opens, as shown in Figure 5-14. The fields are blank and the title bar indicates that you are designing a new form. The only objects in the form are the field objects.

2 Click in the space between **Author** and the **blank data entry area**
Handles appear around the container to show that it is selected, as shown in Figure 5-15. The shaded bands in the horizontal and vertical rulers show the current position of the selected object. The position of the mouse pointer is also tracked on the rulers by small diamond markers.

3 Click the **Author edit region**
Now handles appear only around the data entry area.

4 Click the field label **Author**
Only the field label is selected.

5 Click anywhere in the form outside the objects
The handles disappear from around any selected objects and appear at the borders of the form itself.

FIGURE 5-14: Form Design window

Field label

Click here to select
Author container

Edit region

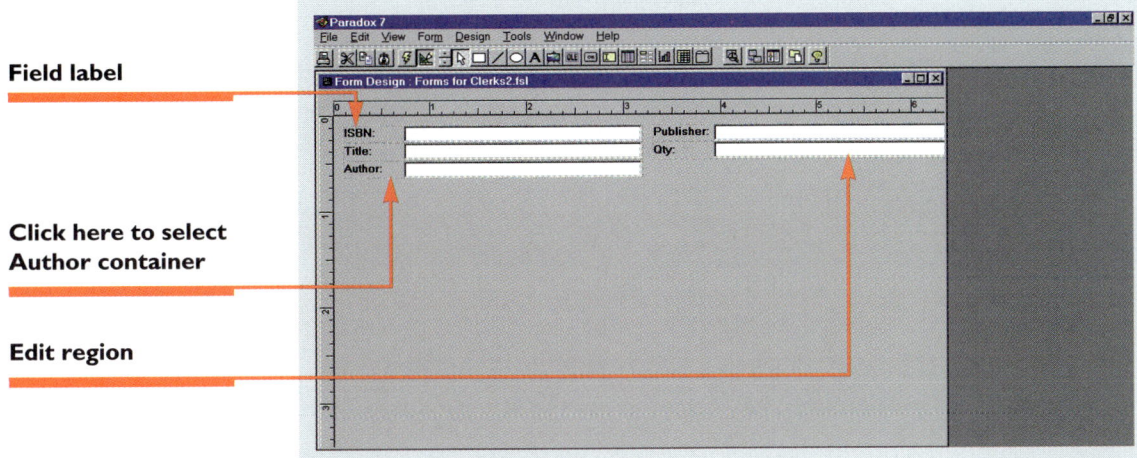

FIGURE 5-15: Form with selected container

Position of selected
object indicated on
rulers

Container is selected

Handle

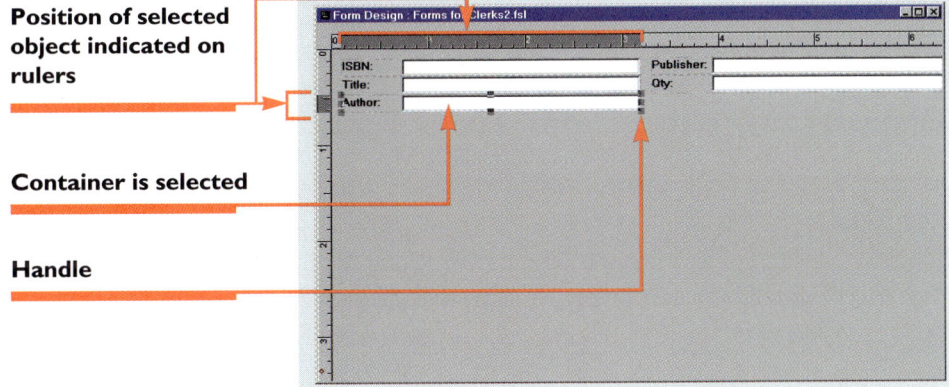

Customizing a Quick Form

You can customize a Quick Form in the Form Design window, just as you can customize a form created using the Form Expert. To switch to the Form Designer from the Quick Form window, simply click the Design Form button 📇 on the toolbar.

Moving objects

In this lesson you will learn how to move objects in your form. To make positioning objects more precise in the design window, Paradox provides a system of horizontal and vertical grid lines that you can display. Even if you don't want to display them on the screen, you can choose the form property, **Snap to Grid**. Then when you add or move an object, Paradox will place it exactly on the nearest (invisible) grid lines. ▶**case** If the fields appear on the screen in the same order as on the paper, data entry should be faster and more accurate. So Zora decides to rearrange the fields in the form slightly to match the paper packing list. Before she begins, however, she decides to use the automatic positioning tool that places objects on the invisible grid lines.

1 Click **Design** on the menu bar
The Design menu appears, as shown in Figure 5-16.

2 Click **Snap To Grid**
The menu disappears and the form design appears, as before.

3 Click the **Author field** to select the container, then click and drag the **container** down the screen to the 2¼" mark on the vertical ruler
Watch the shading in the ruler bars as you move the objects around in the design window.

4 Click and drag the rest of the **field objects** to the positions shown in Figure 5-17
The fields should line up easily because the Snap to Grid property is active. Experiment with moving the objects until you are comfortable doing it. Try placing them in different positions. Just make sure that when you leave this lesson the screen matches Figure 5-17.

FIGURE 5-16: Design menu

Click to align objects with grid lines

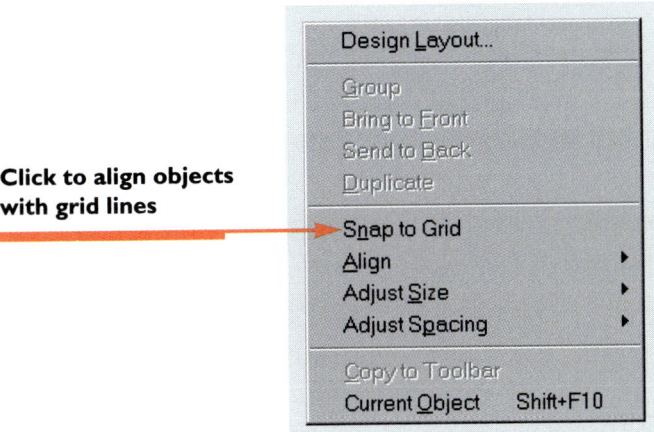

FIGURE 5-17: Form design with fields moved

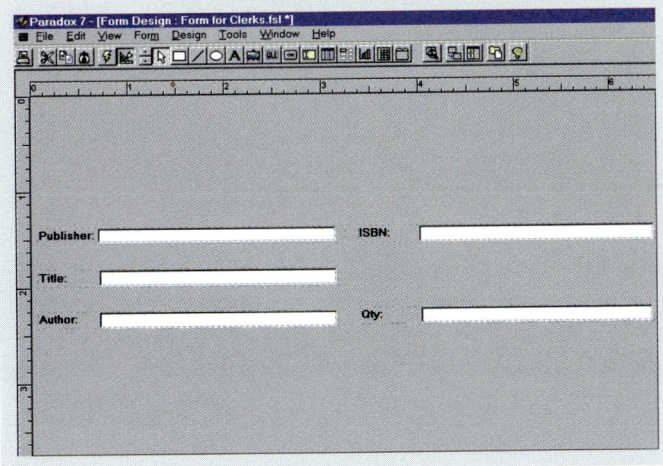

QUICK **TIP**

To switch quickly between the design window and the regular Form window, you can: choose View Data or Design Form from the Form menu; click the View Data or Design Form button on the Form toolbar; or press [F8] to toggle back and forth.■

Resizing objects

When resizing a data entry field in a form, remember that each field has three sections to resize: the container, the field label, and the edit region. You cannot enlarge either the field label or the edit region beyond the boundaries of its container. If you want to make the object larger, you must first resize the container, then the contents. On the other hand, to make the object smaller, you must reduce the contents before you can shrink the container. To resize an object, select it, then click and drag one of the middle side handles to the desired size. To increase both the width and height of an object, click and drag one of the corner handles.

case Zora wants to resize some of the objects in the form. The Publisher and Qty fields are much larger in the form than the length of the data they'll display, so she decides to reduce both of them.

1   Click the **edit region** of the Publisher field
   Eight handles appear around the container, as before.

2   Click the **edit region** again
   Now only the edit region has handles. To make the Publisher field shorter, Zora clicks and drags the right side of the Publisher edit region.

3   Move the pointer to the middle of the right side of the edit region box until you see ⟷, then click and drag the **handle** to the left until the edit region is about ¾" wide
   Notice that as you drag, the pointer changes to ⟵. The Publisher edit region is shorter now, so Zora can shorten the Publisher container as well.

4   Click outside the Publisher field to deselect the edit region, then click the **Publisher field** again
   Handles appear around the container again, which is still its original size, as shown in Figure 5-18.

5   Move the pointer to the middle handle on the right side of the container, then click and drag the **handle** to the left to match the edit region you just resized

6   Repeat Steps 1 through 5 to shorten the **Qty** field to approximately ¾"
   Now the field lengths match the field sizes Zora specified in the table structure. Finally, she decides that the form would look less crowded if she added more space between the Author and Qty fields. The Qty container should still be selected.

7   Click and drag the **Qty container** so the left side is positioned at 3½" on the horizontal ruler, then click outside the Qty field to deselect it
   Your form design should now look like Figure 5-19.

FIGURE 5-18: Resizing the Publisher field

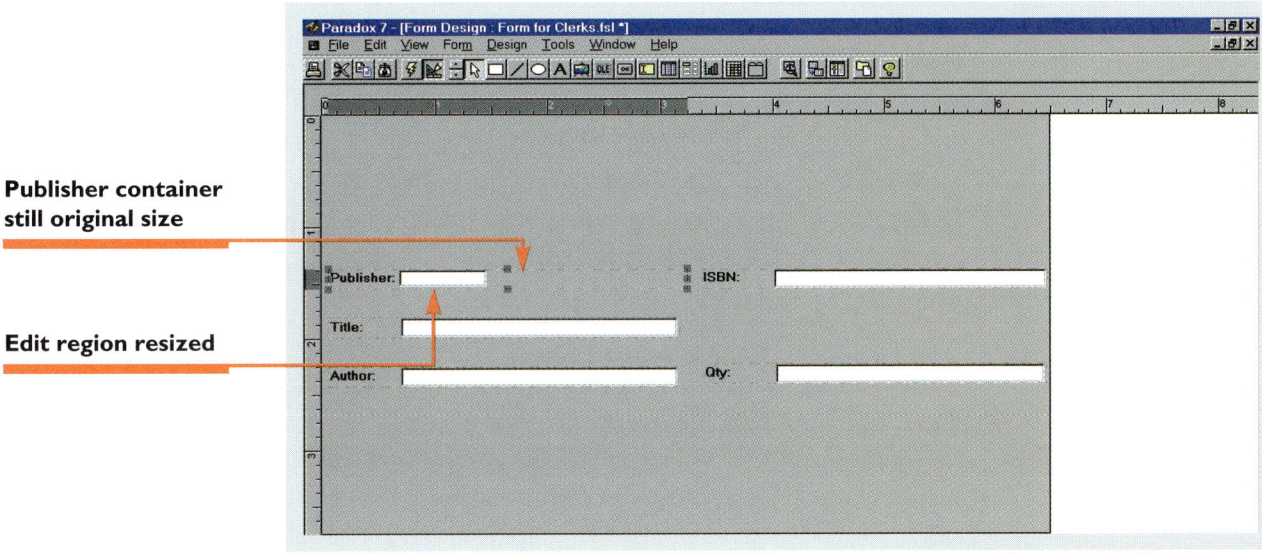

**Publisher container
still original size**

Edit region resized

FIGURE 5-19: Form with fields moved and resized

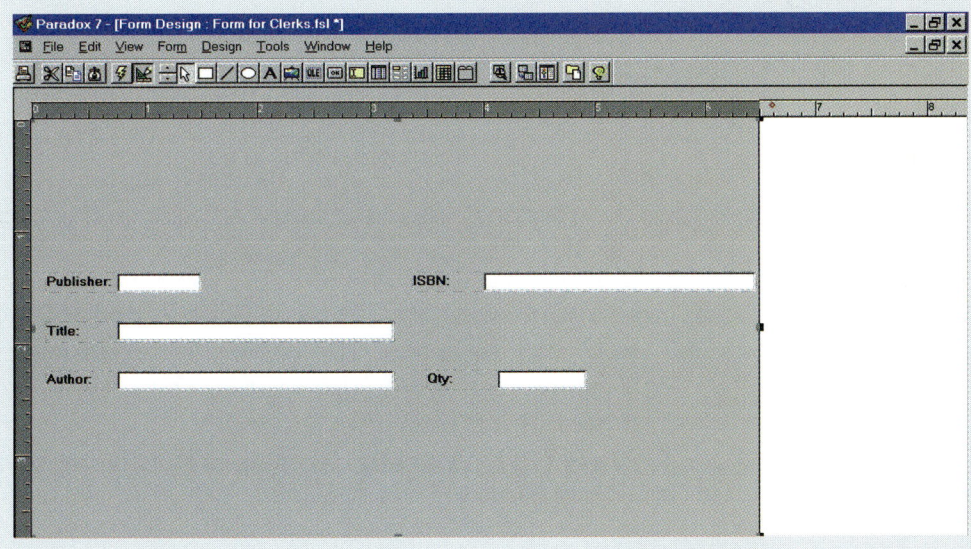

Adding text

To add text to a form, you first add a **text box** (which is like the containers you used in the previous lesson), then type text in the text box. Together, the text box and the text make up a **text object**. After you add a text object to a form, you can change its appearance and size. See the related topic "Other objects you can add to a form" for a description of the other objects you can add. ▶case Zora thinks the form would look better with a title. Also, to make the form as easy to use as possible, she adds a few lines of instructions.

1 Click outside the form area to view the rulers if necessary, then click the **Text tool button** A on the toolbar
   The pointer changes to ⁺A. Zora will use this pointer to draw a text box for the title. She begins by positioning the pointer where she wants the upper-left corner of the text box to appear. To see the location of the completed title text box, look ahead to Figure 5-22.

2 Position the pointer so that the crosshair is at **1"** on the horizontal ruler, about ⅛" down from the top of the form

3 Click and drag the pointer down to ⅜" on the vertical ruler and over to **5"** on the horizontal ruler, then release the mouse button
   As Zora drags the pointer, she sees the text box's outline.

4 Type **The Book Alley**, then right-click the text with the mouse
   The context-sensitive menu appears, as shown in Figure 5-20.

5 Click **Properties**, click **Text tab** to put it foremost, then click the **Center radio button** in the Alignment area
   Compare your screen to Figure 5-21. Now Zora is ready to insert some instructions.

6 Click **OK**, then click A again and draw another text object from ¼" to **6"** on the horizontal ruler and between ½" and 1¼" on the vertical ruler
   You can add text boxes anywhere on a form.

7 Type the following text, pressing **[Enter]** to move to the next line:
   1. Look for the book title before entering a new record.
   2. If found, add new shipment to the Qty field.
   3. If not found, add new record.
   4. Press Ctrl+Spacebar to select Publisher code from list.
   The completed form looks like Figure 5-22.

8 Click outside the text object to deselect it

FIGURE 5-20: Text object context-sensitive menu

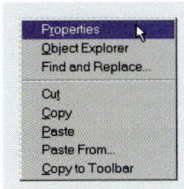

FIGURE 5-21: Text Properties dialog box

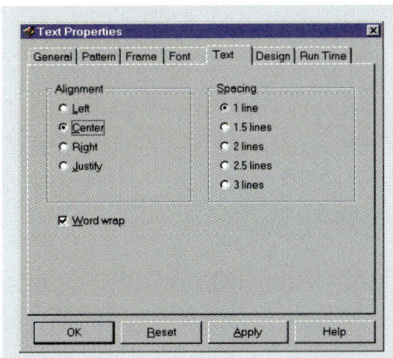

FIGURE 5-22: Completed data entry form

Title text box →

Instruction text box →

Other objects you can add to a form

The design object buttons on the toolbar allow you to add many kinds of objects to your form design. You have already added field objects. In this lesson you are adding text objects. You can also add boxes, lines, ellipses, graphic images, push buttons, other tables, and special fields, such as the date. To do so, click the desired button and draw the object in the design, just as you did with the text objects. Each type of object also has properties that you can change by right-clicking it and choosing from the context-sensitive menu.

TROUBLE?

If the Paradox Text Expert dialog box appears after you draw a text box, click Cancel to leave the Expert and then enter the text. To disable this Expert, click Edit on the menu bar, click Preferences, click the Experts tab, click the top box to remove the check mark, and then click OK.■

QUICK **TIP**

If the top or bottom lines of the text are cut off, you need to enlarge the text box container. Select the text box to display the handles, then drag the handles to enlarge the text box.■

Printing forms

After you create and design a form, it's a good idea to print it and compare it to the paper form you're trying to match. See the related topic "Using the printed form" for information on other uses for the printed form. ▶**case** Zora has finished customizing the form for the inventory table and is ready to print it and compare it to the packing list. First she will view a record in the form.

1 Click the **View Data button** on the toolbar

The first record appears in the form, as shown in Figure 5-23.

2 Click the **Print button** on the toolbar

The Print File dialog box opens, as shown in Figure 5-24. Because Paradox prints only the record that is currently on the screen, most of the print options in the dialog box are dimmed and not available.

3 Click **OK**

Figure 5-25 shows the printed form, which looks like it will be compatible with the paper form. The instructions will help keep the data in the inventory database accurate and complete.

4 Click **File** on the menu bar, then click **Close**

A dialog box appears asking if you want to save the changes to the form.

5 Click **Yes**

The form is saved and Zora returns to the Project Viewer.

FIGURE 5-23: Form with first record

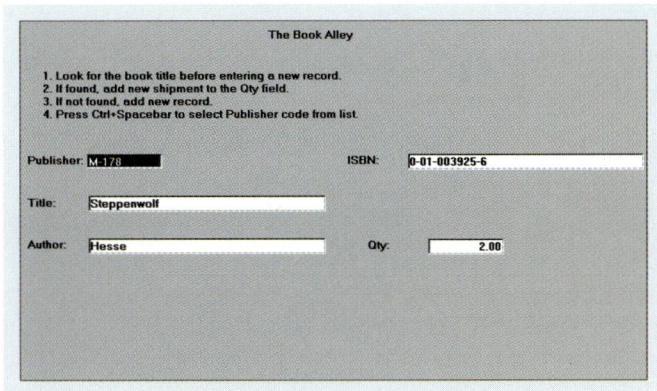

FIGURE 5-24: Print File dialog box

Options not available
when printing a form

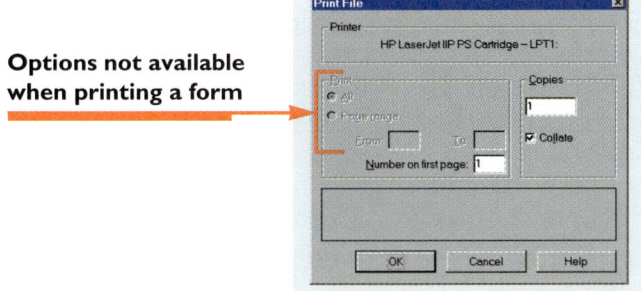

FIGURE 5-25: Printed form

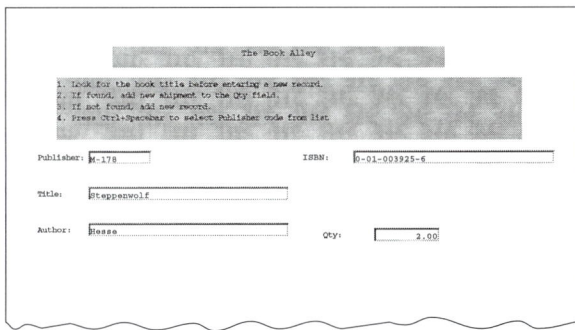

Using the printed form

A blank, printed form design is useful for data collection. You can carry the printed form around with you, write in the relevant data, and then, when you return to your computer, quickly transfer the handwritten data to the on-screen form.

Using the data entry form

Now that you've created a custom form, you are ready to use it! You can use the Project Viewer to open a form, just as you would open any other Paradox file. The related topic "Opening a form" describes four ways to open a form. ▶**case** The Book Alley has received another shipment of books. Some are additional copies of books already in stock, while others are new to the store. Zora asks Mark, one of the store's clerks, to try out the new data entry form. Following the instructions, Mark looks for the book title to see if it is in stock. If it is, he adds the new copies to the Qty field. If it is not, he adds a new record.

1 If necessary, click **Forms** in the Project Viewer to display the list of form files, right-click **Form for Clerks.fsl**, then click **View Data**
   Form for Clerks opens, showing data from the first record in the table.

2 Maximize the screen, then click the **Edit Data button** 🖾 on the toolbar
   Paradox is in Edit mode, as indicated by the message in the status bar.

3 Click the **Locate Field Value button** 🔍 on the toolbar
   The first book title in the packing list is *The Only Problem*. Mark looks for that title.

4 Type **The Only Problem** in the Value text box, click **Title** in the Fields list, then click **OK**
   The data for *The Only Problem* appears in the form, as shown in Figure 5-26. Mark sees that there is already one copy in stock. This shipment includes four more copies, so he changes the Qty field to 5.

5 Click in the **Qty field**, type **5**, then press **[Enter]**
   The quantity is updated. Mark enters the next book on the list, which is titled *On Your Own Terms*.

6 Click 🔍
   The Locate Field Value dialog box opens, as before.

7 Type **On Your Own Terms** in the Value text box, click **Title** in the Fields list if necessary, then click **OK**
   The status bar displays a message indicating that *On Your Own Terms* was not found, which means that the title is not currently in stock. So Mark adds a new record instead of updating an existing one.

8 Click the **Last Record button** ▶ on the toolbar, then click the **Next Record button** ▶
   A blank form opens for entering the new data, as shown in Figure 5-27.

FIGURE 5-26: Record for *The Only Problem*

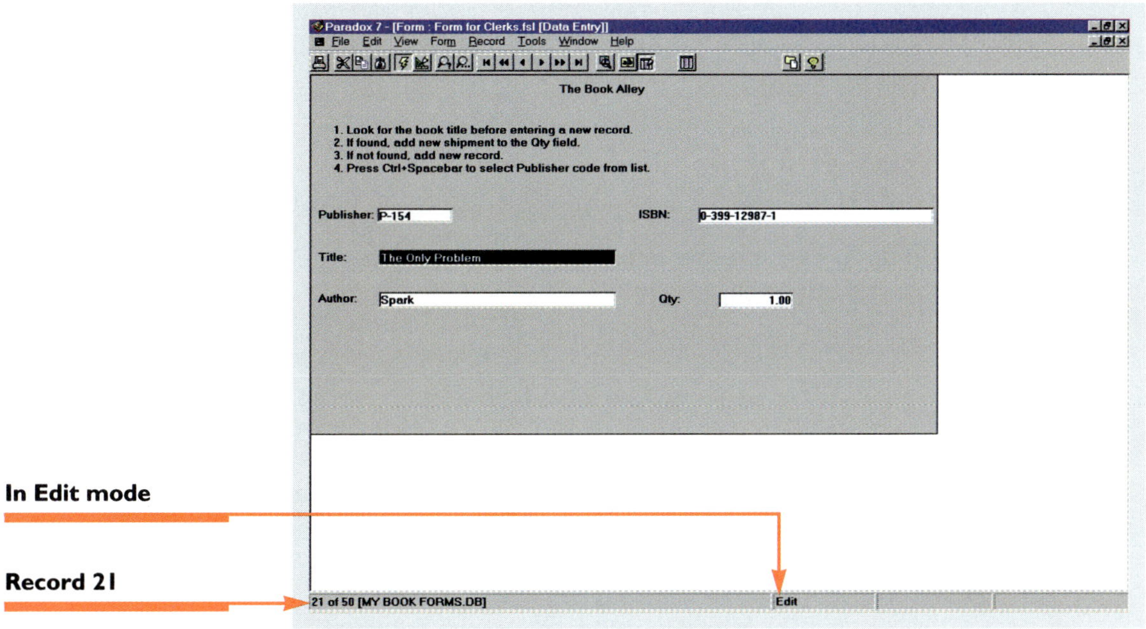

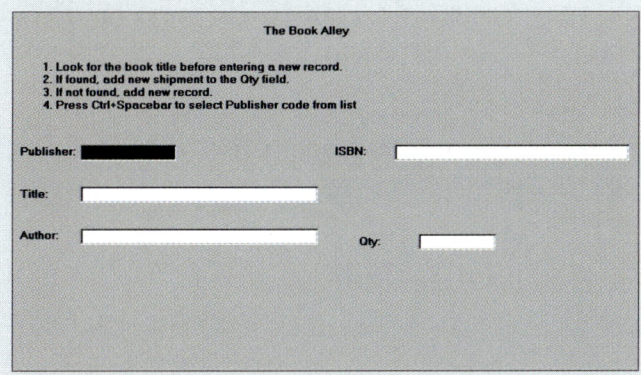

In Edit mode

Record 21

FIGURE 5-27: Blank record

Opening a form

If you have closed the form but want to enter data in it, you can open the form with the Project Viewer by one of the following methods:

- Right-click the form name and click View Data in the context-sensitive menu
- Click the Open Form button on the Project Viewer toolbar, then select the form name
- Click File on the menu bar, Open, Form, then select the form name
- Right-click Forms in the Project Viewer, then click Open and select the form name

The Table View window does not open when you run the form unless you click the Table View button on the toolbar.

Using the data entry form, continued

Mark is ready to enter the publisher data for the new record. According to the directions on the form, Mark can display a list of publisher codes to choose from.

9 Click in the **Publisher field**, then press **[Ctrl][Spacebar]**
The Lookup Help dialog box opens. Mark selects the code for Vintage.

10 Scroll down the list in the Lookup Help dialog box, click **V-130**, the code for Vintage, then click **OK**
The code V-130 appears in the Publisher field.

11 Press **[Tab]** to move to the next field and enter the following data:

ISBN	Title	Author	Qty
0-394-75301-1	**On Your Own Terms**	**Stechert**	**8**

Now that Mark is finished trying out the new data form, Zora displays the Table View window to enter the category and price information for the new book.

12 Click the **Table View button** 🏢 on the toolbar
The My Book Forms records appear in tabular layout, with the Qty field of the last record entered highlighted. Zora is ready to add price information.

13 Click in the **Price field**, type **15.95**, press **[Shift][Tab]**
The default value of SF for category isn't accurate for the new record, so Zora changes it using the lookup table.

14 Press **[Ctrl][Spacebar]**, select **RM**, then click **OK**
The new title, *On Your Own Terms* (record number 21), is completely entered now, as shown in Figure 5-28.

15 Close both the table and the form
You should have already saved all the changes you made to the form, but if you are asked if you want to save changes to the form, respond Yes. You return to the Project Viewer.

FIGURE 5-28: New record in table view

Entered in table view

New record entered
using form

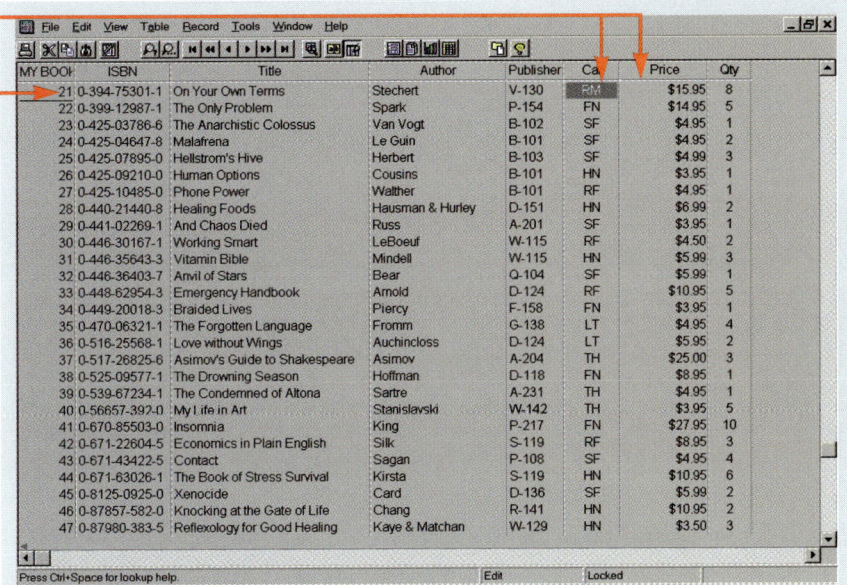

TASKREFERENCE

TASK	MOUSE/BUTTON	MENU	KEYBOARD
Add a text box	Click [A], then drag the pointer ⁺A to create the desired shape		
Align objects to grid		Click Design, then click Snap to Grid	
Create a form		Click Tools, click Expert, then select Form	
Create a Quick Form	Click [▦]	Click Tools, click Quick Form	[F7]
Display table view (from form view)	Click [▦]	Click View, click Table view	[F7]
Enter data in a table using a form	Click [▶], then click [▶] for blank record	Click Record, click Last, click Record, click Next	[Ctrl][F12], [F12]
Move objects	Click the object and drag it		
Opening a form	Right-click the form name in the Project Viewer, then click View Data in the context-sensitive menu or Click [▣], then select the form name or Right-click Forms in the Project Viewer, then click Open, then select the form name	Click File, click Open, then click Form	
Print a form	Click [🖨]	Click File, click Print	
Resize objects	Select the object, move the pointer to the edge until you see ↔ and resize		
Use Form Expert	Click [🔮], then select Form	Click Tools, click Experts, then select Form	
Use Form Design	Click [📝]	Click Form, click Design Form	[F8]
View data in a form (from design view)	Click [⚡]	Click Form, click View Data	[F8]

CONCEPTSREVIEW

Label each element of the Paradox Form Design window, as shown in Figure 5-29.

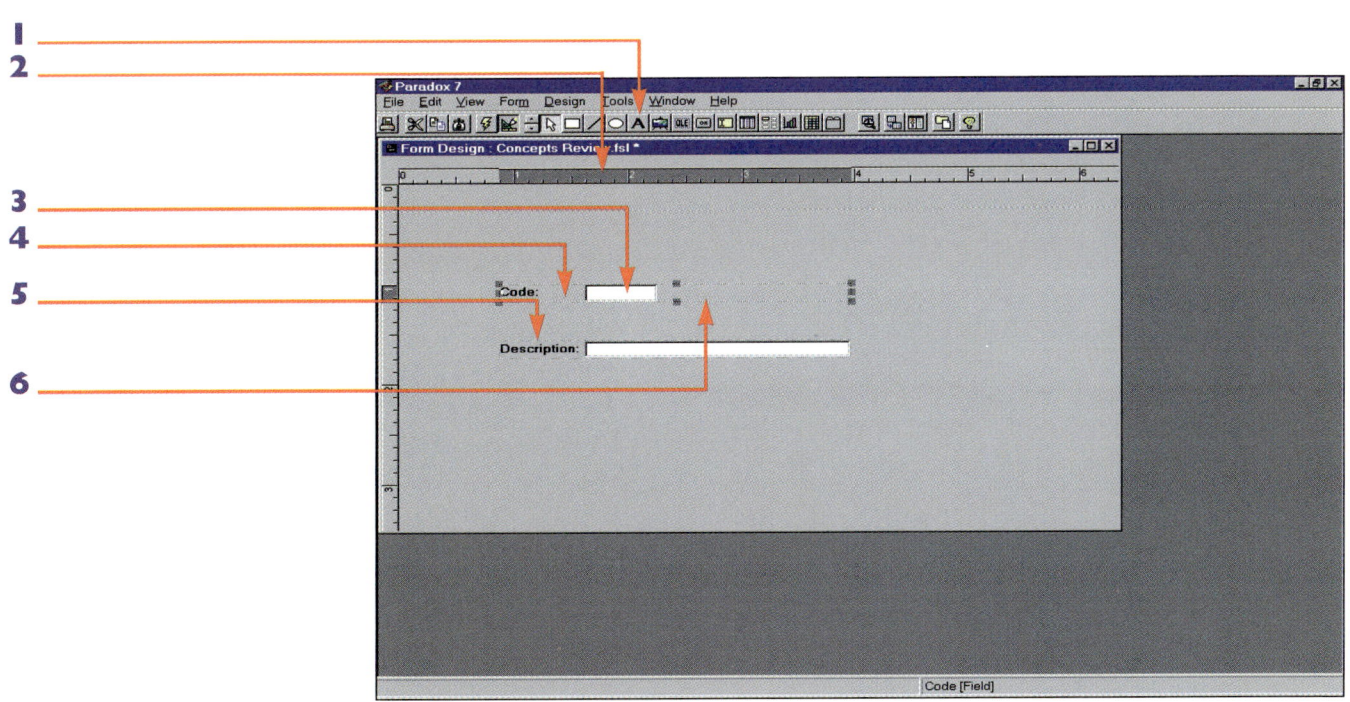

FIGURE 5-29

Match each statement with the term it describes.

7 Allows you to view data in form view

8 Allows you to change the form design

9 Allows you to insert a text object into a form design

10 Shows the record data in a form

11 Drag to move or resize an object

12 Shows the position of objects in the design

13 Contains the field label and edit region objects

a. Design button

b. Rulers

c. View Data button

d. Handles

e. Container

f. Text button

g. Edit region

Select the best answer from the list of choices.

14 In the Form Design window you can move fields
   a. Wherever you want on the screen
   b. Only to existing field locations
   c. Horizontally but not vertically
   d. Vertically but not horizontally

15 Before you can enter or edit data in a form, you must
   a. Save the form design.
   b. Switch to table view.
   c. Switch to Edit mode.
   d. Move to the first record in the table.

SKILLS REVIEW

1 Create a Quick Form.
  a. Copy the PD 5-2.DB file to your working directory with the name My Books Review.DB.
  b. Open the My Books Review table. Create a form using the Quick Form.
  c. Locate the record for the book titled *Vitamin Bible*.
  d. Print the Quick Form.

2 Enter data into the form.
  a. Click the Edit Data button for Edit mode.
  b. Go to the last record, then add a new blank record.
  c. Create two new book records, using data you make up, make sure to use [Ctrl][Spacebar] to look up both the publisher and the category.
  d. Return to the Table View window and locate the new records.
  e. Print the entire table and circle the new records.

3 Use the Form Expert.
  a. Click the Expert button on the toolbar and select the Form Expert.
  b. In Step 1 of the Form Expert, choose data from one table.
  c. In Step 2 choose the layout for one record.
  d. Select the My Books Review.DB table to associate with the form in Step 3.
  e. In Step 4 of the Form Expert, choose to display only the ISBN, Title, Cat, and Price fields.
  f. Accept the default options in Step 5.
  g. Choose the Shadow framed objects style in Step 6.
  h. Name the form Inventory Form in Step 7.
  i. Create the form by clicking Do It! Respond OK when informed that the form is complete.

4 Use the Form Designer
  a. Display the form in the Form Design window.
  b. Select the Price field container, select the Price field edit region, select the Cat field label, select the ISBN field container, select the ISBN field edit region, select the Title field label.

5 Move objects.
  a. Activate the form property Snap to Grid.
  b. Rearrange the fields so they are in one column in the center of the form.
  c. Put the fields in the following order from the top of the page: Title, ISBN, Cat, Price.
  d. Display data in the form to see how the changes look by clicking Form from the menu, then selecing View Data.

  e. Switch to Design Form and save the changes to the form by clicking File on the menu bar, then Save.
  f. Print the current record in the form format.

6 Resize objects.
  a. Return to Design Form from the Form menu.
  b. Reduce the size of the Cat field edit region to about $\frac{1}{2}$", then reduce the Cat container to match.
  c. Increase the Title field container by about $\frac{3}{4}$", then widen the Title field edit region to match.
  d. Reduce the size of the Price field edit region to about 1", then reduce the Price container to match and save the changes.

7 Add text.
  a. Insert a text box at the top of the form, then type the title "Inventory Data Entry," then center the title horizontally.
  b. Add another text box under the fields and type the following message: "Remember to enter the values carefully and verify each number. If you have a question, ask!"
  c. Right-click the message, choose the Font tab from the Properties dialog box, select Bold Italic from the Font Size list, click OK, then save the form.

8 Print forms.
  a. Display data in the form, then print one record in the form layout.
  b. Go to the last record, then click next record.
  c. Print the blank form.

9 Use the data entry form.
  a. If necessary, return to Edit mode, and add four new records using data you make up, using the Inventory Form.
  b. Switch to table view and complete the records by entering data in the blank fields (the fields that are not in the Inventory Form).
  c. Print the table, then close the table and form.

INDEPENDENT CHALLENGE 1

Gino Chelakis wants to start a gourmet mail-order business. He has a catalog nearly ready to print and mail to prospective customers, but he needs to design an order form for his staff. Gino decides to start by creating a form in Paradox. Help Gino design a complete and efficient order form that includes the customer ID number, the item number and description, quantity, and price.

To complete this independent challenge:

1 Copy the PD 5-3.DB table to your working directory with the name My Gourmet.DB.

2 Create a form using Form Expert for entering order information into the table.

3 In Step 2 of the Expert, choose the Multiple records displayed in a table radio button.

4 Display all the fields, choose Shadow framed objects as the style sheet in the Expert Steps.

5 Name the form My Gourmet. Using Design Form, reduce the size of the item number, quantity and price fields. (*Hint:* The container is now the column of the table.)

6 Move the records down and add a title to the form.

7 Enhance the appearance of the form using the Properties dialog box, then save and print the form.

INDEPENDENT CHALLENGE 2

Alice Barton has a new job at Careers Plus, an employment agency. One of her duties is to streamline the process of entering the data for new applicants into the database. Each applicant provides the following information: Name, address, home and business phone, current employment, employment history (last four positions), and education (highest level and any degrees).

To complete this independent challenge:

1 Create a table structure that is appropriate for the information Alice will need to enter. Name the table Careers Plus.

2 Design a form for applicants to complete that is efficient and name it Careers Plus.

3 Design the form so that it displays only one record at a time.

4 Place the most critical and most commonly provided data near the top of the form. Fields that apply to fewer applicants can be placed lower on the form. Make sure to include a title on the form.

5 Enter at least five records, using data you invent, then print the form with one record.

INDEPENDENT CHALLENGE 3

You have been given the task of developing an attractive form to use for entering data concerning cars for sale for use on a Web page. Your mission is to design a form that is easy to use, contains instructions, and has some interesting design elements.

To complete this independent challenge:

1 Make a copy of PD 5-4, saving it as My Autos for Sale.

2 Create a form with the layout of Multiple records, each with records displayed in columns.

3 Display all the fields except number of doors and color, choose Single line framed objects as the style sheet.

4 Name the form Autos for Sale and modify it so that fields aren't needlessly long, then put the price field at the top of the list.

5 Make changes to the appearance to enhance the form. Include a text box with a title and instructions (*Hint:* The text boxes don't have to go at the top of the page.) and save the form.

6 Add at least four records with data from your local newspaper, then go to Table View to enter missing data.

7 Display data in the form, print it, and close the form and table.

INDEPENDENT CHALLENGE 4

You are interested in purchasing a computer but are confused at all the options. You decide to create a database with the most pertinent information and put in the top vendors as gathered from computer magazines.

To complete this independent challenge:

1 Make a copy of the table PD 5-5, saving it as My Hardware.

2 Create a form for My Hardware, with one record displayed in columns, include all the fields, choose any style sheet you wish, and name it Hardware Criteria.

3 Add a text box with a title "Hardware Criteria Form" and the date you create the form, then save it.

4 Add at least ten records from data you've found in computer magazines or newspapers.

5 Print a copy of the form with data, then print a copy of the table from Table View.

6 Close the form and the table, saving any changes.

VISUALWORKSHOP

You are doing a consulting project for a client that involves researching the search engines available on the Internet. You have created a table, Internet Search.DB, and have entered some data. You've gotten a little behind in your work, and so you decide to hire a work-study student to enter additional data. You want to make sure the data is entered accurately and that minimal training is needed for the student, so you create a form. Save PD 5-6.DB as My Internet Search.DB, and create a form using Figure 5-30 as your guide. Save the form as Internet Search Input and print it with record.

```
┌──────────────────────────────────────────────────────────────────┐
│                                                                    │
│    ┌──────────────────────────────────────────────────────────┐   │
│    │           Internet Search Input Form                     │   │
│    └──────────────────────────────────────────────────────────┘   │
│                                                                    │
│    ┌──────────────────────────────────────────────────────────┐   │
│    │Notes to user:                                             │   │
│    │1.   The developer is the name of the company or organization who is currently selling │
│    │the product.                                               │   │
│    │2.   There may not be a Web address if the product isn't a Web product. │
│    │3.   The contact can be a phone number, person, or address. │   │
│    └──────────────────────────────────────────────────────────┘   │
│                                                                    │
│                                                                    │
│    Name of engine:│Alta Vista                                 │    │
│                                                                    │
│    Developer:      │Digital Equipment Corp                    │    │
│                                                                    │
│    Web address:    │http://altavista.digital.com          │        │
│                                                                    │
│    Contact:        │DEC                                 │           │
│                                                                    │
└──────────────────────────────────────────────────────────────────┘
```

FIGURE 5-30

UNIT 6

OBJECTIVES

▶ Create a Quick Report

▶ Use the Report Designer

▶ Add and customize a report header

▶ Group and summarize information

▶ Save and print a report

▶ Create a report from a query

Working
WITH REPORTS

Reports are one of the most varied and versatile products you can create in a database and serve a wide variety of purposes, varying from a simple tabular list of the table data to a complex summary of information. Reports and forms are similar, the major difference between them is that reports are meant to be printed, while forms are meant to be viewed on the screen. **case** Zora finds that the forms she has created are satisfactory for data entry, but she knows that printed reports are the best way to distribute information to others. For example, a manager, Jennifer Chi, needs weekly inventory reports. Sometimes a simple list of all the records is sufficient while other times she needs more detailed information. Zora will use the Paradox Quick Report and Report Designer to produce the reports Jennifer needs.▶

Creating a Quick Report

Quick Report allows you to create a simple report, showing all the records in a table, simply by clicking a button. The Quick Report differs from the printouts you created in earlier units by including a header with the current date, the table name, and a page number. ▶case Zora needs to create a report quickly to allow Jennifer to see the current stock levels. In order to fit all the fields on one page, she prints the report lengthwise on the page, in landscape orientation.

1 Launch Paradox 7, then use the **Project Viewer** to copy **PD 6-1.DB** and save it to the appropriate directory as **My Book Reports.DB**

2 Set the correct working directory, open the **My Book Reports.DB table**, then maximize it
Before she creates her Quick Report, Zora changes the print orientation from portrait to landscape.

3 Click **File** on the menu bar, click **Printer Setup**, click **Modify Printer Setup**, then click the **Paper tab**
A Modify Printer Setup dialog box similar to Figure 6-1 opens. Notice that a sample of the currently selected orientation is shown to the left of the option button.

4 Click the **Landscape radio button**, click **OK** to close the Modify Printer Setup dialog box, then click **OK** to close the Printer Setup dialog box

5 Click the **Quick Report button** 📄 on the toolbar
A message box appears, stating that Paradox is preparing the report. Then the Quick Report opens, as shown in Figure 6-2. Notice the toolbar buttons, which are appropriate for working with reports.

6 Click the **Next Page button** 📄 on the toolbar
The next page of the report appears. The status bar indicates that this report contains two pages.

7 Click the **First Page button** 📄 on the toolbar
Paradox returns to the top of the report. Now Zora wants to see how one full page of the report looks, so she changes the screen magnification.

8 Click **View** on the menu bar, click **Zoom**, then click **Best Fit**
This displays one full page on the screen. Now Zora prints the report.

9 Click the **Print button** 📄 on the toolbar, then click **OK**
The Quick Report prints in landscape orientation, with all the fields fitting across the length of the page. Figure 6-3 shows the first page of the My Book Reports Quick Report. Zora is pleased with the Quick Report. She doesn't save it, because she can recreate it simply by clicking a button.

10 Click **File**, click **Close**, and click **No** when asked if you want to save the new report design, then close the **My Book Reports.DB table**
The Quick Report window closes and Zora returns to the Project Viewer.

FIGURE 6-1: Printer Properties dialog box

Title will depend on your environment

Click to print lengthwise on page

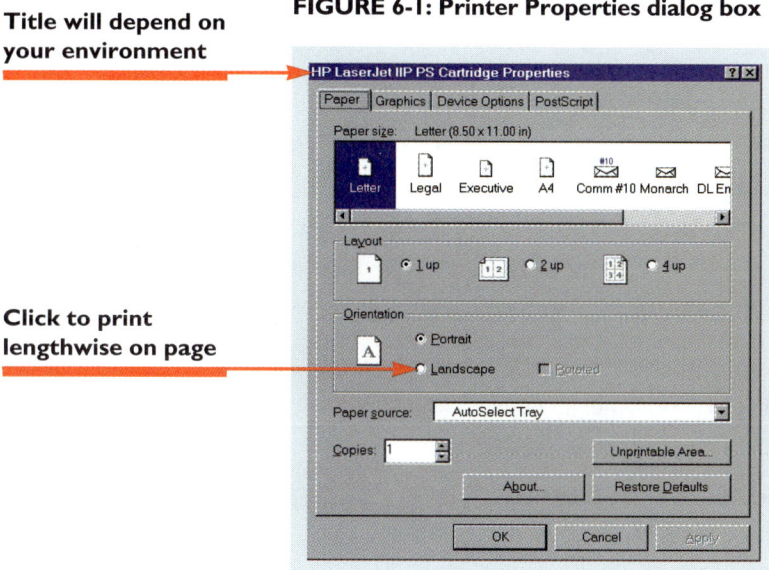

FIGURE 6-2: Quick Report

First Page button

Previous Page button

Last Page button

Next Page button

Table name

Current date (yours might be different)

Page number of report

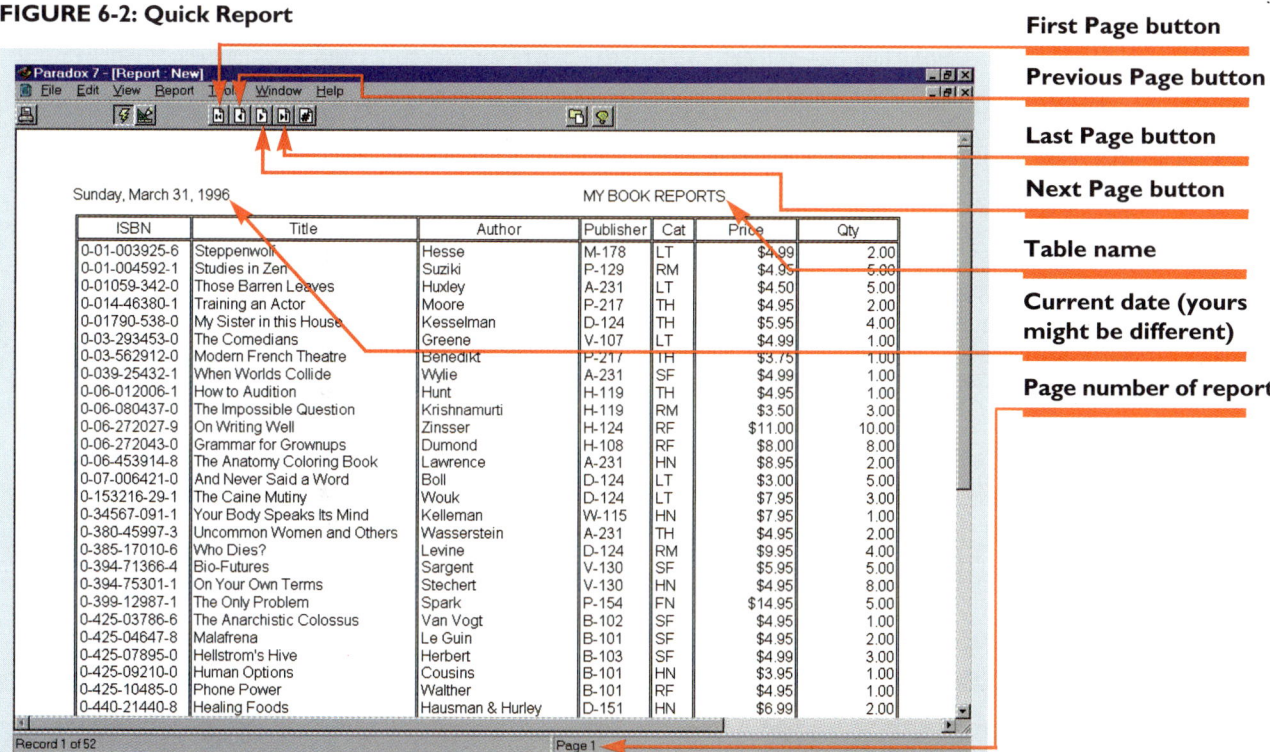

FIGURE 6-3: Quick Report printed in landscape orientation

Sunday, March 31, 1996   MY BOOK REPORTS   Page 1

ISBN	Title	Author	Publisher	Cat	Price	Qty
0-01-003925-6	Steppenwolf	Hesse	M-178	LT	$4.99	2.00
0-01-004592-1	Studies in Zen	Suziki	P-129	RM	$4.95	5.00
0-01059-342-0	Those Barren Leaves	Huxley	A-231	LT	$4.50	5.00
0-014-46380-1	Training an Actor	Moore	P-217	TH	$4.95	2.00
0-01790-538-0	My Sister in this House	Kesselman	D-124	TH	$5.95	4.00
0-03-293453-0	The Comedians	Greene	V-107	LT	$4.99	1.00
0-03-562912-0	Modern French Theatre	Benedikt	P-217	TH	$3.75	1.00
0-039-25432-1	When Worlds Collide	Wylie	A-231	SF	$4.99	1.00
0-06-012006-1	How to Audition	Hunt	H-119	TH	$4.95	1.00

Using the Report Designer

When you need more control over the design of your report, you'll want to use either the **Report Designer** or the **Report Expert**. The two major steps in the Report Designer are selection of the table or tables to use in the report, called the **Data Model**, and selection of the **Design Layout**, including which fields to use. ▶case Jennifer asks Zora to create a report that the store clerks can use when checking inventory on the shelves without price information.

1   Right-click **Reports** in the Project Viewer, then click **New**
    The New Report dialog box opens with four options available. See Table 6-1 for a description of the options. Zora wants help creating the report.

2   Click **Data Model/Design Layout**
    The Data Model dialog box opens, as shown in Figure 6-4.

3   Double-click **My Book Reports.DB** in the File name list box, then click **OK**
    The Design Layout dialog box, which contains style and layout options, opens, as shown in Figure 6-5. Here you can specify the design of your report, as well as which fields to include.

4   Click each of the **Style radio buttons: Single record, Tabular, Multi-record**, and **Blank**
    As you choose different styles, notice how the sample on the right and the options on the left change. Zora prefers the Tabular format.

5   Make sure **Tabular** is selected, then click **Show Fields**
    A list of fields replaces the Style and Layout options list.

6   Click **Price** in the Selected Fields list, click **Remove Field**, then click **OK**
    Paradox displays the new report in the Report Design window, ready for Zora to make further modifications. Zora decides to save the design now, before she makes any modifications.

7   Click **File** on the menu bar, click **Save As**, type **Inventory Report** in the File name text box, then click **Save**
    Paradox automatically adds the extension .RSL. The new title appears in the Design window title bar, as shown in Figure 6-6.

TABLE 6-1: New Report options

OPTION	DESCRIPTION
Blank	A new report that is not connected to a table and contains only minimal design objects: report header and footer, page header and footer, and record band
Report Expert	A new report using the Report Expert
Label Expert	A report designed to be printed on mailing labels
Data Model / Design Layout	A new report using the Data Model and Design Layout dialog boxes; these dialog boxes give you options for giving your report a data model and choosing the primary design objects used to work with the tables in the data model

FIGURE 6-4: Data Model dialog box

Your list might be different

Double-click to choose table

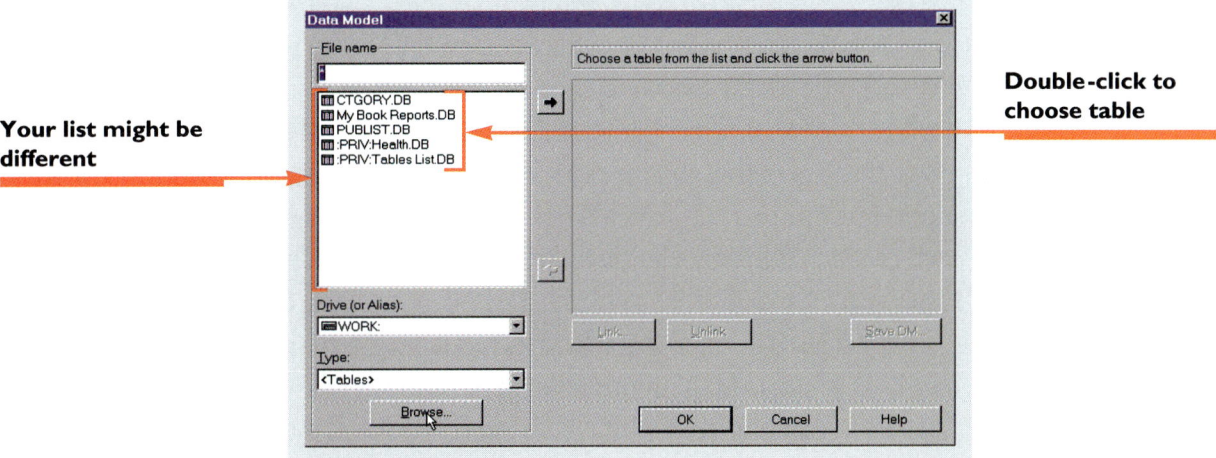

FIGURE 6-5: Design Layout dialog box

Click to display field list

Currently selected layout

Sample tabular design

Click to see other styles

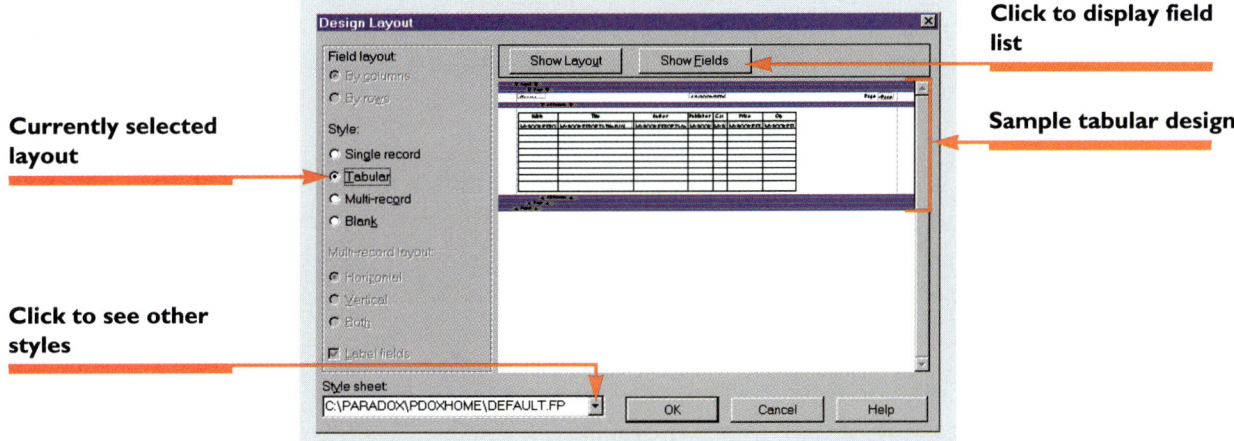

FIGURE 6-6: Inventory Report Design window

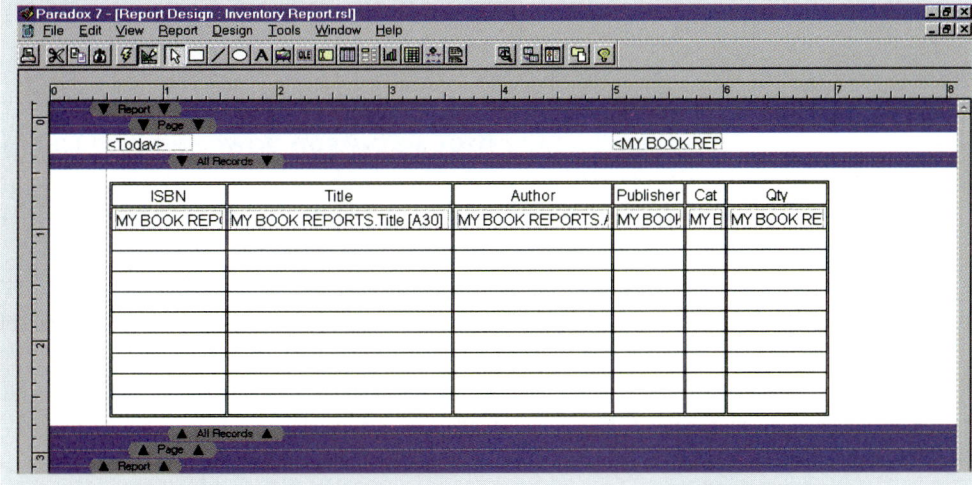

Adding and customizing a report header

The report you created is now in the **Report Design window** where you don't actually see the table data. Instead, you see field objects, such as My Book Reports.Title (A30), which indicate the name of the table on which the report is based, the field name, and the field type and size. The Report Design window, as shown in Figure 6-7, displays the report in three major sections, called **bands**, each of which prints in a particular place in the report. The main band is the **Records band**, which contains the bulk of the table data, and is nested inside the **Page band**. The **Page band** has a **page header** and a **page footer**, which contain information to be printed at the top or bottom of each page. Paradox automatically includes today's date and the inventory table title in the Page header. The Page band itself is nested inside the **Report band**. The Report band also has a **header** and a **footer**, which contain information to be printed at the beginning or end of the report. The horizontal and vertical rulers in the Design window show you the position of the mouse pointer and objects in the design. **case** Zora decides to add a more descriptive title to her report. She uses the Text tool to draw a text box. But first she must make room in the report header for the new title.

1   Click the **upper Report band label** (as shown in Figure 6-8) and move the pointer to the upper boundary between the Report and Page bands until it changes to ↕
    The borders of the Report band change color when clicked and the pointer changes to ↕ when positioned at the boundary, as shown in Figure 6-8.

2   Click and drag the **pointer** down to the ½" mark on the vertical ruler to make room for the two title lines
    Blank space is added to the Report header band when you release the mouse button.

3   Click the **Text Tool button** [A] on the toolbar, then move the **pointer** to the white area of the Report header band
    The pointer changes to ⁺A. Use the **Text Tool** to add text anywhere in a report design. Next, Zora creates a text box in which to type the title and subtitle.

4   Position ⁺A at ⅛" on the vertical ruler and 2½" on the horizontal ruler, then hold the **mouse button** down and drag to draw a box, as shown in Figure 6-9
    After you release the mouse button, the insertion point is at the left end of the box, ready for you to begin typing text.

5   Type **THE BOOK ALLEY INVENTORY**, press **[Enter]**, then type **Books Currently in Stock** inside the text box
    Both titles are in the new text box, but they are aligned at the left margin, as shown in Figure 6-10. If you cannot see all the text, you need to use the handles to resize the text box.

FIGURE 6-7: Elements of Design window

Run Report button

Current date

Report band

Page band

Band labels

Design Report button

Text Tool button

Table name (you can't see the entire title because its container is too small)

Field name, type, size

Records band

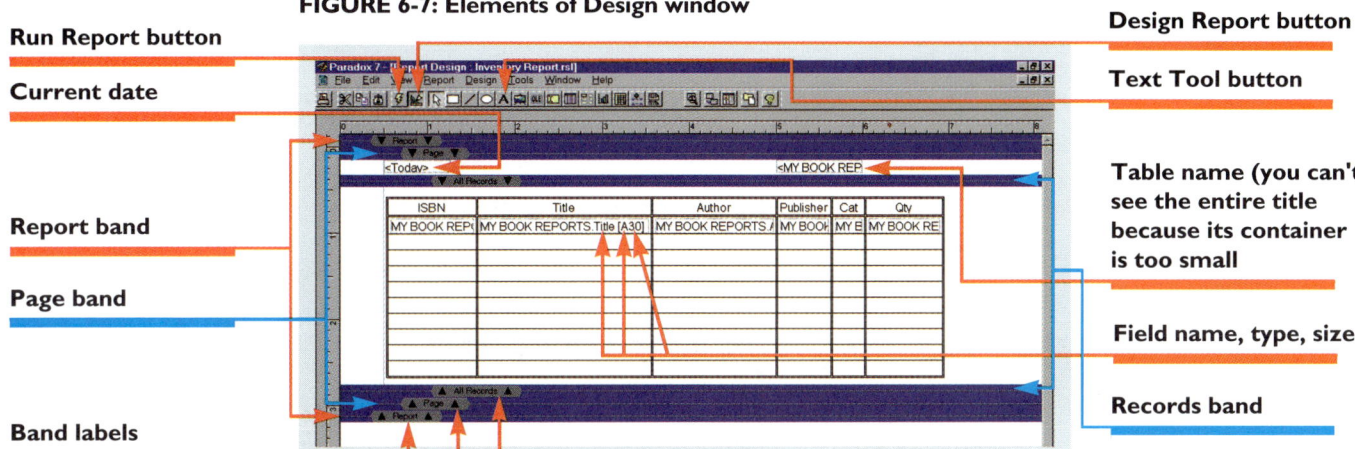

FIGURE 6-8: Enlarging the report header

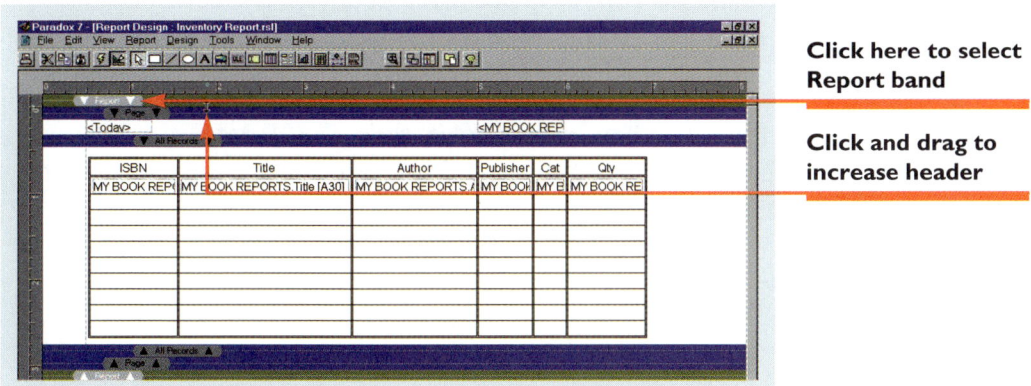

Click here to select Report band

Click and drag to increase header

FIGURE 6-9: Drawing the text box

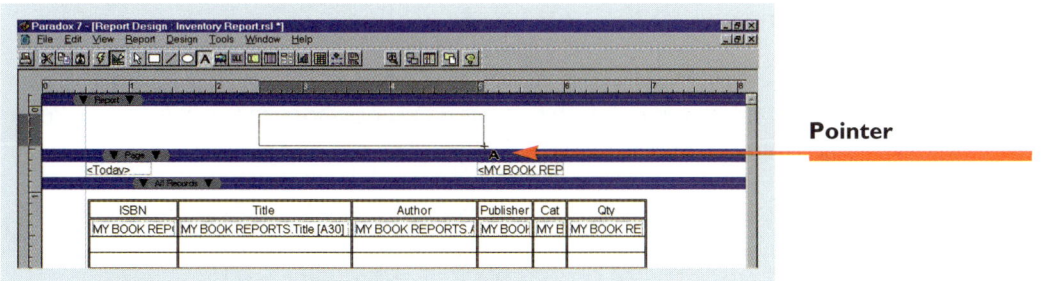

Pointer

FIGURE 6-10: Title in the text box

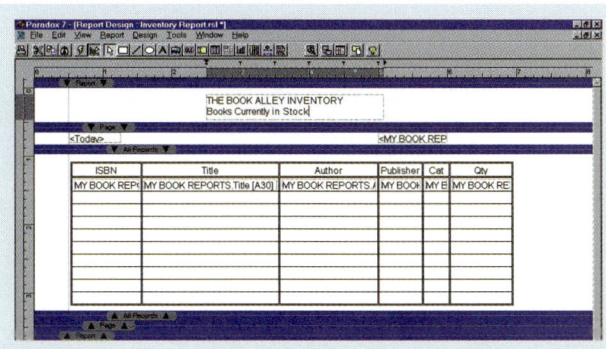

TROUBLE?

If the Paradox Text Expert dialog box appears after you draw a text box, click Cancel to leave the Expert and then enter the text. To disable this Expert, click Edit on the menu bar, click Preferences, click the Experts tab, click the top box to remove the check mark, and then click OK. ■

Adding and customizing a report header, continued

Zora prefers to see the titles centered in the report header and wants to move the page number to the footer.

6 Click at the **beginning of the first line of text** and drag the **pointer** to select the text
All the text in the box is highlighted.

7 Right-click the **text**, then click **Properties**

8 Click the **Text tab**, then click the **Center radio button**
The Text Properties dialog box appears, as shown in Figure 6-11. Now Zora wants to see how the table data looks in the report.

9 Click **OK**, then click the **Run Report button** ⚡ on the toolbar
The book inventory report appears in the View window, as shown in Figure 6-12. The records are ordered by the key field, ISBN.

10 Click **View** on the menu bar, click **Zoom**, then click **Best Fit**
Zora prefers to see the page number at the bottom of the page (in the footer) rather than in the page header. She returns to the Design window to make this change.

11 Click the **Design Report button** 🖼 on the toolbar
Zora returns to the Design window.

12 Click the **lower Page band border** and drag it up about ½"
The page footer is now wide enough to accommodate the Page Number field.

13 Click the **Page Number field** at the top of the page band and drag it from the page header to the page footer at the far left

14 Click the **Run Report button** ⚡ on the toolbar
The book inventory report reappears with the page number as shown in Figure 6-13. Now Zora wants to see how the data looks on the printed page.

15 Click the **Next Page button** 📄, then click the **First Page button** 📄

16 Click the **Print button** 🖨 on the toolbar, then click **OK**
Zora's new inventory report prints.

FIGURE 6-11: Text Properties dialog box

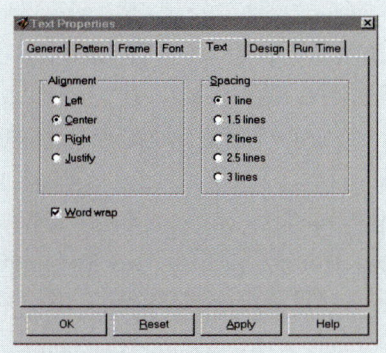

FIGURE 6-12: Text centered on report

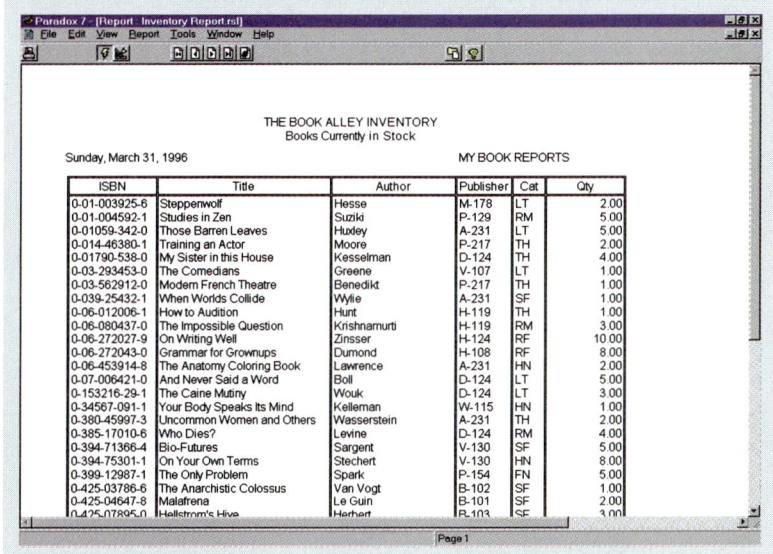

FIGURE 6-13: Modified footer on report

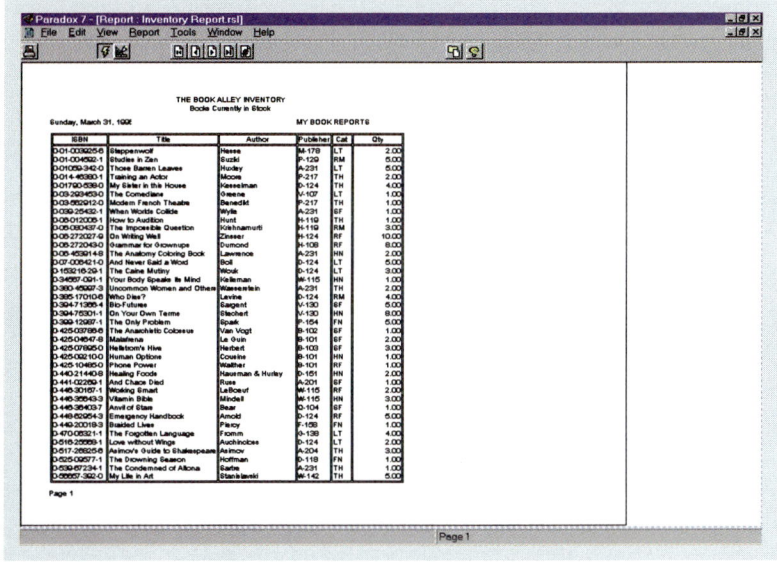

TROUBLE?

If you notice that the Date field does not display the entire date, the container might be too narrow. In the Design window, click the Date field to select it, then click and drag the right handle until the container is the correct width.■

Grouping and summarizing information

It is often easier to form conclusions about data when it is organized into meaningful groups. To group records, you add an additional band to the report design, a **Group band**. The Group band has a **group header** and a **group footer**, where you place information you want printed at the beginning or end of each group. Once you group the data, you can summarize the information in each group, using **Summary fields**. Summary information can be placed anywhere in the report, but it usually appears at the end of a group of records, in the Group band footer. **case** Zora's manager, Jennifer, wants to compare industry statistics on buyer preferences to The Book Alley's current inventory. Zora creates a report that groups titles by category, and counts the number of titles in each category.

1 Click **View** on the menu bar, click **Zoom**, then click **100%**
The report returns to its original size.

2 Click the **Design Report button** 🖾 on the toolbar, then click the **Add Group Band button** 🏛
Zora returns to the Design window and the Define Group dialog box opens, as shown in Figure 6-14. Zora wants to group the inventory records by category.

3 Click **Cat** in the Field list box, then click **OK**
The dialog box closes and Zora returns to the Design window shown in Figure 6-15, where two additional bands, the Group header and Group footer, are visible. The field name "Cat" appears in the group header area so that when the report prints, the Category field value will be printed at the top of each group of titles. Zora wants to see how the report looks now, grouped by category.

4 Click the **Run Report button** ⚡ on the toolbar
The book records are grouped by category, as shown in Figure 6-16. The category code appears in the group header. The groups are arranged in alphabetical order and the records are arranged by ISBN within each group. Next, Zora wants to count the number of titles in each category. She does this by adding a summary field.

5 Click 🖾
Zora returns to the Design window.

FIGURE 6-14: Define Group dialog box

Click to group by category

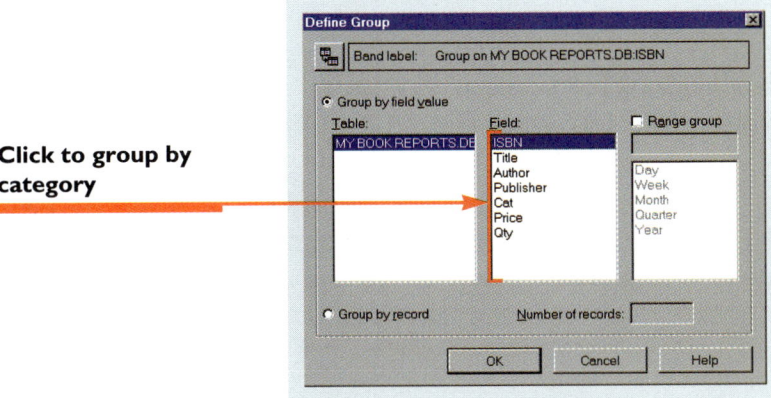

Field Tool button

Add Group Band button

FIGURE 6-15: Report design with group bands

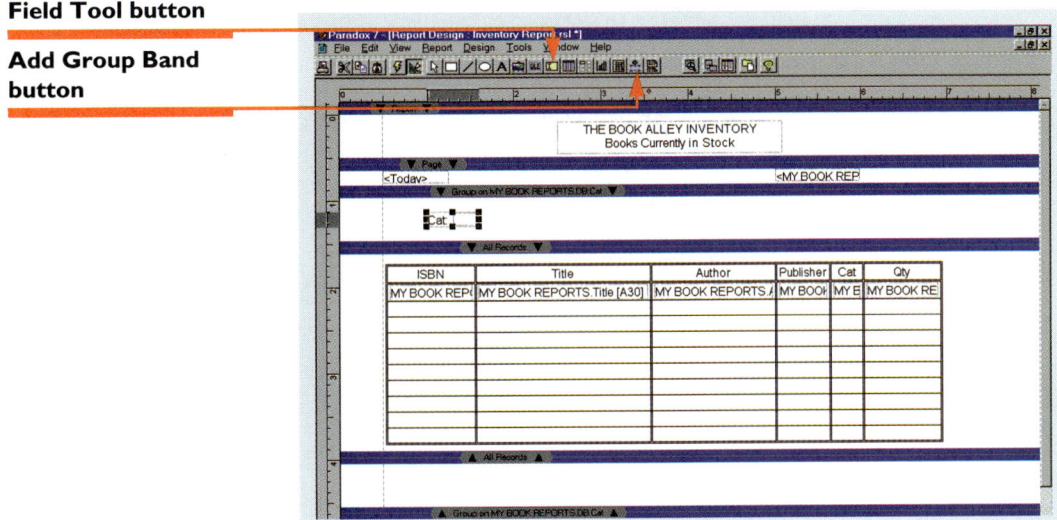

FIGURE 6-16: Report with data grouped by category

Group header

All fiction titles

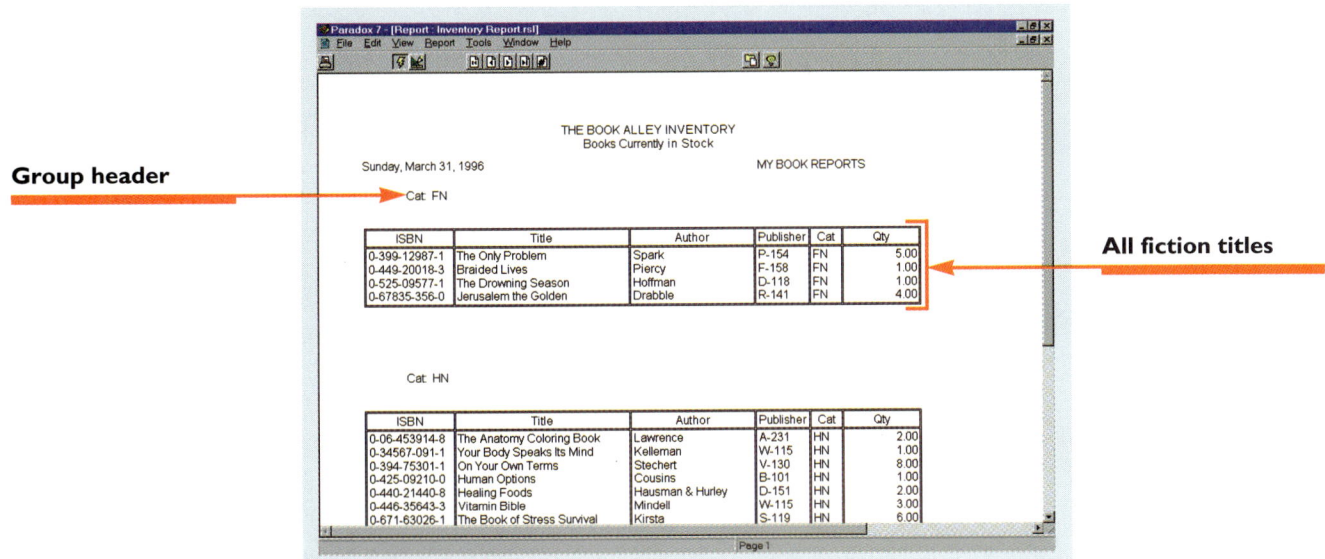

Grouping and summarizing information, continued

Zora wants to include the total number of book titles in each category, so she puts a Summary field in the group header using the **Field Tool button**. The Field Tool button places a field object on a report. Then Zora can reduce the space allocated to the empty group footer.

6 Click the **Field Tool button** 🔲 on the toolbar and draw a **field object box** in the group header, the same way you drew a text box for the title
The new field object appears in the group header, with "LABEL" as the field label. Next, Zora needs to tell Paradox what type of field this field object is.

7 Right-click the **field edit region**, then click **Define Field** in the context-sensitive menu
The Define Field Object dialog box opens, as shown in Figure 6-17. This dialog box allows you to specify which field in your table to use to calculate the Summary field, and what kind of a summary you want. The summary choices available depend on the type of field selected.

8 Click the **My Book Reports.DB list arrow**, then click **Cat**
MY BOOK REPORTS.CAT (meaning the Cat field of the My Book Reports table) appears in the box. Now Zora needs to tell Paradox how she wants the information in the Cat field summarized.

9 Click the **Summary list arrow,** then click **Count**
This tells Paradox to count all the values in each grouping of the Cat field. The Define Field Object dialog box now looks like Figure 6-18. After a summary operator (Count in this case) is selected, the other Summary options become available as defined in Table 6-2. Zora accepts the default, Normal.

10 Click **OK**
The Define Field Object dialog box closes and you return to the Report Design window. Now Zora removes the extra space in the Group band footer.

11 Scroll down to the **group footer** and click in its white space
The Group band label border changes color indicating that it is selected.

12 Position the **pointer** on the **lower Group band border**, then click and drag the **border** up to remove the extra space
The group footer space is removed. Zora decides to see how the data looks in the modified report.

13 Click the **Run Report button** ⚡ on the toolbar
The grouped report appears on the screen. Zora would like to see the entire report.

14 Click **View** on the menu bar, click **Zoom**, then click **Best Fit**
Zora's inventory report, grouped and summarized by book category, appears on the screen, as shown in Figure 6-19. Zora can see that there are 4 books in the fiction category, 12 in the health and nutrition category, and so on.

FIGURE 6-17: Define Field Object dialog box

Click to choose field
to summarize

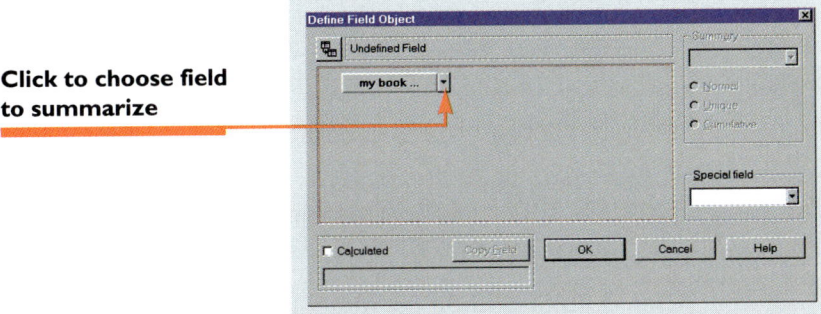

FIGURE 6-18: Cat field defined to count

Table

Field

Click to select
operator

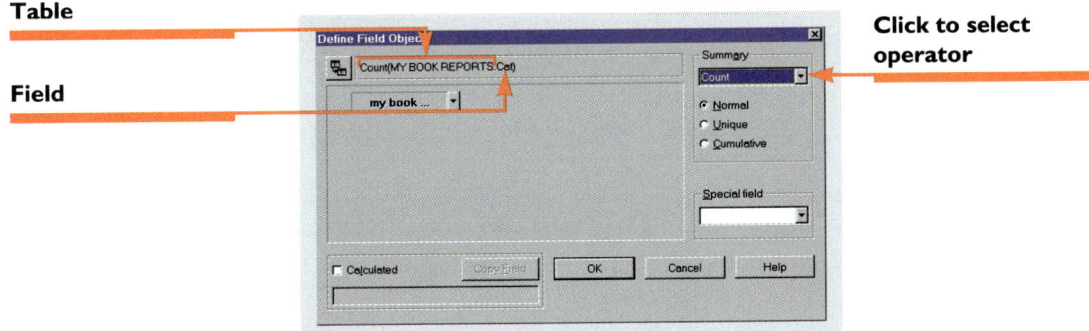

FIGURE 6-19: Book inventory report grouped by category

Count of records in
group

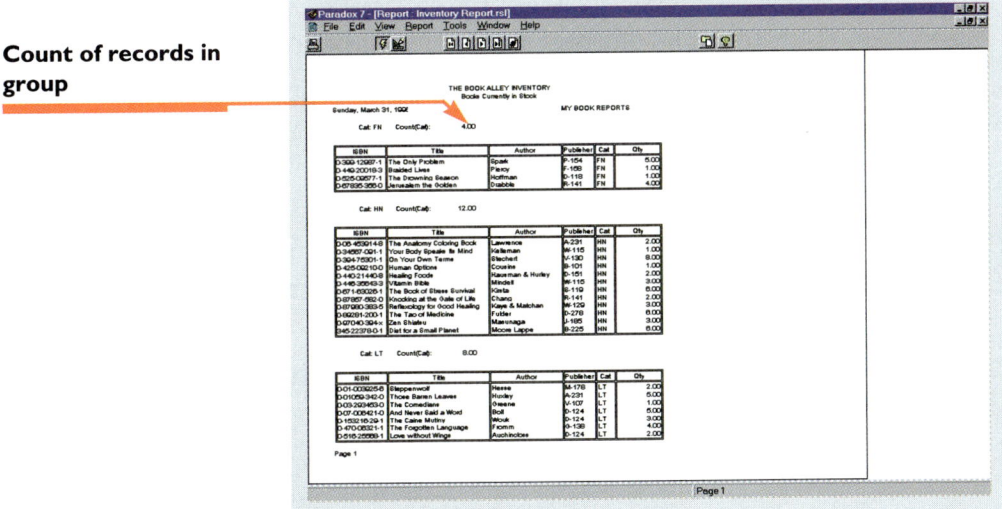

TABLE 6-2: Summary options

OPTION	DESCRIPTION
Normal	Summarizes all the records in each category
Unique	Includes only the first occurrence of the value and ignores duplicates
Cumulative	Keeps a running summary that includes all the summary data from previous groups

QUICK **TIP**

To add the number
of copies in each
category, instead of
the number of titles,
summarize the Qty
field using the Sum
summary operator.

Saving and printing a report

You can print the report from either the Design or the View window, but you must be in the Design window to save it. Keep in mind that it is helpful, when you are designing a report, to frequently print at least one page. This gives you a realistic view of how your data looks, including headers, footers, and font style changes. After printing the report, you might see that you need to change the print orientation in order to fit all the fields on one page. Sometimes you might have so many fields in a report that they won't even fit on one page in landscape orientation. Table 6-3 describes the options for handling this kind of data over-flow in the Print File dialog box. ►**case** Zora wants to show Jennifer a printout of the report she's just created that includes the category groups. She will print her report using standard Paradox procedures. But first she saves the report with a different name, so that she doesn't write over the first report she designed.

1 Click the **Design Report button** 📄 on the toolbar
The Report Design window opens.

2 Click **File** on the menu bar, click **Save As**, enter **Group by Category** as the filename, then click **Save**
The title bar shows the new report name. Before printing the report, Zora wants to set the print orientation to landscape, so that all the fields will fit on one page. She already did this once, using the Print Setup dialog box. This time she'll use a different method.

3 Click **Report** on the menu bar, then click **Page Layout**
The Page Layout dialog box, which contains options affecting the print orientation, paper size, and margin settings, opens, as shown in Figure 6-20.

4 If necessary, click **Landscape** in the Orientation settings, then click **OK**
The dialog box closes and the design appears wider than before because the landscape orientation is specified. Zora is ready to print her report.

5 Click **File** on the menu bar, click **Print**, then click **Report**
A Print File dialog box opens, as shown in Figure 6-21, listing your printing options.

6 Click **OK**
Figure 6-22 shows the first page of Zora's printed report.

7 Click **File** on the menu bar, click **Close**, then click **Yes** to save the most recent changes to the report
The Report Design window closes and Zora returns to the Project Viewer.

FIGURE 6-20: Page Layout dialog box

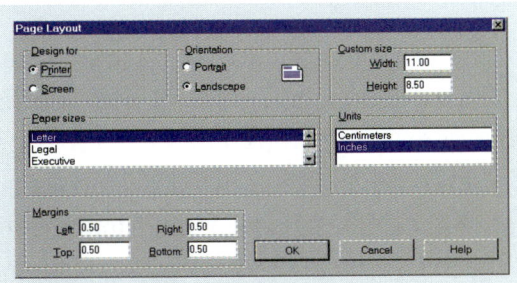

FIGURE 6-21: Print File dialog box

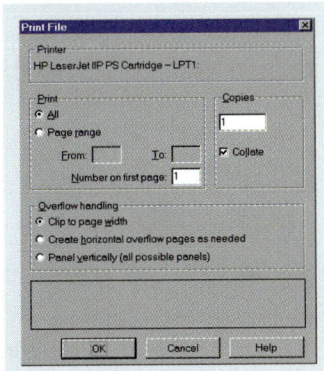

FIGURE 6-22: Printed inventory report, first page

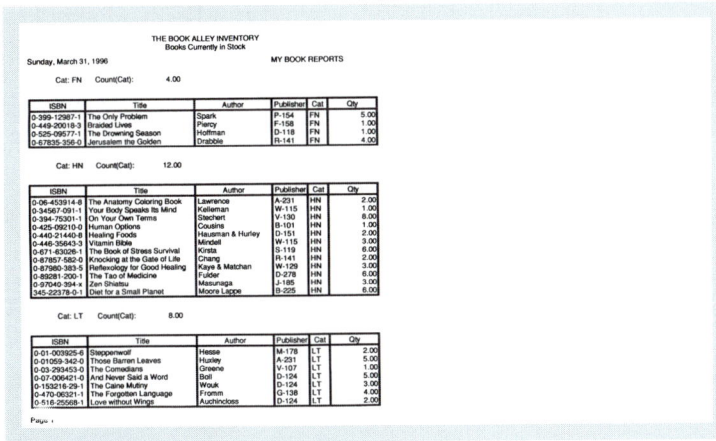

QUICK **TIP**

You can print your report design with no data showing. This is useful for documenting the report design and sketching changes that occasionally will become necessary. From the Design window, click File on the menu bar, then click Print, and you see that you have two choices: Design and Report. Click Design to print the report design.■

TABLE 6-3: Overflow handling options

OPTION	DESCRIPTION
Clip To Page Width	Cuts off (or clips) all data that exceeds the right page margin
Create Horizontal Overflow	Prints extra panels (extra pages containing the data that overflows to the right of the main Pages As Needed report page) only when there is data in that area
Panel Vertically (All Possible Panels)	Prints all panels, whether data exists or not

Creating a report from a query

To limit your report to a subset of information in your table, you first create a query that extracts the information you want, then you design a report based on the resulting Answer table. After you create the query, you should save it. The next time you need a similar report, you can quickly run the query in order to include the newest information in the report. For more information, see the related topic "Other uses for queries in reports." **case** Zora is planning to attend a conference sponsored by the Science Fiction Writers of America. Wanting to be prepared with a list of all the science fiction titles that The Book Alley has in stock, she creates a query to extract all records with SF in the category field. She would also like to see each publisher's full name rather than just the code, so she links the inventory table with the publisher table in the query.

1   Right-click **Queries** in the Project Viewer window, then click **New**
The Select File dialog box opens.

2   Click **My Book Reports.DB** in the file list, then click **Open**
The Query Design window opens with the My Book Reports table skeleton. First, Zora adds the Publist table to the query so that she will have access to the publishers' names.

3   Click the **Add Table button** 🗔 on the toolbar, click **Publist** in the Select File dialog box, then click **Open**
The Publist table skeleton appears in the Query Design window. Now Zora links the tables, using an example element.

4   Click the **Join Tables button** 🗔 on the toolbar, click the **Publisher field** in the My Book Reports table skeleton, then click the **PUBCODE field** in the Publist skeleton
The example element "join1" appears in both fields. Zora is ready to check the fields she wants in the report.

5   Click the **check boxes** for the **ISBN**, **Title**, and **Author fields** in the My Book Reports table, then click the **check box** for the **Name field** in the Publist table
Next Zora limits the books to the science fiction category.

6   Click the **Cat field**, then type **SF**
Finally Zora saves the Answer table, so she can use it as the basis for a report.

7   Click the **Query Properties button** 🗔 on the toolbar, delete the default name (except the .DB), type **SF Category Report** in the Table text box, then click **OK**
The query design is shown in Figure 6-23. Zora saves the query before running it.

8   Click **File** on the menu bar, click **Save As**, then save the query as **SF Category**
Zora runs the query to make sure she has specified the correct records and fields.

9   Click the **Run Query button** 🗲 on the toolbar
The results appear, as shown in Figure 6-24.

Example elements join table

FIGURE 6-23: Completed query

Condition limits records

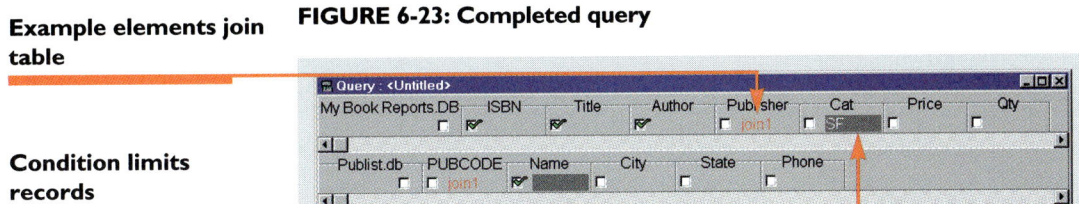

Answer table saved as SF Category Report

FIGURE 6-24: Query results in SF Category Report table

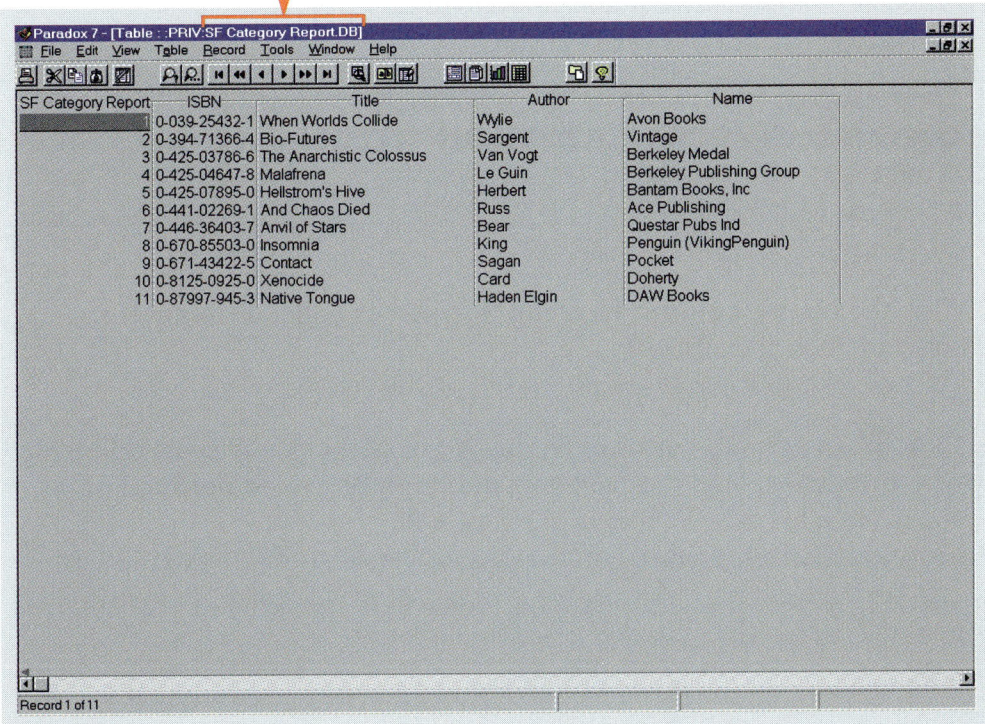

Other uses for queries in reports

You can create a query that limits the data to a range of values, rather than just one specific value. For example, Zora might want to look at the titles of all books in the $15 to $20 price range. She could create a query and specify that condition in the Price field, then base the report on the results of the query.

QUICK **TIP**

When you create a query, you don't need to include the linking field in the Answer table to have the tables linked.■

Creating a report from a query, continued

Zora decides to create a Quick Report for this table, then open the Report Designer to add some custom details.

10 Click **Tools** on the menu bar, then click **Quick Report**

Paradox creates and displays a Quick Report for the table. Zora wants a more descriptive title for the report, so she opens the Report Design window.

11 Click the **Design Report button** 🖼 on the toolbar

The Quick Report design appears in the Report Design window, as shown in Figure 6-25. Zora first deletes the default title (the table name), and then adds a new text box for the title.

12 Click **SF Category Report** (or the portion you can see) in the page header so that the handles appear, then press **[Del]**

The title disappears. Now Zora adds a new title.

13 Click the **Text Tool button** 🅰 on the toolbar, draw a **text box** in the page header, type **SCIENCE FICTION TITLES**, then **center** the text in the box

As before, the new title appears in the Page header band centered in the text box. Zora wants to change the heading "Name" to "Publisher" to be more accurate about the field contents.

14 Click the **Name column heading** three times until only **Name** is selected, then press **[Del]**

The Name column heading disappears. Now Zora adds the Publisher column heading.

15 Click 🅰 and draw a **text box** in the center of the empty column heading, type **Publisher**, then click and drag the **Page Number field** to just above the table data, as shown in Figure 6-26

Zora has finished changing the Quick Report and wants to see how it will look on the printed page. She remembers that she set the page layout to landscape orientation for the previous report. She changes it back to portrait for this one.

16 Click **Report** on the menu bar, click **Page Layout** and **Portrait** in the dialog box, then click **OK**

Zora wants to see how the report will look on the page.

17 Click the **Run Report button** ⚡ on the toolbar, click **View** on the menu bar, click **Zoom**, then click **Fit Width**

Figure 6-26 shows the modified Quick Report with Zora's new title and column heading. She is satisfied with the report, so she saves and prints it.

18 Return to the **Design window**, click **File** on the menu bar, click **Save As**, save the report file as **SF Books**, then print the report

The report design is saved, as shown in Figure 6-27, and printed. As the inventory changes, Zora will run the SF Category query first to extract the data she wants for the report, then run the SF Books report.

19 Close all files and return to the **Project Viewer**

FIGURE 6-25: Quick Report in Design window

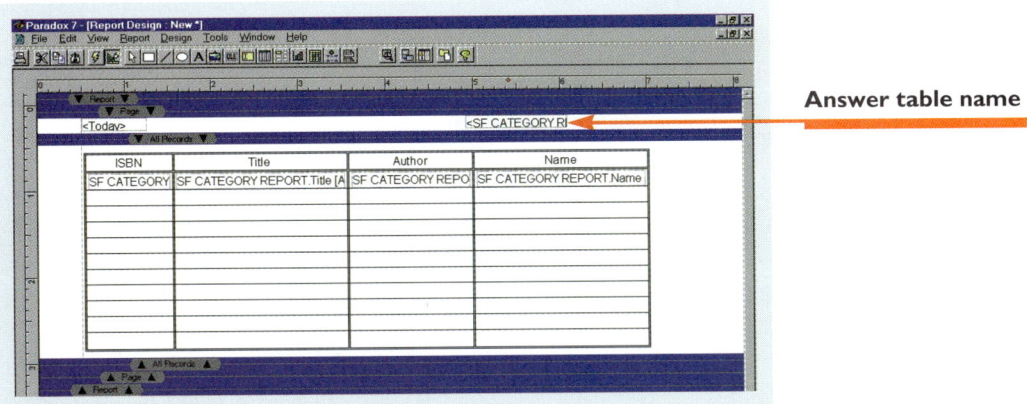

Answer table name

FIGURE 6-26: Modified Quick Report

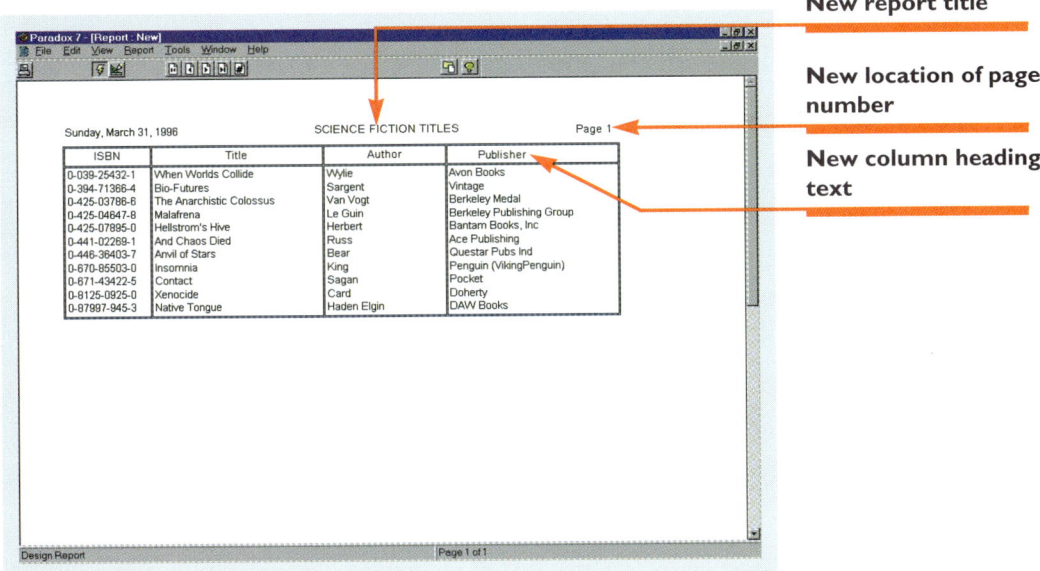

New report title

New location of page number

New column heading text

FIGURE 6-27: Design window for modified report

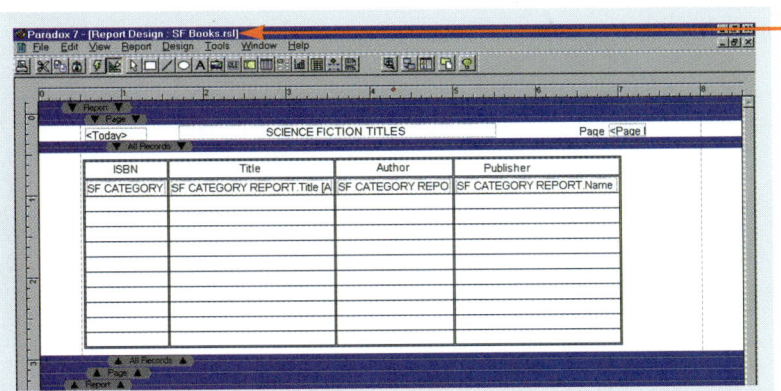

New report name

TASKREFERENCE

TASK	MOUSE/BUTTON	MENU	KEYBOARD
Add text box	Click **A**, then drag the pointer ⁺**A** to the desired shape		
Create a Quick Report (a table is open)	Click 🗐	Click Tools, click Quick Report	[Shift][F7]
Create new report		Right-click Report in the Project Viewer, click New or Click File, click New, then click Report	
Opening a report	Right-click the report name in the Project Viewer, then click Run Report in the context-sensitive menu or Click 🗐 or Right-click Reports in the Project Viewer, then click Open	Click File, click Open, then click Report	
Print report	Click 🖨	Click File, click Print	
Save report	Click Close button, click Yes to save	Click File, click Save As	
Use Report Designer	Click 📈	Click Report, click Design Report	[F8]
View data in a report (from design view)	Click ⚡	Click Report, click Run Report	[F8]

CONCEPTSREVIEW

Label each element of the Paradox Report Design window, as shown in Figure 6-28.

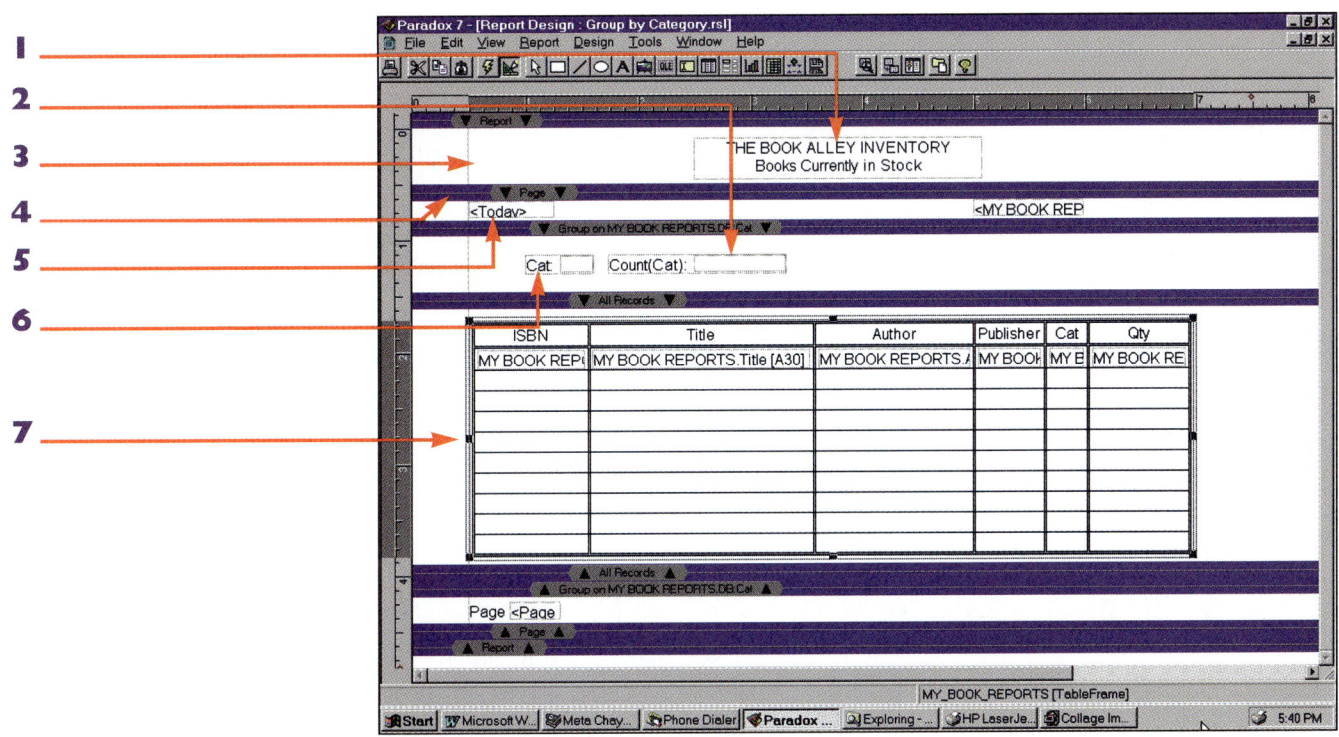

FIGURE 6-28

Match each statement with the term it describes.

8 Provides tools for creating custom reports

9 Creates a standard report

10 Contains table data

11 Changes the report magnification

12 Added to arrange records in logical sets

13 Contains information to be printed at the end of the report

14 Used to add text to a report design

a. Records band

b. Report footer

c. Report Designer

d. Text Tool

e. Quick Report

f. Group band

g. Zoom

Select the best answer from the list of choices.

15 The data model tells the Report Designer

a. Which field to include in a report

b. How the records are to be arranged

c. Which table or tables to use in the report

d. The font size and style to use for the report title

16 Information you want printed at the top of each page is placed in the

a. Records band

b. Report header band

c. Group footer band

d. Page header band

SKILLSREVIEW

1 Create a Quick Report.

  a. Copy PD6-2.DB to Custom Reports.DB.

  b. Open the Custom Reports.DB table.

  c. Change the printer setup to print in landscape orientation.

  d. Run the Quick Report.

  e. Change the screen magnification to see a whole page on the screen.

  f. Print the Quick Report in landscape orientation.

  g. Return the printer setup to portrait orientation.

  h. Close the report without saving it.

  i. Close the table.

2 Use the Report Designer.

  a. Start a new report from the Project Viewer using the Data Model/Design Layout report.

  b. Select Custom Reports.DB from the File name list.

  c. Choose the Tabular style.

  d. Remove the ISBN and Cat fields from the report design.

  e. Save the report as No ISBN or CAT.

3 Add and customize a report header.

  a. Remove the Custom Reports title from the page header.

  b. Increase the size of the report header.

  c. Click the Text tool button and draw a box in the report header.

  d. Type "THE BOOK ALLEY" on the first line and "Current Book Inventory without ISBN or CAT" on the second.

  e. Center the text in the box.

  f. Save the report as Custom Title.

  g. View the report with data.

  h. Print the custom report.

4 Group records in your report.

  a. Return to the Design window and add a Group band.

  b. Choose Publisher as the field to group by.

  c. Define a field and add a summary field in the group header to count the titles in each group.

  d. View the report design zoomed to fit the page width.

5 Save and print a report.

  a. Save your report as Group by Publisher.RSL.

  b. Run the report.

  c. Print the report.

  d. Close the report.

6 Create a report from a query.

  a. Create a new query to link the Custom Reports table with Publishlist by the publisher code fields.

  b. Set a selection condition to extract health and nutrition titles.

  c. Check the ISBN, Title, Author, Cat, Price, and Name (publisher) fields.

  d. Rename the Answer table HN Query.DB.

  e. Save the query as HN Query.QBE.

  f. Run the query.

  g. Create a Quick Report.

  h. Open the Report Designer and change the report title to "Health and Nutrition Titles."

  i. Center the title in the text box.

  j. Save the report as HN Query.RSL.

  k. View the data in the report design.

  l. Return to the Design window and change the page layout to landscape.

  m. View the data in the report design.

  n. Print the report.

  o. Close all files, saving any changes.

  p. Exit Paradox 7.

INDEPENDENT CHALLENGE 1

You are the manager of a growing hardware store. The regular customers filled out information forms when they signed up to receive your catalogs. The information includes each person's name, current address, phone number, and sign-up date. You want to enter this data into a Paradox table and print a report that lists all the people in your database, ordered by their sign-up date. You also want the report to group the records by month of sign-up. Your Student Disk includes a table named PD6-3.DB, which contains the records of your regular customers.

To complete this independent challenge:

1 Copy the PD6-3.DB file to your working directory as Customers by Signup.DB.

2 Create a Quick Report of the data.

3 Add a Group band that groups the records by the range of sign-up date. (*Hint*: Click Range Group in the Define Group dialog box, then click Month.)

4 Eliminate the extra space in the group header and footer bands.

5 Change the title to "CUSTOMER LIST BY SIGN-UP DATE" and center the title.

6 Change the page layout to print in landscape orientation. Save the report as Customers by Signup.RSL and print it.

INDEPENDENT
CHALLENGE 2

Your manufacturing company has a database with tables that contain a variety of information. One table contains the company sales representatives and sales activity information. Another table contains details of strategic planning and sales projections. A third table contains a list of current products and their component parts. You can link two or more tables to access information from more than one table.

To complete this independent challenge:

1 Create the table structures and save them as Products.DB, Sales.DB, and Market.DB.

2 Enter at least 10 records into each table using data you invent.

3 Design a report suitable for specific recipients. Create one report for each of the following groups: a client, a potential employee, upper management, a material supplier, and the personnel office.

4 Print and save each report.

INDEPENDENT
CHALLENGE 3

You are preparing a report of available cars based on information downloaded from a Web page. You want to include only the pertinent information for potential customers. You identify make, year, model, color, and price as key variables in customer decisions. You also want to group the data by price information.

To complete this independent challenge:

1 Make a copy of PD6-4, saving it as My Auto Report.DB.

2 Create a new report by right-clicking Reports from the Project Viewer. Choose the Data Model/Design Layout option.

3 Choose a tabular layout and remove appropriate fields so that only make, year, model, color, and price are displayed in the report.

4 Add a Group band that groups on year.

5 Name the report Auto Report, orient the page in portrait mode.

6 Add a title, "Automobiles Currently Available," in Arial Black, bold, 12 points (resize the text box to fit).

7 Display data in the report, print it, save all changes, then close the report and table.

INDEPENDENT
CHALLENGE 4

As the supervisor of the Sports Unlimited sales force, you need to be provide reports to the sales representatives by state. For example, you need a report that lists customer information for customers who reside in the state of California. You have the necessary data in the PD6-5 and PD6-6 tables, so you create a query that links the tables, extracts the data, and then creates a report from the Answer table.

To complete this independent challenge:

1 Make copies of the PD6-5.DB and PD6-6.DB tables, name them My Sports Customers and My Sales Force respectively and save them to the appropriate directory.

2 Create a query that links the two tables by Sales Rep Code, extracts the names of customers who reside in California, and displays the company, phone number, first contact date, and Sales Rep name. Name the query and Answer table California Customers.DB.

3 Create a Quick Report, then customize the header in a way you choose.

4 Add a Group band and group on Sales Rep name.

5 Save the report as California Customers.

6 Display the report with data and print it.

7 Close the query and the report, saving any changes.

VISUALWORKSHOP

You have seen many local bookstores go out of business but you and your former professor of marketing have decided there is a niche for a bargain bookstore in your home town. You have a table that lists a shipment of books that you have received as reviewer copies for a nominal fee. You need to produce a report that lists the books by category and counts books within the category. Using Figure 6-29 as your guide, create a report. Use the tables Bargain Books.DB and Category.DB using Category as the common field for linking. Save all objects (query, Answer table, reports) as Bargain Books. (*Hint:* Use the line tool on the Design window toolbar to draw the line under the title.)

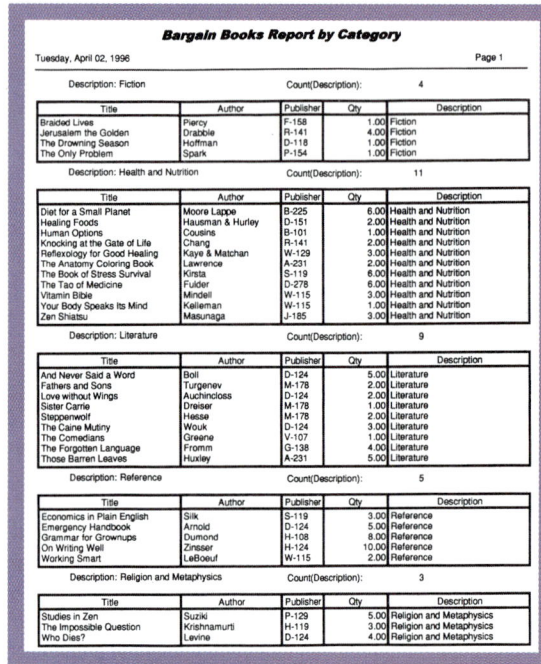
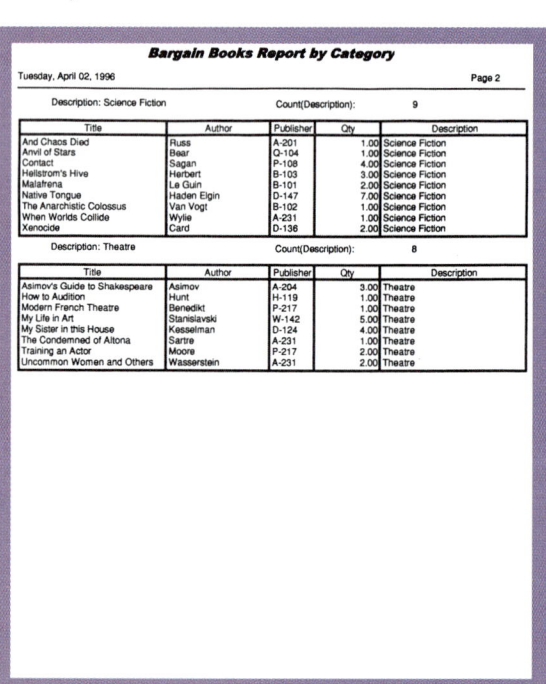

FIGURE 6-29

OBJECTIVES

▶ View Paradox experts

▶ Create a table with Table Expert

▶ Modify a table generated with Table Expert

▶ Use Mailing Label Expert

▶ Create a report using Report Expert

▶ Modify a report generated with Report Expert

Using EXPERTS

Paradox experts provide a step-by-step approach to commonly performed tasks. Each step is a screen with options to choose regarding the task. Often there is a sample displaying the results of the various options. The steps are easy to follow and help guide your thinking about the Paradox task. Paradox experts can save you valuable learning time and ensure that you have performed a task correctly. You can always modify the results of an expert, as you can with any Paradox object. **case** Zora has been asked to be the contact with the publishing houses that supply books to The Book Alley. She needs to communicate with them and report on their activities. Since she must perform some tasks that are new to her, she decides to use Paradox experts. ▶

Viewing Paradox experts

Paradox offers nine experts to guide you through different tasks. In addition there are two experts available as preferences: Text object and Startup Expert. For more information on these experts, see the related topic "Experts Page Preferences." To use an expert you can either click the Experts button or choose Tools from the main menu and then click Experts. **case** Since Zora is not familiar with the range of Paradox experts, she begins by viewing the choices.

STEPS

1   Click the **Experts button** 🔆 on the toolbar
The Paradox Experts dialog box opens on the toolbar as shown in Figure 7-1.

2   Click each of the **nine experts** and read the description at the bottom of the Paradox Experts dialog box
The nine experts are also described in Table 7-1.

3   Click **Cancel**
The Paradox Experts dialog box closes. Zora is interested in other ways to see the experts.

4   Click **Tools** on the menu bar, then click **Experts**
The same dialog box opens. Zora now is introduced to the experts and knows two different ways to see them.

5   Click **Cancel**
Now that Zora understands the options, she decides to use the Table Expert to create the table with publisher information.

Table 7-1: Paradox experts

THIS EXPERT	HELPS YOU
Chart Expert	Create a chart of your data
Database Expert	Select a ready-made database and customize it to meet your needs
Form Expert	Create a form that displays data from one or two tables in a variety of predefined layouts and styles
Launcher Expert	Create a small tabbed form you can use to open or launch selected forms, reports, queries, scripts, and executable files with the click of a button
Mailing Label Expert	Create mailing labels in a variety of standard mailing label formats
Merge Expert	Merge data from a table into a form letter using a variety of word processors
Report Expert	Display and print data from one or two tables in a variety of predefined layouts and styles
Table Expert	Create a new table from a list of table templates
Text Import Expert	Import fixed length or delimited text into Paradox tables

FIGURE 7-1: Paradox Experts dialog box

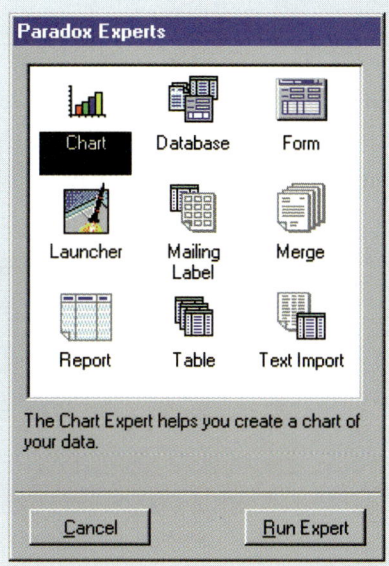

FIGURE 7-2: Experts tab of Preferences dialog box

Make sure these aren't checked when you leave this dialog box

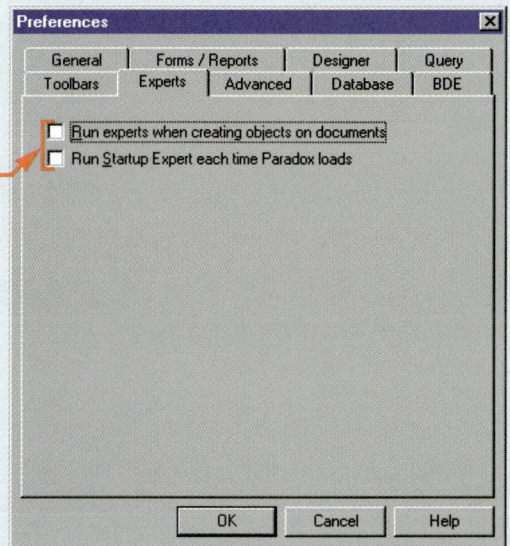

Experts Page Preferences

Two additional experts can be selected from the Preferences dialog box, as shown in Figure 7-2. To open this dialog box, choose Edit from the menu bar, click Preferences, then click the Experts tab. In this dialog box you can select the first option, which will invoke an expert each time you use a tool to create a chart, button, field, or text object in the Form Design and Report Design windows. If the second option is checked, the Startup Expert appears each time you start Paradox. From the Startup Expert you can choose to either use the Database Expert to choose a predefined database structure for your data, use Table Expert to name and create your own database, name an existing database, or open an existing database. Make certain that both options are NOT checked when you leave the dialog box.

Creating a table with Table Expert

Using the Table Expert can be a handy way to create a table if there is a table template that approximates the table you want to make. Paradox offers 21 different table templates to choose from, covering a variety of industries and business, for example, customer, Automatic Teller Machines, and material tables. ▶**case** Zora must send notices to each of the publishing houses that supply books to The Book Alley to inform them of an upcoming change of address and phone number for The Book Alley. She knows she needs to send mailings throughout the year so she decides to create a table for the data.

1 Click the **Experts button** 🐵, click **Table**, then click **Run Expert**
The Paradox Table Expert - Step 1 of 4 dialog box opens. Here you choose the table template that most resembles the table you want to create, then you choose the specific fields of the table to include. After clicking through the various table templates, Zora decides that the Vendors table most resembles what she needs.

2 Scroll down and click **Vendors**, then click 〉〉 to include all the fields
Compare your screen to Figure 7-3. Notice that [Full Address] expands to include the details in the Fields in my table list. In the next step Zora chooses to let Paradox assign a key.

3 Click **Next**, click the top radio button (if necessary), then click **Next**
It is easiest to let Paradox assign a key. Now you are in the Step 3 of 4 dialog box. Zora knows that she needs to sort on Publisher Code and Name, so she chooses the closest Vendor field names.

4 Click **Vendor ID** and **Vendor Name**
Compare your screen to Figure 7-4.

5 Click **Next**
The Paradox Table Expert - Step 4 of 4 dialog box appears. Since Zora knows that she wants to make some changes to the structure, she chooses to modify the structure.

6 Type **Publisher Data** in the file name box, click the **Edit the table's structure radio button**, then click **Do It!**
Make sure you save the table in the correct directory. Use the Browse button to change directories. Compare your screen to Figure 7-5.

FIGURE 7-3: The Paradox Table Expert - Step 1 of 4 dialog box

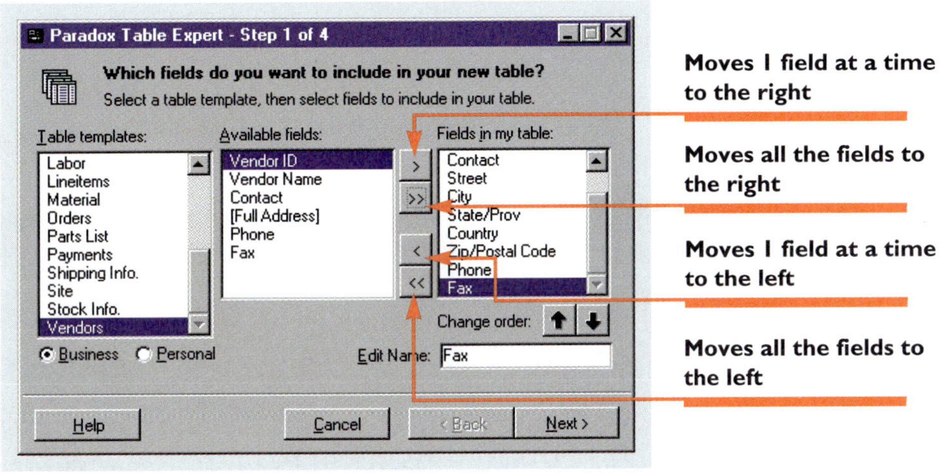

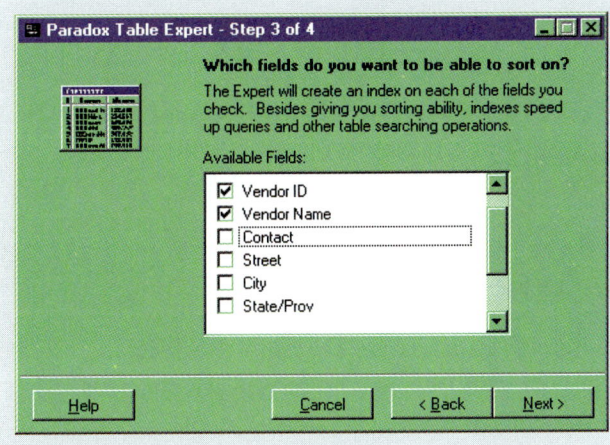

Moves 1 field at a time to the right

Moves all the fields to the right

Moves 1 field at a time to the left

Moves all the fields to the left

FIGURE 7-4: The Paradox Table Expert - Step 3 of 4 dialog box

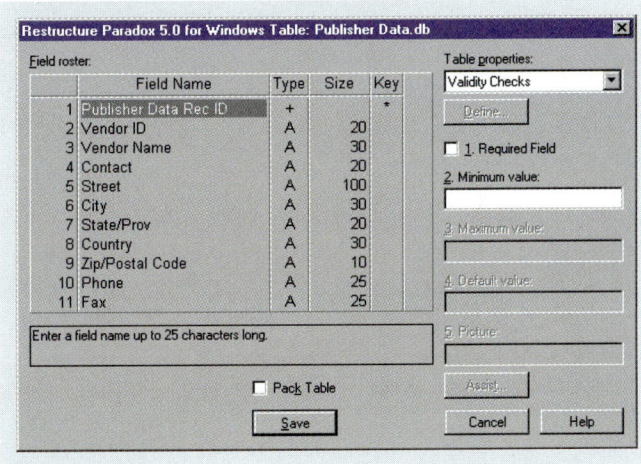

FIGURE 7-5: Restructure dialog box

TROUBLE?

If you accidentally remove some of the fields in the Step 1 of 4 dialog box, you can use the other arrow keys to move fields between lists. ■

Modifying a table generated with Table Expert

As good as the templates are that Paradox supplies, rarely is one an absolutely perfect fit. Luckily, it's easy to modify the table structure to meet your needs. It's easier to modify a structure than begin a table from scratch. **case** Zora knows that Publisher Code is a common field with the other book tables, so she renames Vendor ID.

1 Click **Vendor ID** to select it and type **Publisher Code**
Changing a field name is as simple as retyping it.

2 Rename **Vendor Name** to **Publisher Name** in the same way
The names are more appropriate now for the Publisher table, as shown in Figure 7-6. Zora notices that some fields are unnecessarily large.

3 Change the size of **Publisher Code** to **6**, then change the size of **Street** to **30**
The sizes of Publisher Code and Street change. Zora decides that Publisher Code is the key.

4 Move to **Publisher Data Rec ID**, press **[Ctrl][Del]**, then press **[Spacebar]** in the key area of Publisher Code
Compare your screen to Figure 7-7.

5 Click **Save**, answer **Yes** to all restructure warnings
You are ready to enter data.

6 Double-click **Publisher Data** in the Project Viewer, click the **Edit Data button** 📝, then enter the following records using **[Tab]** to move between fields:

Code	Name	Contact	Street	City	State	Country	Zip	Phone	Fax
A-201	Ace Publishing	George Alertson	100 Main Street	Tacoma	WA	USA	98402	206-535-2974	206-535-2976
A-204	Avenel	Mary Ramsey	2332 6th Street	NY	NY	USA	10007	212-555-2379	800-555-2378
A-231	Avon Books	Penelope Prittchet	1005 5th Avenue	NY	NY	USA	10023	800-238-0659	800-238-0658
B-101	Berkeley Pub Grp	Edgar Williams	235 Broadway	NY	NY	USA	10001	212-631-8572	212-631-8571

Compare your screen to Figure 7-8.

7 Close the table
Zora is ready to prepare a mailing list for this table.

FIGURE 7-6: Changes to field names

New names

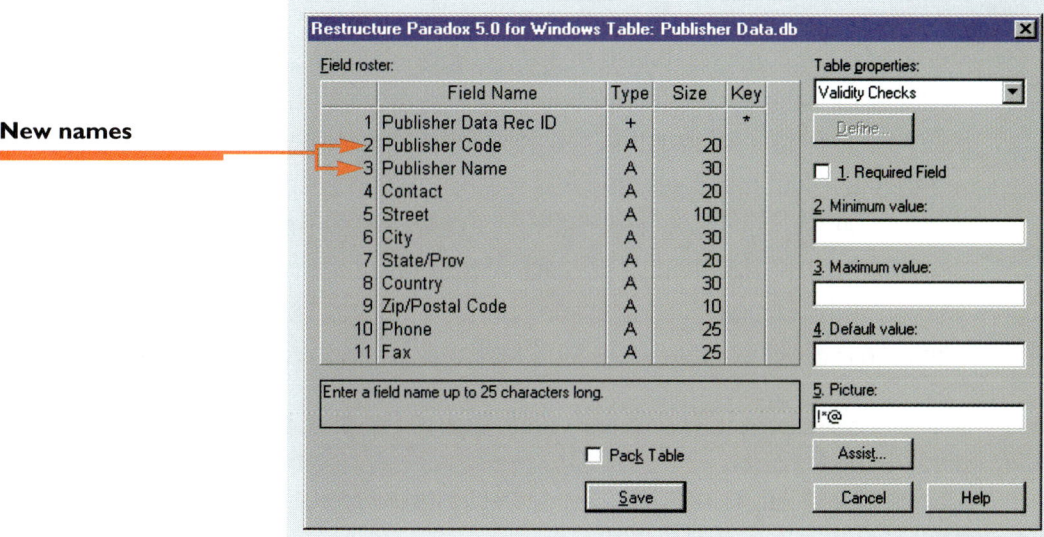

FIGURE 7-7: Changes to structure

Changes to structure

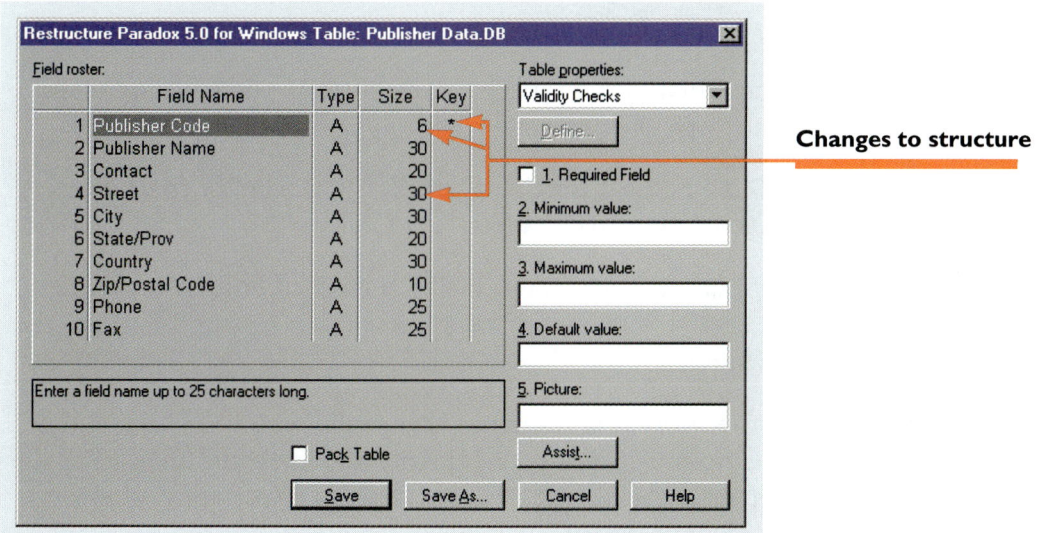

FIGURE 7-8: Records added to new structure

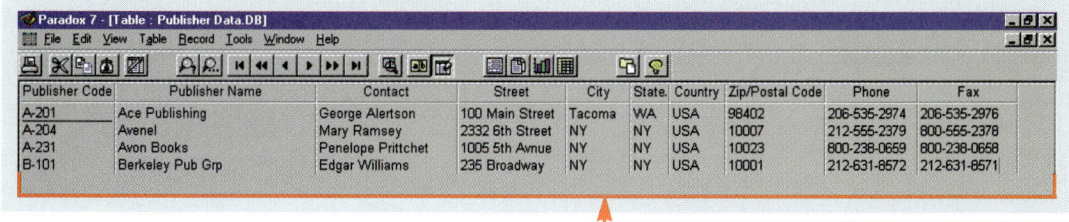

Columns are narrowed here to display all fields. Your screen only shows part of a record at a time.

Use Mailing Label Expert

Sending correspondence to lists of a wide range of people, customers, clients, and vendors, for example, is a common task and using mailing labels makes it more efficient. For more information, see the related topic "Keeping your mailing list up-to-date." Mailing labels are just a special kind of report. Paradox Mailing Label Expert makes this job easy, especially if you are using a standard label form.

case Zora must send notices to each of the publishing houses to inform them of an upcoming change of address and phone number at The Book Alley. She uses a standard Avery label and so uses Mailing Label Expert to create the labels.

1 Click **Tools** on the menu bar, click **Experts**, click **Mailing Label**, then click **Run Expert**
The Paradox Mailing Label Expert - Step 1 of 6 dialog box appears. Because Zora is using Avery label 5160, she accepts the default.

2 Click **5160-Address**, if necessary, then click **Next**
The Step 2 of 6 dialog box appears. Zora uses the publisher information she just created but has been added to by her assistant.

3 Select **Publisher Information.DB** from the list
Compare your screen to Figure 7-9.

4 Click **Next**, click **Arial** in the font list, click **Bold** in the style area, click **12** in the size list, then click **Next**

5 Click the **Left Side radio button**, if necessary, then click the **Left-to-right radio button**, then click **Next**

6 Click **Publisher Name**, click **Place Field**, then click **line two** of the sample label
The publisher name appears on the first line.

7 Add the rest of the address in the same way; make sure to put a comma and space after City, and spaces between City and State and Zip
Compare your screen to Figure 7-10.

8 Click **Next**, type **Publisher Mailing** in the Report name box, click the **View the labels onscreen radio button**, then click **Do It!**
It takes a few moments to create the labels, which is a special kind of report. You see the report design onscreen first, then the data in the labels. The labels appear, as shown in Figure 7-11.

9 Click **OK**, print the labels, then close the report

FIGURE 7-9: Paradox Mailing Label Expert - Step 2 of 6 dialog box

Your list may be different

Use this button to search directories if necessary

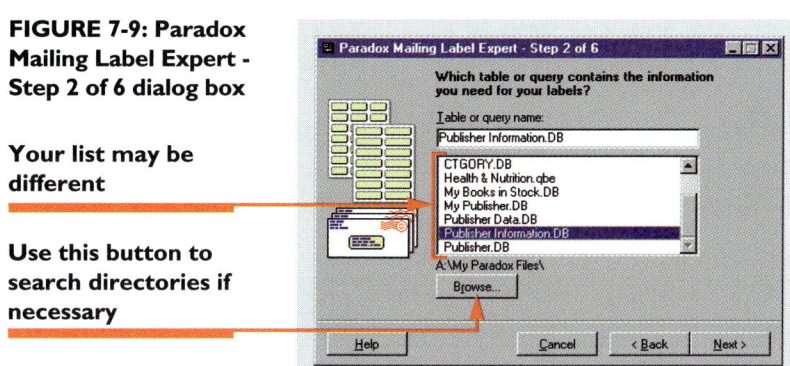

FIGURE 7-10: Paradox Mailing Label Expert - Step 5 of 6 dialog box

Remember to put in comma and space

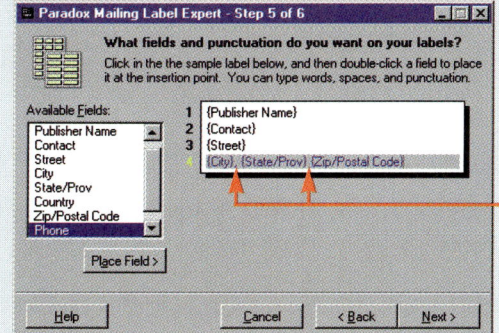

FIGURE 7-11: Mailing Label Report

To switch to Design view

Name of report

Print button

Buttons to move around report

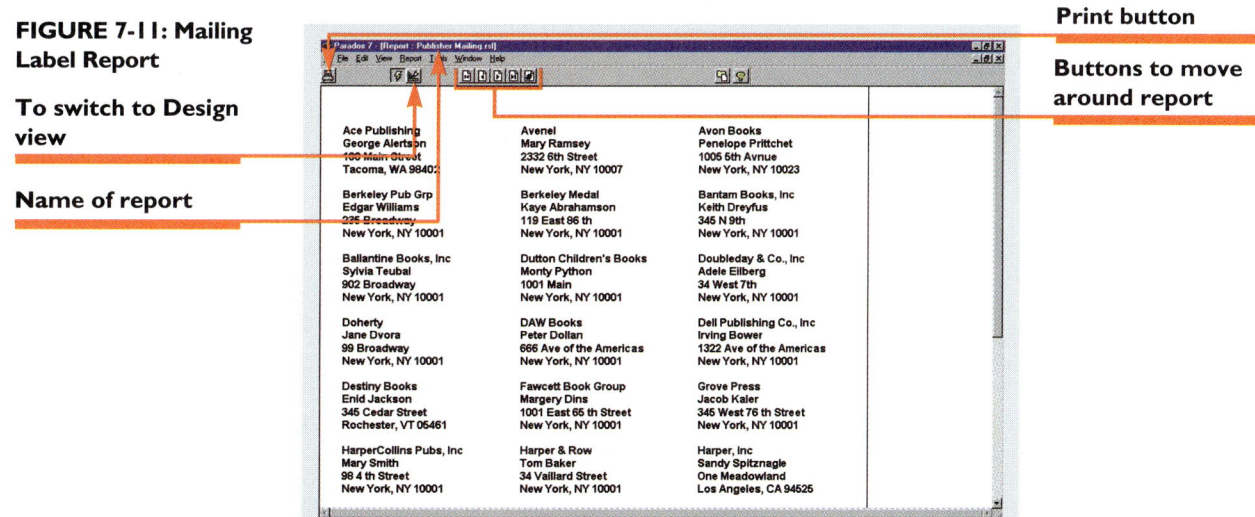

Keeping your mailing list up-to-date

Mailing labels are efficient ways to send correspondence to large numbers of people. But a major task that is often overlooked is maintaining the table that is used to generate the labels. Addresses change, names change, and people ask to be removed from the list with some frequency. Make sure if you are using a list that it is current and that you request any change of addresses the post office receives as a result of forwarding. That way you can keep the table up-to-date.

Creating a report using Report Expert

Reports are one of the most useful features of a database program. Even with the predictions of a paperless society, paper, or hard-copy, is still widely used and circulated in today's business world. By guiding you through the process, Paradox's Report Expert helps you to quickly create reports. **case** Zora needs a report to use when she calls the contacts at the publishing houses. She uses Report Expert to create a report of publisher information.

1 Click the **Experts button** 🔍, click **Report**, then click **Run Expert**
The Paradox Report Expert - Step 1 of 8 dialog box appears. This step defaults to using one table for the report. Zora accepts the default.

2 Click **Next**, click the **One record per page radio button**, then click **Next**
Even though you select one record per page, Paradox will display as many records as will fit on a page, but make it easy to insert page breaks between records. The Paradox Report Expert Step 3 of 8 dialog box appears.

3 Select **Publisher Information.DB**, use the **Browse button** if necessary to locate the table
Compare your screen to Figure 7-12.

4 Click **Next**, then in Step 4 of 8 select **Publisher Name**, then click ▶ to move it to the **Display these fields box**

5 In the same way, move the available fields **Contact**, **City**, **State/Prov**, **Phone**, **Fax** to the **Display these fields box**
Compare your screen to Figure 7-13.

6 Click **Next**, in Step 5 of 8 click **Printer** in the Target output area, if necessary, click the **portrait radio button**, then click **Next**

7 In Step 6 of 8 click **Framed objects** in the style sheet area, then click **Next**
In Step 7 of 8 you can add a special title and the time and date to the footer or header. This is handy especially if you think you might create more than one version of the report and you want to be able to tell which report is the most current. Zora wants a title and time/date stamp.

8 In Step 7 of 8 click **Title text check box**, press **[Tab]**, type **Publisher Contact Information** in the title box, click **Display date**, click **Display time**, click **Center** in the footer
Compare your screen to Figure 7-14.

9 Click **Next**, type **Publisher Contact Information**, click **Run the report** if necessary, then click **Do It!**

10 Click **OK**, click **View** on the menu bar, click **Zoom**, then click **Fit Width**
The report appears, as shown in Figure 7-15. Zora reviews the report and decides she needs to make some changes to it.

FIGURE 7-12: Paradox
Report Expert – Step 3
of 8 dialog box

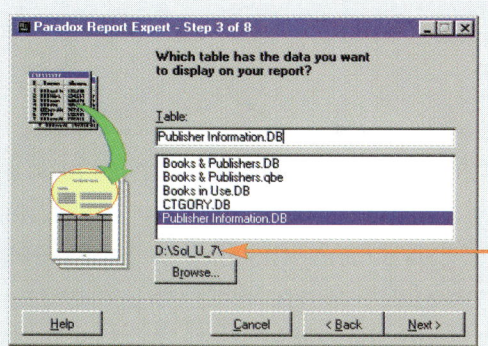

Your directory may be different

FIGURE 7-13: Paradox
Report Expert – Step 4
of 8 dialog box

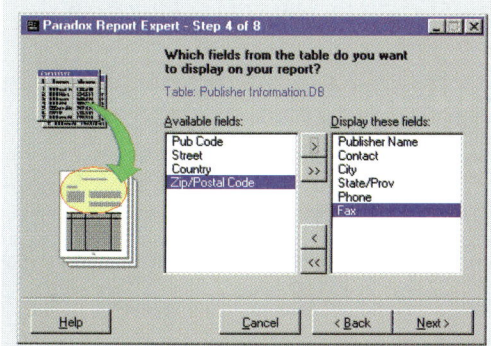

FIGURE 7-14: Paradox
Report Expert – Step 7
of 8 dialog box

Notice sample

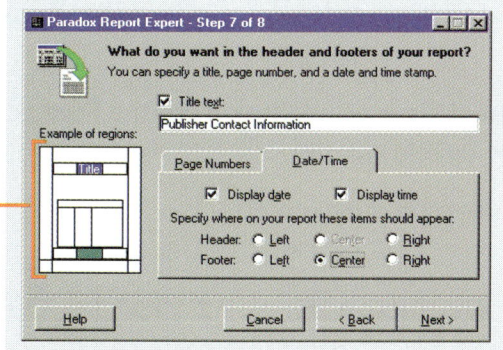

FIGURE 7-15:
Publisher Contact
Information report

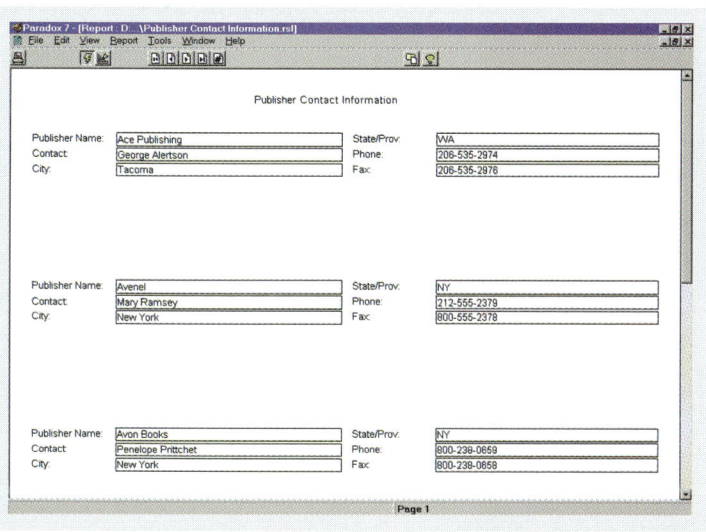

QUICK **TIP**

You might want to print a specific page or pages of a multi-page report. Remember you can print specific pages in the Print File dialog box by clicking Print range and then typing in the number of pages to print in the From and To boxes.

TROUBLE?

If you make an error in a step of an Expert, you can always go back as far as you want by clicking Back.

Modifying a report generated with Report Expert

Often you will want to start with Report Expert to create a basic report and then modify it to match the specific needs of your business situation. The reports you create with Report Expert can be modified by using the Design Report view. It is important to become facile with modifying reports because business needs change and reports must change too. ▶case Zora wants each record on a page by itself so she can take notes as she calls the contacts. Because she chose the one record per page layout, it's easy to insert a page break after each record.

STEPS

1 Click the **Design Report button** 🖼
Zora wants to add a place to write notes as she contacts the publishing houses.

2 Click the **Text Tool button** 🅰, draw a text box under **City**, then type **Notes:**
Compare your screen to Figure 7-16. You can put any text you'd like in a text box on a report. Next, Zora wants to insert a page break so that each record is on a page by itself.

3 Click the **Insert Page Break button** 🖼, then click **under the text box**
The page break appears as a solid line, as shown in Figure 7-17. The line can be moved by dragging it, or deleted by selecting it and pressing [Del]. Next Zora wants to remove the time/date stamp.

4 Select the **Timestamp container** from the Page band, then press **[Del]**
The date and time is no longer inserted at the bottom of each page of the report.

5 Click the **Run Report button** ⚡
The report appears with data. Zora looks through the report.

6 Click **Go to Page button** 🔲, type **2**, then click **OK**
Compare your screen to Figure 7-18.

7 Print pages **1** and **2** of the report, then close it, saving the changes

FIGURE 7-16: Text box added

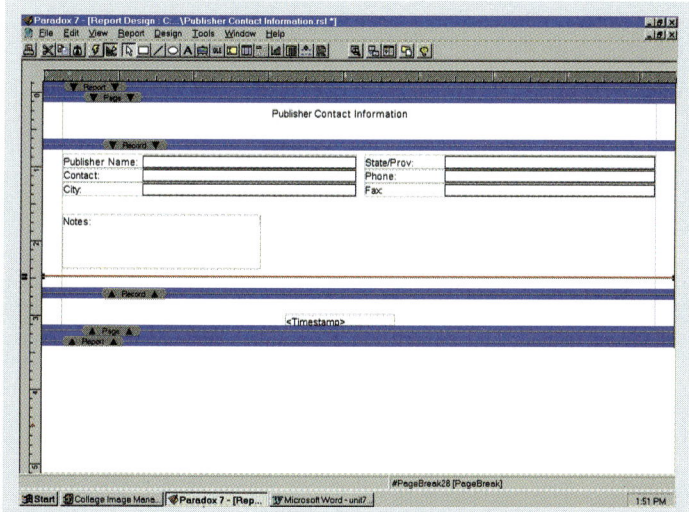

FIGURE 7-17: Page break added

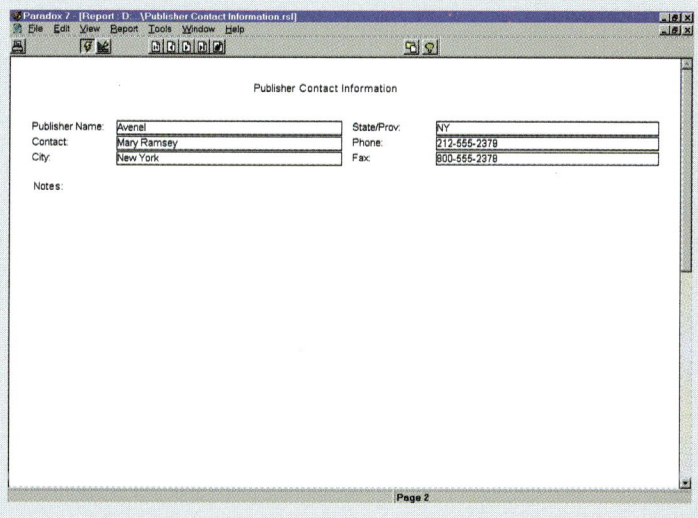

FIGURE 7-18: Modified report

QUICK **TIP**

If you are viewing a report with data, you can quickly go to Design view by pressing [F8].■

TASKREFERENCE

TASK	MOUSE/BUTTON	MENU	KEYBOARD
Insert a page break in Design view	Click then click where you want to place the break		
Modify the design of a report	Click	Click Report, click Design Report	[F8]
Modify the design of a report from the Report Expert	On the last Report Expert step choose the last radio button, open the report in a design window so you can modify it		
Restructure a table from the Table Expert	On the last Table Expert step choose the last option button, edit the table's structure		
Start an expert	Click , then double-click the expert of your choice	Click Tools, click Experts, double-click the expert of your choice	

CONCEPTSREVIEW

Label each element of the Paradox Report Expert – Step 4 of 8 dialog box, as shown in Figure 7-19.

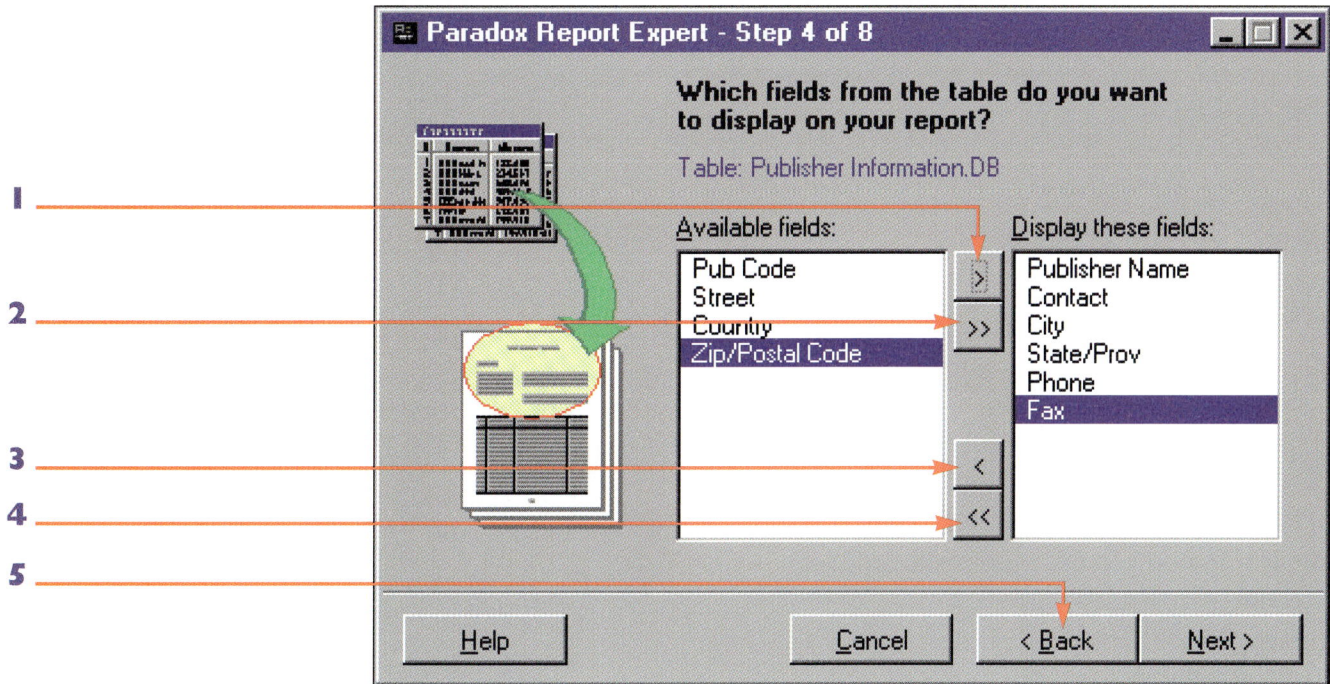

Figure 7-19

Match each statement with the term it describes.

6 Provides step-by-step process for creating mailing labels

7 A pre-designed table

8 Used to turn on Startup Expert

9 The button used to return to a previous step in Expert dialog boxes

10 The button used to add a new field tool to a report in the Design view

11 The button used to change directories in Expert dialog boxes

a. Preferences dialog box

b. Browse

c. Mailing Label Expert

d. Table template

e. Field Tool

f. Back

Select the best answer from the list of choices.

12 Which of the following is not a Paradox expert?

a. Text Import

b. Report

c. Startup

d. Setup

13 To run experts when creating objects on documents you

a. Choose Document Objects from the Experts dialog box.

b. Choose Creating Objects from the Experts dialog box.

SKILLSREVIEW

1 View Paradox experts.

a. Click Tools on the menu bar, then click Experts.

b. Review each of the experts, reading the description.

c. Click Cancel.

d. Click Edit on the menu bar, then click Preferences.

e. Click the Expert tab to make it foremost.

f. Review the options, make sure both are cleared when you leave the dialog box.

g. Click OK.

2 Create a table with Table Expert.

a. Click the Experts button on the toolbar.

b. Double-click the Table Expert.

c. Select the Table template Labor.

d. Move all fields to your table, then remove Project Title, Estimated Hours, and Employee Number.

e. Move Social Security Number to the top of the list and move Last Name to the second in the list.

f. Define the key as the Social Security Number.

g. Create indexes on Social Security Number and Last Name.

h. Name the table "Labor for Book Alley."

3 Modify a table generated with Table Expert.

a. Click the Restructure button on the toolbar.

b. Rename Social Security Number to SSN, rename Middle Name to M_Name.

c. Make the field size of M_Name, 10, and First Name, 25.

d. Save the structure, answering Yes to all validity and data loss questions.

e. Enter four records.

f. Print the table in landscape orientation and close it.

4 Use Mailing Label Expert.

a. Click Tools on the menu bar, click Experts, double-click Mailing Label.

b. Choose the label type as 5260-Address.

c. The table that contains the information is Customer List.

d. Choose font Times New Roman, style bold, and size 11.

e. Accept the default for how the label sheet is fed into the printer.

f. Put Company on the first line, Street on the second, City, State and Zip on the third line.

g. Name the report "Customer Mailing List."

h. View the labels on the screen.

i. Print and close the report.

5 Create a report using Report Expert.

a. Click Tools on the menu bar, click Experts, double-click Report.

b. Display only one record per page.

c. Choose to use only one table, Customer List.

d. Display all the fields.

e. Accept the default printer and screen settings in Step 5 of 8.

f. Choose the bold text style sheet.

g. Title the report "Customer List," click the Page number tab and select the Page N of M radio button.

h. Name the report "Customer List" and view the report on the screen.

i. View the report in Best Fit mode, and print the last page.

6 Modify a report generated with Report Expert.

a. Press [F8] to view the report in Design view.

b. Add a Group Band to group on State.

c. Remove extra space in all bands.

d. Remove the State field because the records will be grouped by state and that data is redundant.

e. Move the record band fields to eliminate extra space.

f. Run the report.

g. Print the second page.

h. Close the report saving all changes.

INDEPENDENT CHALLENGE 1

As the manager of a growing software consulting company, Hi Tech Soft Touch, you need to stay in touch with clients. You notice that the table template Shipping Info has most of the information you need to build a table of your clients.

To complete this independent challenge:

1 Use Table Expert to create a table using the Shipping Info template using all the fields except Department field.

2 Let Paradox Expert create a key, and identify Last Name and Zip as fields to sort on.

3 Name the table "Hi Tech Soft Touch Clients."

4 Edit the table structure to rename State/Pro to simply State, size of Street 30, and State 2. Save the structure and add at least four records.

5 Use Mailing Label to create labels to send to clients. Use 14 pt, Arial Narrow, Bold formatting.

6 Name the report "HTST List," print the labels, then save and close the report.

INDEPENDENT
CHALLENGE 2

You have data in a table concerning food for your catering business, but you need to be able to present it in a report format and distribute it to potential clients. You want a report quickly and so you begin with Report Expert and then modify the report to match your needs.

To complete this independent challenge:

1 Create a report using Report Expert and one table and display multiple records at a time.

2 Use the table from your Student Disk, Food Listing.

3 Display all the fields, choose the Shaded objects style sheet, then assign an appropriate title.

4 Run the report then go to Design view to modify it.

5 Add the date to the bottom center of the page, then shorten the fields so that the report fits on one page.

6 Change the format of the numbers to remove inappropriate decimals, then center align the columns Servings and Vegetarian.

7 Print and close the report saving changes.

INDEPENDENT
CHALLENGE 3

As marketing manager for a local used car dealership, Autos are Us, you have a table of people who have called or stopped by the office and expressed interest in vehicles listed by Autos are Us. You also have a table of currently available vehicles. You must send a report to the people who have expressed interest. You decide to use experts for both the vehicle and mailing reports.

To complete this independent challenge:

1 Create a report using Report Expert and the Vehicle table from your Student Disk. Name the report "Vehicles Listed."

2 Display one record per page, put the date in the center of the footer, and create a title.

3 Make the report visually interesting to the potential client by modifying the design using shading, frames, etc. Print the final report and save it.

4 Create a mailing report using the Leads table, name it Leads Mailing List, then save, print and close it.

INDEPENDENT
CHALLENGE 4

You've been asked to keep track of membership payments received for your local Windows user group. Your user group, Windows Power Users, is very active and adds new members often. You will use a laptop to record payment received, usually $25, and print a receipt for the new member.

To complete this independent challenge:

1 Create a table using Table Expert and the Payments template and name it "Windows Power Users Payments."

2 Use all the available fields and define Check/PO number as the key, then restructure the table to change Check/PO number to Check number.

3 Add a field for the Member Number (this will be the common field with the Member Table), then add six records.

4 Create a report for a receipt using Report Expert. (*Hint:* Use the layout for one record per page and then insert a page break after the record band.)

5 Put a welcome message in the footer of each receipt. Save the report as "Receipt for New Members," then print and close the report.

VISUALWORKSHOP

You have been assigned the job of hosting a reception for the publishing contacts for The Book Alley. One of your tasks is to create name tags for each of the contacts. Using Figure 7-20 as your guide, create name tags using the Mailing Label Expert. Use the Publisher Information table and save the report as "Name Tags for Publishing Contacts." (*Hint:* The Label category, "Avery Specialty Labels" contains label templates for name tags.)

FIGURE 7-20

Glossary

Answer table   A temporary table that contains the results of a query.

Bands   Horizontal sections of a report design that specify the placement of design elements in the printed report.

Best fit   A zoom (viewing) scale that adjusts the data so it will all fit on the screen at once.

Chart Expert   An expert that guides you through creating a chart of your data.

Check box   In a query, the small box under a field name in the table skeleton that indicates whether the field is to be included in the results of the query.

Check mark   In a query design, a symbol used to indicate that a field is to be included in the results.

Child table   The secondary or detail table that is linked to a parent or master table.

Comparison operator   A symbol used in queries to compare two values ($<,>,<=,>=,=,<>$).

Composite key   A key composed of two or more fields.

Composite secondary index   An index containing two or more fields.

Container object   An object that surrounds and controls the behavior of the objects inside it, usually the label and edit regions.

Database   An organized set of related information arranged in one or more tables.

Database Expert   An expert that allows you to select a ready-made database and helps you customize it to meet your needs.

Data model   The table or tables used in a report design and the relationships between them.

Design objects   Elements of a design, including data entry and other fields, text, graphic images, lines, and boxes.

Desktop   The main Paradox workspace between the toolbar at the top of the screen and the status bar at the bottom.

Dynamic record update   Changes you make to the records in a table occur as soon as you leave the record, not at a later time.

Edit mode   The operational mode in which you can add or change table data.

Edit region   The area in a form in which table data is entered.

Example element   In a query design, a character or group of characters that specifies the fields that link two tables together.

Experts   Paradox experts provide easy-to-follow steps that help you quickly perform common Paradox tasks.

Field   An item of data in a table, or a column of data.

Field condition box (area)   In a query design, the area in a table skeleton in which you enter selection conditions to limit the records that will appear in the results table.

Field label   The field name that appears adjacent to the data field in a form or report.

Field name   Attributes of a table, describing the information stored in the field.

Field object   A design element that can be added to a report or form design, often a special field such as Date or Page Number, or a summary field such as Count or Total.

Field roster   The part of the Create Table dialog box that contains the field specifications.

Field size   The maximum number of characters that can be stored in a field.

Field tool   The button to use in Design view to place a field object on a report or form.

Field type   The designation that determines the kind of data that can be entered into a field.

Field value   The data contained in a field of a record.

Field view   An extension of the Edit mode that allows you to edit the contents of a single field, character by character.

Filter   A method of limiting table records to a subset of the total for viewing or editing.

Fit width   A zoom scale that reduces the data to fit the screen width.

Form   A way of viewing and entering table data that displays one record at a time.

Form Designer   A Paradox window that contains toolbar and menu options to help create custom form designs.

Form Expert   A Paradox tool that presents form design options in a series of steps.

Form layout　　The specification of the number and arrangement of records to be displayed on the screen at once.

Form view　　The display of table data one record at a time.

Grid lines　　Horizontal and vertical lines available in a Design window that help place objects in a form or report design.

Group band　　An optional horizontal section of a report design that defines the grouping of records.

Group footer　　The information that is to be printed at the end of each group of records in a report.

Group header　　The information that is to be printed at the beginning of each group of records in a report.

Handles　　Small black squares that appear around an object when it is selected.

Index　　A file that specifies the order in which records are to be displayed or accessed.

Join　　The process of defining a relation between two tables. *Also called* link.

Key　　A field or combination of fields that provides a unique value for each record in a table. Also used to order records in a table. *Also called* primary key or primary index.

Key violation　　An error that occurs when an invalid or duplicate value is entered into a key field.

KEYVIOL　　A temporary table containing records that do not meet newly imposed validity checks.

Landscape orientation　　A printing option that rotates the text to print lengthwise on the page.

Launcher Expert　　A Paradox tool that creates a small tabbed form you can use to open or launch selected forms, reports, queries, scripts and executable files with the click of a button.

Link　　The relationship between two tables that specifies the corresponding fields.

Locked records　　Paradox automatically makes a record unavailable to another user (locks it) when you are editing a record.

Lookup table　　A list ot valid field entries that can be linked to a data entry table to speed entry and validate new data.

Mailing Label Expert　　An expert that guides you through creating mailing labels in a variety of standard mailing label formats.

Master table　　The primary table of interest in a table relationship. *Also called* parent table.

Menu bar　　The area across the top of the screen that contains commands relevant to the current activity.

Merge Expert　　A Paradox tool that helps you merge data from a table into a form letter.

Navigation buttons　　A group of six toolbar buttons that move the cursor among records in a table or form view.

Object inspector menu　　A list of properties or actions appropriate to the selected object. Opened by right-clicking the selected object.

Objects　　Any entity that can be manipulated by Paradox, including tables, queries, reports, forms, etc.

Operator　　A reserved word, character, or symbol used to combine conditions in queries, such as AND and OR.

Page footer　　Information that is to be printed at the bottom of each page in a report.

Page header　　Information that is to be printed at the top of each page in a report.

Parent table　　The primary table of interest in a relationship. *Also called* master table.

Portrait orientation　　The standard printing of text across the width of a page.

Primary index　　An index on the key field or fields that determines the order in which the records are stored. *Also called* key or primary key.

Project Viewer　　A Paradox tool that helps you work with and manage files.

Properties　　Characteristics of an object that determine its appearance or behavior.

Query　　A question you can ask of a Paradox table that extracts fields and records that meet the specified criteria.

Query image　　The graphical display of the question asked of a table, indicating which fields to include, the filter conditions, and the record order.

Quick Form　　A simple default form created by clicking a toolbar button or selecting from the Tools menu.

Quick Report　　A simple default report layout created and printed by clicking a toolbar button or selecting from the Tools menu.

Record   A row of data in a table that contains a group of related fields of data.

Record set   A specific number of records that can appear on the screen at once in the table view; the exact number depends on the screen size.

Records band   The central section of a report that contains the bulk of the table data.

Relational database management system   Software that stores data in two or more related tables so that the data can be accessed from all the tables for a single report, form, or display.

Report   Printed table data.

Report Designer   A Paradox window containing toolbar and menu options to help create a custom report.

Report Expert   A Paradox tool that presents report design options in a series of steps.

Report footer   The information that is to be printed at the end of a report.

Report header   The information that is to be printed at the beginning of a report.

Report layout   The number and arrangement of records in a report design, one of the steps in the Report Expert.

Restructure   The process of modifying a table structure.

Run a form (or report)   To view actual data in a form or report design.

Scroll lock   An icon at the bottom of a table view that can be used to keep one or more left columns from scrolling off the screen.

Secondary index   An expression containing one or more fields that allows you to view records in an order other than the key or primary index order.

Selection condition   In a query, an expression entered in a field that limits the records that are included in the results of the query.

Snap to Grid   A feature available when working with objects that automatically places objects on the nearest (invisible) grid line.

Status bar   The area across the bottom of the screen that displays information about the current activity and other messages.

Style sheet   A predefined set of appearance options for a form design, including frames, colors, and three-dimensional effects.

Summary field   A report design element that presents summary information about the data in the report, such as the total number of records in a group or the total or average of the values in a field.

Table   An arrangement of data in rows and columns.

Table Expert   A Paradox tool that helps you create a new table from a list of table templates.

Table name   The name you assign to a table file when you save the structure.

Table skeleton   In a query design, the display of field names in which you can specify the fields to include in the results and enter any selection conditions that will limit the records.

Table structure   The specification of a table that includes the field names, their types and sizes, and, optionally, indicates the key field, secondary indexes, and validity checks.

Table view   The display of table data in rows and columns.

Table view properties   Characteristics that determine the appearance of a table on the screen.

Text box   The container for text in a form or report design.

Text Import Expert   An expert that guides you through the process of importing fixed length or delimited text into Paradox tables.

Text object   A design object consisting of a text box with text.

Text object Expert   An expert that guides you through creating objects on documents.

Text tool   A toolbar button used to add text objects to a design.

Title bar   The area across the top of a window that displays the name of the application and changes color when the window becomes active.

Toolbar   The area below the menu bar that contains buttons and tools for frequently performed tasks.

Toolbar buttons   Icons on the toolbar that provide quick access to many commonly used menu commands.

Tooltip   A bubble that appears above or below a button that describes it as you move the cursor over the button.

Validity checks   Limitations on or specifications of values or formats that can be entered into a field.

View scale   The degree of screen magnification.

Wildcard   A symbol or symbols that represent any character or group of characters.

Working directory   The directory that Paradox opens automatically when you start a session and in which your files are stored during the session.

Zoom   The process of changing the scale of a design or viewing screen.

Index